College for All

The Foundations

Sawtry Village College
1963-1984

Maurice Dybeck

College for All

Maurice Dybeck

Sawtry College Warden
1963-1984

Winston Churchill Fellow

Ex Trustee: Brathay Hall Trust

Ex Chairman: Young Explorers' Trust

Author:
Study Geography (with Rushby & Bell)
The Village College Way
A Broad River (Brathay History)

Director/Scriptwriter:
over 50 films for **Explorer Films**
and over 100 published articles

First Published in 2010 by Sawtry Community College
Fen Lane, Sawtry, Huntingdon PE28 5TQ
Copyright © Sawtry Community College 2010

ISBN: 978-0-9566537-0-3

Designed by Mike Cooper
Printed in England by Reeds Printers, Penrith

Contents

THE RT HON SIR JOHN MAJOR KG CH

FOREWORD
BY THE RT HON SIR JOHN MAJOR, KG CH

In times gone by, rural areas typically had a focus. During much of the time I was the Member of Parliament for Huntingdon, Sawtry Village College was a primary focus, not only for the village, but for a much wider area.

There were many reasons for this, not least being the community involvement of the Warden, Maurice Dybeck, and his wife, Marjorie. Maurice has now written a history of the first 21 years of the College, delving back to its modest origins in 1963.

At that time, few could have imagined the profile it would achieve. It was a small school surrounded by much larger institutions to the North and South: Sawtry was undaunted.

The philosopher and politician, Edmund Burke, wrote of the "little Platoons" that made up society. Sawtry Village College was one such Platoon that grew and spread its influence. Maurice Dybeck's part history/part memoir traces its growth. It is more than the growth of a school: in microcosm, it is the growth of a community, whose story is told by a man at the very centre of much of what was achieved during those 21 years.

The College continues to thrive. Those, like me, who know and admire it hope it will long continue to do so.

John Major

May 2010

Why I wrote this book

There is much to be said about our first 21 years and, like many older men, I feel the urge to record something of the challenges and responses of those times.

Is this an unjustified indulgence? Who would want to read something about times long past, living in such a different world?

Although I continued to reside in Sawtry for many years after retirement from the College, I was aware that changed circumstances meant changed responses. There was a risk, at that time, that to write about 'those early days' could be implied as some criticism of what had happened subsequently.

Twenty three years on I no longer hesitate to write because, thanks to a 2008 visit and the hospitality of current staff, I am aware that the confidence and enterprise of the present staff are more than a match for any boast I might make about the past. And I know they will not mind me observing that not a few of the solutions we adopted in those days are again coming to the attention of educationists who wish to try them in this new age!

This is not a full account of all that went on. I have omitted much that is normal and common to all schools: exams, concerts, meetings, successes, and concentrated rather on things that are sometimes a little out of the ordinary – things that might amuse and, maybe, inspire! You never know.

I am grateful to Sir John Major for writing such a supportive Foreword. He was our MP and, thanks to his Government, the College achieved the Comprehensive Sixth Form that had eluded me. But while Sawtry went from strength to strength in many new ways, it is sad to note that, nationally, Secondary Education is as confused as ever.

I see no coherent way forward while the focus for development remains on *Schools* rather than *Communities* within which and for which they exist.

Is it too much to hope that some of the suggestions herein might help our current leaders?

Maurice Dybeck.
Warden 1963-1984

Part one
Early Years

THE OFFICIAL OPENING OF

SAWTRY
Village College

MONDAY 14 OCTOBER 1963

at 3 pm

HUNTINGDONSHIRE COUNTY COUNCIL

EDUCATION COMMITTEE

01 **Early days**

One hundred years of Sawtry schools

I begin with a glimpse into the year 1976:
from my Report to Governors...

Sawtry Board School opened in May 1876. On 1st May 1976, suitably attired, I presented Fraternal Greetings to Mr John Garner, the Head of Sawtry Junior School, whose school is celebrating the centenary in grand style with many pupils dressed in period costume. Later that day my wife and I walked to Glatton and also honoured Mr Bill Hall, the retired Head, who had done so much for education in Sawtry. In the last 13 years his school has been joined by the Village College, the Agricultural and Homecraft Centres, and the Infants' School, reflecting the expansion of the area, and accommodating an ever-increasing range of facilities.

In the past decade Sawtry has lived through many upheavals: two county amalgamations, the transition to Comprehensive education, the struggle of Sawtry Village College as a small school amongst large well-established 'giants', the campaign for a Sixth Form, and the trebling of the village population. Far from harming us, these struggles have given us a strength and a confidence founded upon the need to justify every action. So the end of this first century of state education sees the Sawtry community well-placed to deal with the future.

The Village College has always tried to create patterns of working which are appropriate to the needs of both pupils and community. Sometimes this has been inconsistent with general County policy. More often, and increasingly so, our patterns and suggestions have been adopted as pilot schemes which can ultimately benefit schools in general.

In reporting to the Governors I went on to list examples: Sixth Form bids, Joint Library, Self-Budgeting, Economic Lettings, Refreshment Facilities.

Growth at Sawtry is more akin to growth of a family than to empire building. Growth in an empire, in politics or industry is usually something in which central control is strong. But growth in a family comes through the people themselves. As members of that family grow up and find their feet, they become independent, argue a bit, perhaps, and eventually move out into their own fields. We encourage this. We encourage self-help and responsibility. In return we expect, and get, support from the 'parents' of our family: the Village College.

Before 1963

When the college was founded in 1963 England was in the final stages of transition into 'Secondary Education for All', a movement prompted by the 1944 Education Act.

We need to remind ourselves of the general situation Post War. For most people, Secondary Education meant passing 'the scholarship' and getting to Grammar School. Only about 20% of the nation achieved that goal. Most of the rest stayed on at the Council School until the leaving age of 14 or, later, 15. Most Council schools were all-age extensions of the Primary school, run by the Local Education Authority or, in many cases, by the churches. Gradually, these schools were being replaced by Secondary Moderns.

In 1957, I was a new teacher, appointed at the opening of one such Secondary Modern school on the edge of Birmingham. The optimism and the excitement at the wonderful new facilities stimulated staff and pupils to create a learning community. This did much to make up for the fact that all the entrants were Eleven-Plus Failures. In the coming years our pupils' successes enabled them to hold their own in any comparison with their Grammar School neighbours, both at school and later on.

Starting up

September 1963

The opening of Sawtry Village College took place in a similar wave of optimism. In our case the institution went one step further. It was not just a bright new secondary school, but a school for the whole community based on the ideas pioneered by Henry Morris in Cambridgeshire over the previous forty years. The first Village College was opened in 1930.

However, we were not set up by Cambridgeshire but by one of Britain's smallest counties, Huntingdonshire, whose population had one of the lowest per-capita incomes. *(Survey by Chase Manhattan Bank 1962)* Following the 1944 Act, the government required all counties to draw up Reorganisation Plans, closing all-age schools and putting every pupil over age 11 into specialist secondary education. For a full modern curriculum, secondary schools had to employ specialist staff and this, in turn, demanded not just new premises but also, to be economic, a minimum pupil population. The Sawtry catchment area was 90 square miles enclosing 21 villages or hamlets. Even so it only had within it, in 1963, some 220 eligible youngsters, after 60 or so had been creamed off to Grammar Schools.

Henry Morris faced similar problems of scattered population in Cambridgeshire in the 1920s and '30s. By founding his Village Colleges ahead of the national demand for secondary education for all he was able to provide a good standard of education for rural children. Small schools can be expensive but Morris was able to persuade his councillors and supporting charities to finance them by augmenting what they offered with facilities for the whole community.

My job interview

We candidates didn't communicate much with each other; nobody wanting to show off what talents they thought they were bringing to the job. So conversation swung to what we knew of this place, Sawtry. One man seemed to know a lot about the area and it turned out he had done much of the campaigning to get the college built. He was a local Head and although he didn't get the job, which must have been a great disappointment to him, we worked profitably together in the years ahead. At interview I was asked if, after a former exciting job in the mountains of the Lake District, and experiences at Gordonstoun, I would mind coming to work on the edge of the Fens. *"I suppose I'll get used to it"* probably earned me good marks for frankness but *nul points* for tact !

Staff Appointments

The first task of any Head is staff appointments, and here we were looking for not just good teachers but ones with a commitment to the ideals of a community college. This worked out well although, strictly speaking, most of them were only being paid for their work as teachers of the pupils. Evening classes merited a fee of course, but most other involvement, and there was plenty, was voluntary. We were lucky to have a gem of a local youth leader, Jim Green, who had a loyal following for his club in the British Legion hut. So it was logical and right to offer him the move to our, his, new Youth Centre. Some evening classes already existed organised by Bill Hall, the Headmaster of Sawtry all age school. These were held in a mixture of premises: Women's Institute Hall, the school, and farms, for Farm Welding classes. Most of these could now move into our many classrooms and practical rooms and be augmented by a much wider range of skills training. And, thanks to the special evening buses, people could come from many of our surrounding villages. Few people came by car. All this work was organised by the Deputy Warden, Peter Jones, and David Marshall, my first Youth/Community Tutor, who had a tiny office next to mine.

The College Badge

In the 1960s few schools had logos or straplines but everyone had a badge. I based our badge on a representation of the school's large catchment area. A couple of bold lines up and down to represent the Great North Road, which divided us in two. Blue to the right to signify fen country, and yellow to the left for the corn in the rolling farmland. And a large **S** across it all for Sawtry. If it looked a little like a dollar sign then so be it; the largest community within our area was an American Air Base. The hills on our left were the only ones between our area and the Urals, so, in a winter east wind we 'knew it' as they say. In the school entrance we had a large cutout panel outlining our catchment and painted in the same blue and yellow, the school colours. On it I got each pupil to place his admission number in the correct geographical location. Thus, although we were a scattered rural area, all could see where they were situated in relation to others. The builders had, as a parting gift, donated a fine flagpole and so I took the hint. We had a blue and yellow pennant, courtesy of the Swedish nation, which we flew on most days. And the Union Jack on high days.

Being the only village college in Huntingdonshire I felt that I was under no obligation to follow slavishly the Cambridgeshire pattern. A tour of those establishments, wonderful as they were, convinced me that a new approach was called for. In essence I felt that the Cambs colleges were paternalistic, following a fairly set pattern which recognised the needs of communities living not far from a famous university town. In contrast we were well and truly rural. Sawtry itself had a population of under 1,000 and the chief means of movement was by bus or tractor. But Ian Currey, our Director of Education, was well aware of the differences and had persuaded his council to give us support to match these particular needs. This included a generous staff ratio and buses not only to bring in most of the pupils, but also free buses to bring in great numbers of adults to evening classes and youngsters to the youth club.

Premises

In the Brochure for the Official Opening, the County Architect spells out the logic of his design. Central and adjoining the entrance was the large hall off which were the adult rooms, the library, kitchens and a servery. Movable screens allowed for flexible use and a wide range of activities. We were lucky to get, behind the hall and its well-equipped stage, a gymnasium – not a requirement in a school this size but something of immense additional benefit to youth and community. Not for us the school hall with badminton court lines blazoned on the parquet! I was told that the gym provision was possible because they had economised on the roof materials – thin sheet metal. But more of that later. The Youth Centre was separate but close to the gym and changing rooms. I asked why we were the first place in the county to get a Youth Centre. *"Well I was asked to design a Village College and they all had youth centres. So that's what you got!"* ...said the architect. Do I believe that?

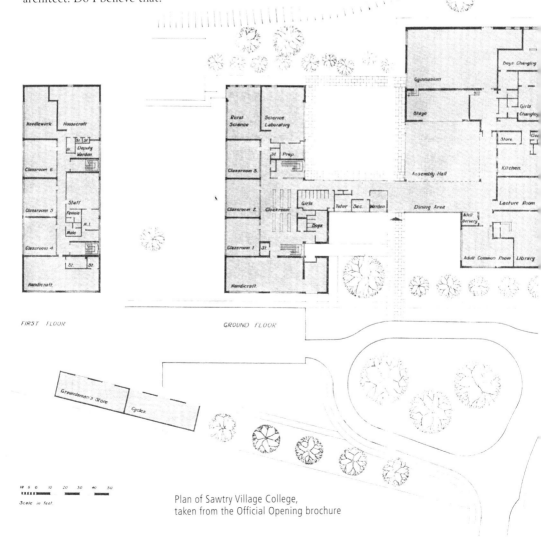

Plan of Sawtry Village College,
taken from the Official Opening brochure

It was a pleasant surprise to see the college buildings recognised in Pevsner's 'Buildings of England'. The college was sited in the centre of the village, thus giving practical expression to its aim to be at the heart of the community. People criss-crossed its paths and fields in their daily movements and experience showed that familiarity with the place, and an 'open door', bred respect rather than vandalism.

So, in Sawtry, the small school had an additional two rooms dedicated to adult use, a youth centre, the first in the county, and some staff with a brief to facilitate all these supplementary activities. As Warden, I was committed to see that the place fully lived up to its role as the education hub for the whole community.

There was a similar optimism to that which I had found near Birmingham. *"Best thing that's happened to us since they stopped the night soil collection"* said Parish Council Chairman Newton at the official opening by Chris Chataway, Secretary of State for Education. And my Governing Body, most of whom were farmers, gave me a breathtaking brief: *"Mister Doybeck, you just do what you think is best and we'll back you"*

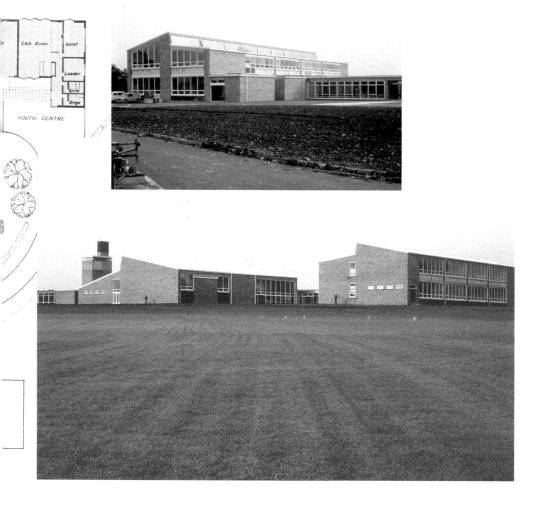

YOUTH CENTRE

What is a Warden?

Since a village college is more than a school, the title Headmaster was felt to be not quite right. Henry Morris, who founded village colleges, dubbed us Wardens; a title he knew was used by some of the 'proper' Cambridge colleges. This puzzled people, and here are some of the alternatives that came up in my postbag over the years:

Warder. No, we were never a prison, I hope! That address came from an organisation whose label said they existed for the 'mitigation of suffering throughout the world' So, perhaps they did think I was a Warder!

The Headperson. Oh, here we are getting quite early on into the politically correct age. Hold back a bit!

The Promoter. Is this what the staff thought I was when Responsibility Allowances were up for grabs?

The Principle. Well, I hope I had those. And that one came from the army, in an HMSO envelope: 'Certified Official'. Yes sir.

The Meadmaster. We helped found the Sawtry Winemakers quite early on, so maybe this was them welcoming me to Join the Club. Cheers.

Head of Resources. Adult Literary Co-Ordinate College.(sic) This from a group promoting Literacy! Ah, but we had plenty of resources.

To all the staff (c/o Mr Dybeck). I liked that one. Of course I took care of them all.

Sawtry Village Collage. This from our own county. So even they think we are just a hotch-potch patchwork!

The Headteacher. Ugh. I got out before this became common. No more sex?

Chief Executive. That's more like it. Though I hope we never became just a business.

The Headhamster. The one I liked best. That puts you in your place. Or was it that they realised I had once been a 'Desert Rat'? – Commissioned into the Seventh Armoured Division in Germany in 1949. The Jerbil was their symbol.

02 **The School**

The secondary modern years

Although we were a small school we needed to remember that most of our youngsters were coming from even smaller schools and that many of them lived in scattered rural communities. Despite the glitz there was apprehension. Parents of pupils from Stilton were grumpy. They had been promised transfer to this bright college a year ago in 1962 but there were building delays. Nevertheless, the upper parts of Stilton (all age) school were phased out at that time. Those over age eleven were sent to Orton Longueville Secondary Modern School, on the edge of Peterborough. And they had bought blazers and kit for that school! They had been told that they could retain these blazers at Sawtry. But I decided that a new image was required for a new school. And buying another lot of new kit did not go down well.

Other schools that were losing their 'top' with the formation of the college were Holme and Sawtry. Alconbury, Great Gidding and Folksworth had already lost their senior pupils by transfers to nearby Stilton and Sawtry.

Technically the school opened on Sept 1st 1963, the day my third child was born, but, for pupils, work began on Sept 10th. There were 220 pupils in all and a teaching staff of twelve. I recall that the Director of Education, Ian Currey, and the Chairman of the Governors, Alderman Hoefkens, who was also Chairman of the County Education Committee, came and supported us at our first school Assembly. There were no steps on to the stage so I had to leap up using my old school tuck box. But, thanks to prior training, we had a school orchestra who were to support the singing and soon to do their stuff at the official opening on October 14th.

We were two-form entry with eight classes to cover the four years of compulsory secondary education. It needs to be remembered that a school leaving age of 15 allowed pupils, at that time, to leave school at the end of the term in which they became 15. So 4A and 4B could decline in size by a third at the end of each school term. The first challenge, then, if the new school was to be seen as attractive, was to persuade potential leavers to complete the planned courses by staying on until the end of their fourth year. This worked well with many potential leavers, despite the lure of full employment in local jobs.

Our Aims

These were formulated when we began and, despite all the coming changes, they stood, I hope, the test of time.

1   *To provide a sound general education for all children according to their age, ability and aptitude.*

2   *To set before children high standards in work and play and to encourage them to reach for these standards at all times.*

3   *To create opportunities for enlarging their experience of the world around them.*

4   *To develop in all children a responsible attitude towards other people, encouraging generosity, unselfishness and courtesy.*

The School Curriculum

As Head, it was up to me and the staff to choose and set the courses of work for our eight classes to cover in the next four/five years. Looking back from after 1990 when so much of what schools teach has been firmly defined by government decree it is both exciting and frightening to realise how much responsibility was given to schools in choosing what to teach. In 1963 it was not an expectation that most pupils would take GCE, although the requirements of that exam were always in mind when planning the broad curriculum.

Guidance came from many sources. There was even a book: *'The Secondary Modern School: Schemes of work'* which set it all out pat. It was published in 1950, but I felt we had come quite a long way since then. Our small county of Huntingdon had few Advisers, not yet called Inspectors, and none of them had direct experience of village colleges. But their support at staff interviews was invaluable. *(I think particularly of Mr Wellington, Mr Lumley and Mr Ross)* With plenty of applicants to choose from, the appointed teachers were men and women of vision. They came with their own fund of experience indicating what, in their view, was best taught in our bright new school. And my own experience of what had succeeded in the first Secondary Modern I taught in proved useful. Educational thought in those days, as expressed in the press, was in a fair turmoil. Are we to turn our kids into the white hot scientists and technicians for a bright tomorrow? Or are they still just hewers of wood and drawers of water? Are we educating for Jobs? Which jobs? For Leisure, or for Life?

In the end, like most new schools, we had to push debate to one side and just get on with the job, following the generally agreed pattern of teaching in the majority of schools of our kind. Having said that, here are a few of what might, in hindsight, be seen as interesting deviations. 'Innovations' is what we would call them!

1   Something called **Modern Maths** was just beginning and, with a keen teacher, John Yates, we embraced this wholeheartedly. The new approach sought to make maths less of a routine drudge and more exciting, spacial, and tactile. John covered his walls with pentagons and the like, and pupils made models of strange mathematical shapes. He wanted to buy a 'calculator' and the one he wanted, and got, was a special import from Sweden. Sawtry was going ahead in computing from Day One. All calculations were to be metric and school rulers, issued to all, were 30cm long. In later years we were rapped by Peterborough engineering firms for not doing fractions and inches. You can't win.

2   One aspect of maths that we developed was **Statistics,** which became a CSE subject. Peter Jones championed this one as something that helps the layman to see the truth that lies behind all those facts and figures which constantly bombard us these days. *(eg If 50% of children are always below average, is that statement perjorative? Or simply factual?)*

3   **English** is all about expression and communication and quite early on we made sure that this included Spoken English. The popular view of country farm kids not being as communicative as cockneys had to be countered. We put on big school productions, but also held form dramas and a speaking competition. Through the joint PTA we encouraged our contributory Primary schools to put on their own little shows. The CSE exam was just being set up and we fully embraced its Spoken English option. In this we were regularly

chosen as the school to which others looked when standards were being set for this exam. And we worked closely with the English Speaking Board. We never did much about a school magazine but Andrew Clifton's **'Leaves'**, a fully pupil effort, gave many a chance to express themselves in their own way. There was also **'Bones'** – a humerus magazine *(grr)*. And we often included school literary efforts in the periodic **Eventsheets**, to be seen by the whole community. Fascinating to note that this last 'opening' encouraged adults to counter with their own poems! Education for All?

4   I will let **Physical Education** speak for itself in the various success stories scattered through these accounts. Ian Tait was always diligent in giving me Sports Reports to read out in Assembly. The best general lesson that our competitive teams learned is that size isn't everything. Although for many years we were less that a third of the size of any other secondary school, we frequently won matches. It was a great morale-booster – and not only in PE – to see that Sawtry could hold its own against all comers. On the community side these notes will show that PE was not just a school matter. Local youth used the facilities to the full, and it was the community's enthusiasm and support that led to the building of the swimming pools.

5   **Domestic Science,** as a subject, has had its ups and downs in recent years. We taught all the basics from Day One but we took the 'domestic' aspect a stage further by including, under Mrs Baxter and others, what we termed **Child Care.** And we wonder how many later mothers have been glad of the practical and psychological instruction that we were able to include. Our students sat the exam of the National Association for Maternal and Child Welfare. We were visited and encouraged by their top Parentcraft Adviser: Lenora Pitcairn. And it goes without saying that cooking and needlework were not something that was confined to the girls.

6   **Rural Studies.** We were, in 1963, very much a farming area. The County recognised this by building next to us the County Agricultural Education Centre. We had good relations with them and Course links. Some of our pupils would later go there for further training. On our own site Dick Tuplin, i/c Rural Studies, had one of our two science labs. The County turned down our request for special units but it was not long before we acquired, for him, a redundant 'Prefab' (£150) for livestock. But the stories of Dick's hens and sheep are not for recalling here!! For a while we had, like most secondary moderns, a plot of arable land for crops. As we grew in size, and permanent extensions were slow in coming, these plots got covered with another kind of 'prefab': the transportable classroom. At one time we had seven of them!

7   **Outdoor Education.** This was not even a subject on the curriculum of most schools but I, and many of my colleagues, were familiar with the great social value of much that could be done outside the formal classroom. For my part I had been on the Outdoor Education Advisory Committee of the Ministry of Education for some years besides having been, in an earlier incarnation, Chief Instructor at the Brathay Hall (Residential) Centre in the Lake District. Although, as country children, our pupils were quite used to open spaces, many of them had not travelled far and one of our objects was to literally widen their horizons. The accounts that follow allude to much of this work out of doors.

8   **Practical Studies.** From 1970, our curriculum was organised under three major groupings -Sciences, Humanities and Practical Studies – with a senior graduate teacher in charge of each group. Brian Parkin came to us to bring

together, in 1969, all that we called Practical Studies – Woodwork, Metalwork, Needlework, Domestic Science and Art, and he renamed the grouping 'Craft, Design and Technology', advertising its presence on the outside wall as Sawtry Craft Centre. The unity of purpose throughout these disciplines was picked up and admired by government inspectors in 1980 when the work was described at length in a Ministry Booklet: *'Craft, Design & Technology – some successful examples.'*

Brian always spoke of CDT as a 'think' subject and this was borne out by the mantra posted on his wall giving the stages in any design process:

Start – *identify the problem – write it down – list considerations – offer six outline solutions – select one – sketch it – show how it's made – cost it – make presentation drawing – make it – test it – evaluate/improve it – stop*

And that's something you could apply to many of life's activities.

9   **Foreign language** teaching can be a problem in small schools with limited resources but we embraced French from the beginning. We were arrogant enough to suggest that our contributory Primary schools 'laid off' it until they came to us. This was not always popular but it allowed us to start from a level playing field, as we now say. Language laboratories were becoming the vogue in the 1960s but they were expensive and often meant dedicating one room to a set of cubicles. Under John Lemon we compromised with a more mobile system which was then 'networked' round an ordinary classroom with an excellent cabling job by our lab technician.

10   **Religious Education** was not an easy subject to staff and, since I had been Head of RE in my former school, some of this work initially came my way. Later, in this role, we had a Spanish priest, an Anglican trainee and the voluntary services of our local Rector. Later, under Mrs Anderson, our syllabus attracted much praise and was used in the 1980s in the formulation of the new county Agreed Syllabus. It is unusual for pupils to show such interest in a subject that, unfairly, is often bottom of their popularity poll. In the upper years pupils regularly chose RE as an exam option.

11   **Traffic Education,** like Child Care, was not a subject on many school curricula. But we felt it had a lot to offer in making young people, especially boys, aware of the dangers of modern living. So we prepared and had accepted our own *'Mode Three'* CSE syllabus. And thus a CSE pass could give them skills for real life and confidence where it might be needed. And *'Safe on a Moped'* was filmed at Sawtry for the County Road Safety Team, and distributed nationally.

12   **Typing and Office Practice** was something we included for senior girls, who would take the popular RSA examinations in the Fourth Year. Our village college status allowed us to acquire and share typewriters with Evening Classes. The rise of the computer might seem to have made these some of these skills redundant. But note how few people nowadays make proper use of that keyboard. And do we not still need those filing skills and telephone disciplines?

13   Are **School Assemblies** part of the school curriculum? At a time (1970s) when full school Assemblies were becoming a thing of the past we always had daily Assemblies seated, on chairs. In early years we were fortunate in that, having a large school hall, we could assemble the whole school every day. I always regarded this event as the prime responsibility of the Head, though of course others, staff and pupils, shared in the work. We always sang hymns

with the redoubtable Pam Pettifor at the keyboard. As a spiritual occasion, I hope that we fulfilled both our legal and moral obligations, although, even in the '60s, this sometimes meant an uphill struggle. Soon pictures and music came to the rescue, drawing on personal resources from far and wide. For a good response, one had to have good blackout and this was only achieved after much contriving. The back-of-hall skylights were permanently blocked off, "incidentally saving heat-loss", I told the architect. Setups on the 'Multi', our portable Audio-Visual base, minimised the fuss involved. *"Can we have the lights please?"*

Assemblies are also the time when Heads 'hold forth'. It was marvellous in a small school to have this direct face-to-face contact with them all. But it was not to last. As the school got bigger we still had daily Assemblies but subdivided into half school groups, or Year groups. We met in a series of contrived larger spaces throughout the buildings. But even when we got to over 500, we would, on occasion, have a Full School Assembly, usually at the start and end of terms, when we would slide back the screens, bring down extra chairs and ask the kitchen staff not to bang the saucepans. Then we could have a brief feeling of this community to which we all belonged.

So much for the curriculum. Now we had to link it to the customers.

Form organisation for the older pupils

As a Secondary Modern school (1963-1970+) our educational brief was to provide teaching appropriate to that 80% on the population who had not gone to the Grammar School. With the older pupils the challenge was to see how many of them valued education enough to stay on for a fifth year. Some national exams were available at 4th or 5th year levels: RSA and UEI offering various typing and commercial qualifications, but as yet there was no Certificate of Secondary Education (CSE). There was the prospect of going on to 'the Tech' in Huntingdon or Peterborough, equidistant from Sawtry, at ten miles each, and taking higher qualifications. But the ultimate goal for the 'brightest' ones would be to emulate the Grammar Schools and take subjects in the General Certificate of Education (GCE). There was a growing feeling, nationally, that the cutoff provided by the 11 plus examination was unrealistic and that the potential of many borderline pupils was greater than at first thought. At one point we were required to give up our 'best' pupils at age 12 handing them over for late Grammar School entry. *(See Case Study below.)*

But soon the real challenge for most pupils of this level was to be the Certificate of Secondary Education, introduced nationally in 1965. This was perfect timing for us. Pupils stayed on to take this exam in increasing numbers so that by 1969 over half the year group stayed on as Fifth Formers. (28 out of 48) They achieved, overall, some 90 subject passes. The following year this doubled to 180.

Our first Sixth Form: 1968

Meanwhile interest, nationally, was growing for a larger number of pupils to take GCE O level. At first we felt it best that such pupils stayed on for an extra 'Sixth' year to reach that level. So a Sixth Form of six pupils was started in 1968 for the specific purpose of allowing GCE O level work to develop. GCE courses were offered in English Language, Mathematics, Statistics, Physics, Biology, History, Geography, Religious Education, Woodwork and Art, and pupils were passing in up to nine O levels. Sometimes, as a safeguard, it was wise for some pupils to do GCE in tandem with CSE work, even though a Grade One CSE was accepted as a GCE equivalent. However, this meant taking a double dose of exams. Later, in 1970, when it became clear that pupils could manage O level in five years, we moved this work into the Fifth. We retained our embryo Sixth Form and it was extended over the next five years so that, in the end, we also offered **A levels** in the following subjects: English, Maths, French, History, Geography, Domestic Science and Art. By 1974 we had 18 pupils in the Sixth Form – almost a quarter of the original Secondary Modern intake.

So much for the 'infallibility' of the eleven Plus!

The Newsom Report

Despite these aspirations towards exam success it is worth remembering that the original vision was for the Secondary Modern school to be clear of the limitations of purely academic work and to concentrate instead on what the Greeks called 'The Whole Man'. To this end the government produced, in 1963, in the same month as we opened, the Newsom Report: *'Half Our Future'* to give focus to such aspirations. In tune with its recommendations I note that early on I wrote, of our curriculum policy, the following:

The success of the education of most children can only be measured by asking:

1   *How far have they succeeded in finding worthwhile employment and becoming a credit to their employers?*
2   *How far have we prepared them for adult life so that they can understand and cope with the social and commercial pressures that surround them?*
3   *How far have we prepared them for married life, for leisure, and for becoming responsible members of the community?*

Our implementation of Newsom ideals took many forms. But in fact they were not really a response to Newsom since, as the above notes indicate, we already had many of them in mind!

Exam success: Case Study

In the days of the Eleven Plus the county had a scheme whereby if we had promising pupils in the first year, who might have just missed getting a Grammar School place, we were to yield them up to the Grammar School at 'twelve plus'. One year, about 1965, we had two, a boy and a girl, in this category, and I was due to take them both to the Grammar School by car for interview. Yes, they had to pass that hurdle, too. But the boy refused to go and I was left taking the girl (alone!) to interview. Four years later I looked at the GCE results of both these students. I think the girl got three O levels. The boy, who stayed with us, got five!

Pastoral Care

The Form Base

In their small primary schools pupils had been used to being with one teacher for much of the day. Work in a secondary school necessitated moving around from lesson to lesson to many different teachers. So it seemed important that all pupils had a home base in which to start each session and to be with a form teacher who was their mentor and friend. In 1963 school desks, with holes for inkpots and room under the lid for all your books, were still the order of the day, although they made little sense if most lessons were taken elsewhere. Soon, we arranged that every child would have, in or outside his classroom, a personal locker, with his own key which he was entrusted to look after. This in itself was an educative exercise! The communal school cloakroom, a smelly damp melee of bustle and duffel coats, was soon abolished, and each class had its own peg space outside its base classroom. The hope was that we could persuade the young to be tidy and systematic and avoid the all-too-common sight of hundreds of pupils traipsing round the school all day burdened with all their belongings.

The Year Group

As the school grew - 1970 – we brought in another layer of pastoral care: that of the Year Group with each of the school years having a Head of Year. This teacher would become the first point of reference with parents in many matters. The Year Group would also, in time, become the unit that met for the daily school Assembly.

Legally, all schools were expected to assemble as a body at the start of every day. With our big school hall this was indeed the pattern throughout our early years. As Headmaster it gave me personal contact with them all. The staff, all of whom I had just met for our daily five minutes in the staff room - their pastoral care - would place themselves strategically along the hall sides and all the pupils would be seated on chairs. Never just standing.

As the school grew bigger we sought to retain the 'as-a-body' feeling through these Year Groups. This was not easy when those Year Groups were 70 or 80 in size. But we did manage, eventually, with much ingenuity, to carve out spaces for simultaneous Year Assemblies throughout the school. One Year met in the Youth Centre. One in the Adult Lecture room, another in the large Drama room, one in the 'Amphi' (see below), and one in a room made bigger by removing a wall. (!) On most days I still ran Hall Assemblies for different combinations of years: senior years, junior years, or top year, and adjusted the content of the meeting to that age group.

The Community Group

One last aspect of pastoral care which relates particularly to a village college. Pupils were never the only occupants of the place. There might be a daytime adult typing class in one room, or a Primary school group using the swimming pool. There might be a County meeting in the lecture room, or an over 60s club or a Ladies' Afternoon in the Adult Common Room. Some others might be sharing school dinners. Or the hall might be full of prostrate blood donors. For our pupils, school was not a place apart. It was in the community. They saw others and learned to live respectfully with others.

Two boys in the corridor:
   "What dey doin in dere?"
   "Takin' blood!"
   "eeugh!"

Work Diaries

These were a manifestation of our desire to keep parents in the picture about school lessons. Many schools now have these diaries but we were one of the pioneers, having copied the idea from the well-known Crown Woods Comprehensive School in London where Marjorie Thomson (later Dybeck) was Head of the Sixth Form. The diary listed the homework timetable, the work set and a pupil response. And there was room in it for parents to respond. However, despite good intentions, we found, as do all teachers, that responses at both pupil and parent level were, how shall we put it? 'varied'!

Looking after our senior pupils

Pupils who stay on after the official leaving age deserve the best we can give them. In our early days, people could leave during or at the end of the Fourth year and so the top year was the Fifth - people who chose to stay on for exams. We were pleased that quite a few did so while others went to the 'Techs' at either Huntingdon or Peterborough.

As we grew, and demand for qualifications increased, a few pupils stayed on for a further year to take either O levels or, later, some A levels. This was still in our Secondary Modern years.

But where could we put this extra class? The first idea was to use the side room within the new 'Music Suite', our ROSLA extension. This was space given for extra numbers after the Raising Of the School Leaving Age from 15 to 16. But soon this proved to be too small. Since there was no other planned space for this additional class we had to make space! One end of the Adult Common Room was double the required height and so, with a bit of ingenuity, an upper room was contrived and, within it, each of our Sixth Form students was given their own dedicated space in the form of a Carrell. In the late sixties Carrells had become the 'in' thing for school study. In our d.i.y. design, they consisted of a table with a fitted three tier bookshelf above it. In later years, when we lost our Sixth Form we turned this room into a Careers room, with the staircase access shifted from the Adult Common Room to the Library. This, in turn, made room for us to add an outside door to the space underneath which became the Community Association's fitted Bar.

Senior pupils played an active part in many of the jobs of running the school. After early trials we felt that the Prefect concept was rather passé, where a privileged few could lord it over their fellows. At Gordonstoun, where I had spent a term, they called the Head Boy the Guardian and his team the Helpers. But that seemed a bit too precious. We sought to give ALL senior pupils in the Fifth and Sixth some responsible role. Duty Assistants, we called them. And this worked well. I recall one occasion in the days when we still had the Whole School Photo, and pupils stood in long rows all stacked up; almost the whole of the organisation for this was done by three of our senior boys.

Aerial photo of the college in October 1964.
courtesy of USAF Alconbury
The 'Purley' Pool is on its 1964 site before being incorporated into the building. The first ten foundation blocks for the main swimming pool structure are shown in place. The rough area to the south became the Dual Use field and Bowling Green in 1974.

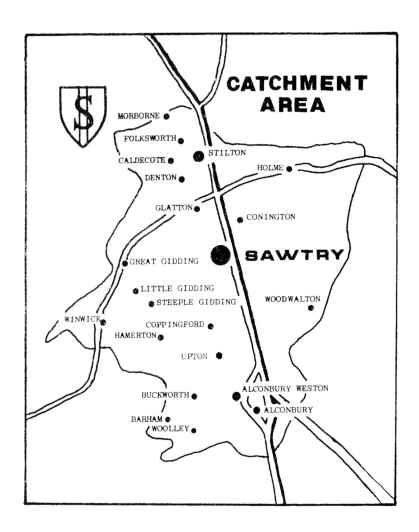

Sketch of the college catchment area.

We used this in all of our literature, so as to make the people in all those surrounding villages feel that they were a part of the whole village college community.

03 **Youth & Community**

Adult Classes

In a Village College the Warden's first responsibility, after the school, is Evening Classes. In 1963 there was already a small core of this work, directed by Mr Hall, Head of the Sawtry all-age School. Classes took place wherever he could find space, in his own school, in homes or, for welding, in farms. Most of this work now shifted to the college, with farmers' courses going to the Agricultural Centre when it opened in late1963.

Cambridgeshire Village Colleges usually had two 'Tutors' one for Youth and one for the Adult (FE) work. We had just one, and the non-school administrative burden fell on myself, Peter Jones, Deputy Warden, and David Marshall the Youth Tutor.

Here is a list of the classes we offered in September 1963.

Classes tutored by school staff:	Other classes:
Keep Fit for Men	Shorthand & Typewriting-2 classes
Basic Dressmaking	Judo for Men
GCE Maths	Music Group
Pottery +1	Advanced Dressmaking
Cookery	Art to Enjoy
Woodwork +1	Radio Engineering
Ladies' Keep Fit	Ballroom Dancing
Film Making	(Astronomy)
Ideas of Freedom	(Local History)
Choral Singing	(Motor Maintenance)
(Square Dancing)	
(Plant Growing)	
(Decorative Metalwork)	
In Folksworth: Mrs Youles ran	Dressmaking
School staff also offered 'Clubs':	Film Society
ie Fees fixed by members:	Badminton
	Chess
The Agricultural Centre	Farm Welding - 2 classes
ran the following:	Tractor Maintenance
	The £ s d of Farming
	Animal Health & Hygiene

Brackets = non-starter +1 = popular, and so an extra class was opened

Class sizes varied from 4 to 19. Judo for girls was added because of demand. Metalwork was in demand but could not start as the room was not ready. Overall, some 222 students participated.

Local organisations which soon became linked to the college included: Young Farmers Club, Badminton Club, Cricket Club, Tennis Club. Other associated organisations which had their own venues included: Women's Institute, British Legion, Guides & Brownies, Air Training Corps, Football Club, Threescore Club.

Our brief, as a college for the 90 square mile catchment area, meant that many of our Evening Class customers hailed from villages far and wide. For them, the county provided a free bus service on two nights a week. This was in the days when few people had cars and there were no regular bus services to most of our 21 villages. The college bus service was also a great boon to the youth of the area coming into the Youth Centre.

Besides drawing people IN we sought to provide some classes OUT in the villages themselves. Usually these happened in the Primary schools but could also be in village halls or homes. Over the years we ran or sponsored classes in: Alconbury, Buckworth, Folksworth, Gidding, Stilton and Woodwalton.

Early growth of Evening Classes
Including classes at the Agricultural and Rural Domestic Economy Centres

Autumn Term	1963	1964	1965	1966	1967	1968	1969
Classes offered	34	31	30	25	22	35	34
Classes held	27	17	26	21	20	28	28
Enrolments	222	229	236	270	313	361	446

The Youth Centre

Youth provision was an essential part of the village college, but the form of that provision was always being extended. From the start, Jim Green was the obvious leader and his club moved in naturally. In 1963 they had a membership of 55 with meetings on at least 2 nights a week plus sports at weekends. By 1968 the club was at capacity with 154 members, and there was a junior club with a further 50. Scouts had another night and later there were also Cub Scouts. Overall, in the catchment area it looks as if youth involvement was of at least 50% of the relevant population against a national average of 30%. This, in spite of transport problems for many of them.

Sport was an attraction, with the school gym, the playground (with member-built floodlighting) and the school fields. Later, the Youth Club had their own special evening in the swimming pool and, even later, use of all the facilities of the Sports Hall.

With a catchment area that covered so many villages and hamlets our Community Tutor had a brief to encourage clubs in them. These sometimes came and went, depending on volunteer leaders; there were usually clubs in Stilton, Gidding, Alconbury, Holme and Hamerton. We were responsible for them in association with the area Youth Officers, and we would publicise them in our literature.

As with the school the youth clubs were able to benefit from home-made extra provisions: murals, bar counters, and storage spaces. When the time came for the first of the 'school' expansions I was able to arrange that some of this took the form of a partitioned-off extension to the club room. In the daytime this new space and its surrounding 'offices' would be the school's Music Suite. But at night it would give the youth club a much bigger room. We even had a switching device so that the inevitable loudspeakers could be equitably shared! Then in the daytime, on most days, the 'youth' side of the partition would be the home of Mrs Nash's Nursery School, something that was established many years before these kind of facilities became commonplace. Then again, as we grew, the enlarged club room became a base for one of the weekly Year Assemblies.

Footnote on shared use of the Youth Centre and the Music Suite. I now add a tribute to music teacher Pam Tuplin (nee Pettifor) who accepted this arrangement uncomplainingly. Having a playgroup or a health clinic on the other side of a folding partition was not always ideal. But the alternative could have been a much 'meaner' music suite, and a smaller club for burgeoning.youth activities. Pragmatism won.

The Agricultural Centre
In 1963/4 we were not the only new premises on the campus. The Huntingdon County Agricultural Education Centre was being built: a reminder that we were in the heart of an agricultural county. All but two of my governors were farmers. The centre provided day release and evening classes in rural subjects and we worked closely with them for both FE work and for wider experience for our older pupils. Those inclined towards farming would have some of their lessons over there. Later, some of our older pupils ended up there for part of each week on day release after they went into farm employment.

In 1965, in a double mobile classroom, the Centre expanded to include a Rural Domestic Economy 'Homecraft' Centre (RDE) which gave us a further range of useful links. *(People were intrigued to note that Ag. Centre staff had some very appropriate surnames: Lawn, Bartter, and Frost.)*

In the early days, before they were fully operational we were able to offer meals and rooms for their students, and we always advertised their courses. But when the Homecraft Centre got going there was some overlap of offerings. This did not matter in the daytime, when we were fully occupied with the school. But it was wasteful that they sometimes ran similar evening classes. In the end, their only evening offerings were lace making and flower arrangement. As part of our liaison, when the college governors were granted a place on their governing body, they invited me to be their representative.

With changing national employment patterns, we were to outlive both of these institutions. However, their demise helped future developments of our own, with the Homecraft Centre becoming the base first for the Community Printshop and then for the many activities of CARESCO, (see page 132). The Agricultural Centre building, after some years as a county store, became a base for Youth Work.

Community Involvement
Youth Clubs and Evening Classes were not the only aspects of our community involvement. In fact they were only the beginning. Look round any community and you will find a wide range of voluntary-run organisations, large and small. In the youth field there will be Scouts and Cadets, in the sports field: football, cricket and tennis clubs. There will be Women's Institute, men's groups, social clubs and carers' groups for the old and the young. Then there will be a variety of church organisations. While many of these groups have their own premises they might welcome the advent of a village college for two reasons. First of all some might see the college as a place where they could regularly meet. And almost all of these organisations could be looking to the college as somewhere for their larger gatherings: dances, conferences, sports days, displays or Feasts. As I saw it, my role was to investigate their needs and see how we could, with our wonderful premises, support them and so enrich their experiences. Common sense told them that the place they, as taxpayers, had provided was there to be used.

I just had to see that it was used properly and responsibly. Responsibility implied that they should not see themselves as tenants – hirers of rooms – but as groups with a shared involvement in the total use of the place. At its lowest, the logic behind this is that if one group has a raveup and smashes windows then all need to be aware that the next lot might have a draughty evening. At its highest, if some annual dinner makes a profit they might be persuaded to donate proceeds towards new stage curtains or school equipment.

It was George Chaney, our second Community Tutor, who, in 1969, harnessed this sense of responsibility by inaugurating our Community Association. Whether he had learned to do this out in Nigeria where, on Government Service, he had earned his MBE, I know not. But he ensured that all 'outside users' signed up to become members of our Community Association.

'What's in it for us?' they would say. The first lure was insurance cover. The small print on the county hire form could be daunting. But, by arranging our own college group premium, we were able to reassure all members on this count.

Then there was priority of booking – something that became important when our popularity rose. For example New Year dances could be - and were - booked by members fifteen months ahead. Then there was the right that we gave them to control membership. And with an eventual membership at over 70 organisations this was significant. Should they welcome member groups from outside the catchment area? We were rapidly becoming a county centre despite our rurality. Should they expel unruly groups? One role they took very seriously was that of reining in-groups that caused trouble at dances because of inadequate supervision. It was significant that this work was done by an elected community group rather than some paid administrator in a school or County office.

There was that wonderful occasion when the football club was hauled up before the Association because of under-age drinking at a dance. It was the club leader, the local 'bobby', who had to answer the charges. And, making the judgement on behalf of the Association: their Chairman, who happened to be a local publican! Our Community Association was unique in that it was the only one, nationally, to be based on a school. It is gratifying to note that, in later years, the pattern we set has been widely adopted in other schools in many parts of Britain. The Community Association got its fingers into many pies. Debates at meetings were often lively and sometimes went well beyond the parish pump. I recall one evening when a local clergyman sought to get us to pass a resolution: *'to stop the Americans bombing North Vietnam'*. We lost our nerve on this one. But George Chaney, ever one to stir people into new projects, never sought a quiet life. His pet phrase, when things got a bit hot, was to urge people on and to go for *'the creative use of conflict'*.

From a handout

A Community Association

- Puts users at the centre
- Gives them running powers
- Gives a collective voice in local affairs
- Provides a foundation from which to expand

Some Clubs

Among the many clubs that found a home at Sawtry Village College some of the most prominent deserve a mention.

Young Farmers Club

This club predated the Village College under the tutelage of Mr Hall the Head of what was then the Sawtry all-age school. There were many young farmers in the area but the YFC embraced a wide clientele: all keen young people out for fun and activity coupled with regular more serious meetings. Dick Tuplin, from the College staff, became their leader and they met regularly in our Adult Common Room and were always game for joining in a useful project. We have to thank the Young Farmers for putting up the swimming pool building – basically an agricultural barn, something they were used to erecting. Later, they set to work fitting out the Adult Common Room with wood panelling. All Cambridgeshire Village Colleges had wood panelled Common Rooms but, proudly, only ours was a diy community job. Whenever we had a big summer festive event we could always rely on the Young Farmers to put on a show; in fact the Sawtry branch had quite a prominent reputation for 'get-up-and-go' throughout the county.

Sawtry pupils on a farm visit

Scouts

Early on in 1968, two people who had recently moved to the village, Mr Johnson and Mervyn Donne came to me about the formation of a Sawtry Scout group. As a recognised youth organisation they could claim use of the Youth Centre, which gave them a good start. We also contrived, over the years, to give them storage space for their tents and camp gear, first in a redundant swimming pool pump house, then in a split-off half of the youth club office and later, thanks to a bit of discreet carpentry, under the school stage. Many school pupils joined the Scouts and soon, also Cubs and Beavers. The Swimming pool hosted their popular county galas and the college field became the focus for vast county rallies, patronised once by the Chief Scout.

(Top) Judo Club

(Right) The Hall, set up for
a Film Society evening

Judo Club

This started as an evening class in our very first year. We were able to give a home to that very necessary piece of equipment – the judo mat – so they had, so-to-speak, a stake in the place. Mr W O'Reilly was the first tutor but some years later it was Mrs Thirtle. Whenever her youngsters got awards she would send me a report and this would be published in the *Eventsheet* for all to see. At no time did this become a 'school' activity but it is true that a great many of our pupils, and some from other schools, benefited from this good work.

Film Society

This popular society started in February 1965 and was organised by staff - Dick Tuplin and Frank Wiseman - and senior pupils. It ran for many years. We used the excellent school stage resources: big screen, coloured lights, interval music et al and two 16mm projectors, one of which was lent to us by the Primary School, so that there was no break after each reel. Remember, this was in the days when few people had television, none of it in colour so these evenings became quite a social occasion. I used to reckon that the half-way refreshment interval was a good time to catch up on what my former pupils were doing. In its heyday the Society ran up to 20 shows a year. This included a Saturday morning show with different films for the younger element. Those were the days when every town had its Saturday morning film club for the kids.

Drama

In the nationwide school building boom of the 1950s and '60s it was normal to provide schools with a well-equipped stage, with tabs, curtains, lights, the lot. We had our allocation and this was doubly valuable to us as a community college. Not only did it encourage good school productions of which we had quite a few but it also drew in local community drama. The Stilton Players were not all from Stilton. Neither were Glatton Drama all from Glatton. The names were just the start. One or more of these groups met regularly for rehearsals and then put on a well-attended show. In many of these productions school staff gave support or played a lead. The stage with its plain white back wall cyclorama made an excellent backcloth for our Film Society cinema. The range of use of the stage was further extended when the Sawtry School of Dancing produced many young ballet dancers putting on such shows as *La Fille Mal Gard*. In later years we were able to extend drama provision by converting the old Art Room into a drama studio with blackout, lighting, stage blocks and even a soundproof control booth for use with our own TV setup. Few other schools had such a room at that time: 1976.

Sketch by Brian Parkin
of our diy Drama Room

Many drama events demand the use of a piano and ours was something of a bargain. It was a full size Concert Grand acquired for us by Youth Tutor David Marshall. His uncle had been Bursar at Kings College London. Their Medical School had long ago acquired their piano from the Wigmore Hall. I did a check on dates and I reckoned that it could have been the very piano on which William Walton's Facade had first been performed! In our humbler environment we had to give it a strong beer-proof cover so that it could safely survive many a weekend 'celebration'. It did.

But I am getting ahead.

04 **Networking**

The Need for Good Publicity

We used to call it 'Communications' but I had better use the current jargon. It is very easy for a school to become isolated and bound up solely with its own clientele, communicating largely through the direct contact between staff and pupils. The village college approach is quite different and from the earliest days I was aware not only that we needed to tell the world what we were about. Equally important was to discern what 'the world' expected of us, and how we could meet those expectations.

The Annual Brochure

One thing I learned from the Cambridgeshire Colleges was the importance of an annual brochure. But whereas the Cambridgeshire brochures were addressed largely to the potential evening class attendees I planned that our brochure would, from the start, embrace all that the college was there to provide. This meant telling readers quite firmly that at the heart of it all was the school. And that without the school there would be no 'college'. I had a feeling that in the Cambridgehire colleges the people who came to evening classes or club events had few links with the school. It was not the parents of the school kids who came in the evening; it was commuting university lecturers, and parents whose children went to Grammar School or, breathe it not, fee paying establishments. Much of this division would disappear later on when we went Comprehensive and when the school status had eventually been fully accepted by all of the community. So, the brochure went out to all parents and all organisations in the area as an encouragement for all and sundry to join things. And they did, in great numbers.

Communication with Parents

Looking first at how the parents saw us:

As we were a brand new secondary school, parents' expectations were high. With such good facilities we could meet many of those expectations. But not always. In 1963 parents complained that they had not all been given an invitation to the Official Opening. In this I was entirely on their side, but could only point out that the event was 'a County matter'. From then on, such things were handled from Sawtry!

We had links to Heads and staff of our six contributory Primary schools, and these links soon extended to the parents of those schools. Primary school parents are not a separate breed to 'our' parents; in fact many would have children in both stages of education and would see the transition from one school to the next as part of growing up. This was something that eventually could, ideally, become even more natural under the Comprehensive system. Not for them the traumas of so called 'parental choice'. So it was not long before we had a joint primary/secondary Parent Teachers Association for mutual support and the discussion of common issues. These links first grew out of the practical co-operation stimulated by the building of the Swimming Pools. Meetings focussed on matters of interest at all levels of education. Schools were also keen to display their prowess, so we had an annual Primary Schools' evening, which was very popular and had a turnout of 400 or more. They scheduled the performances by the smallest ones early on, so they could get off to bed. But the most popular event of the year was always Folk & Fireworks, when the College staff, with the explosive resources of the redoubtable Rev. Lancaster, put on a *Spectacular* on

the field. This was long before group events of this kind had caught on and our aim was, of course, to allow people to enjoy fireworks safely. There was a 'Guy' competition and, after all the bangs, people retired to the school hall for the *'Occasional Few'* Folk Group to run a fun dance aimed at the kiddies. Plus hot dogs, crisps, the lot. For the older ones, there was a disco in the Youth Centre. These events always raised a huge amount of money for equipment for all the schools in the joint PTA. Lastly, in order to seal our links with college parents, we arranged in 1965 for one of the PTA to be nominated on to the College Governing Body. This was many years before this requirement became legal, following the Taylor report of 1973. It is interesting to note that, through some of their other roles, by 1984, over half the Governing body were in fact past or present college parents

There was, however, a dark side to providing, through the joint PTA, a forum for parents of all our contributory Primary schools. In 1970, on the eve of the switch to Comprehensive education, there was a rather vocal body among those parents who resisted the idea of being sent to a small Comprehensive, and one that lacked a Sixth Form. These parents felt that in regarding the transition at 11 to Sawtry as a natural progression we were in fact somehow suppressing their 'choice' to go, instead, to the Comprehensive 'up the road' that was based on the old Grammar school. As one would expect, the press made a field day out of this. But, thanks to LEA support, we survived, strengthened in our desire to make a success of the transition.

The EVENTSHEET

Links to Youth and Community were given practical expression in the EVENTSHEET. This began in 1971 as a termly update to our annual brochure. It was open to anyone to include events that needed publicity. In fact, most of these events were member group events at the college – many of them taking place every week. EVENTSHEETS would go out to via Community Association member groups, of which there were soon over 50. We had no costs for postage as their representatives visited their college pigeon-hole (former Post Office sorting racks) to pick them up. All School parents got one, and this would sometimes combine with one of our regular parents' newsletters. In this way parents were made aware of all else that was going on. Conversely, the community at large became aware of what was happening 'in school'. Finally there was also a distribution of EVENTSHEETS to villages via school pupils so that nobody was missed out.

The Entrance Hall

Long before it became commonplace in schools we sought to make our main entrance a place of welcome and information. Straight ahead was a bold notice telling people that this was far more than a school (see page 51). Then there was a *'What's On'* board with all the Special Events of the week. All the regular events were listed outside the community office a few yards to the left. To the right, at the back of the hall, were easy chairs, a low table and the latest handouts. This was a convenient place to wait to meet someone. There was a cabinet with displays of work - school or community - and moveable panels along the back of the hall for some current exhibition. These panels were adapted from American air base surplus. In this way we hoped to ensure that everyone entering the building felt at ease, despite the continuous comings and goings that must be part of the life of any community college.

Gatherings

Annual fun events soon became part of our way of communicating. One year, 1971, the bizarrely named *'Sa-Ha-We'* was a church-led Sawtry Harvest Weekend. Sawtry Feast Week every June was already well-established but we were able to give it full support including hosting their annual old folks' supper and entertainment. But the really big annual event was the **SAWTRY SHOW** – where all organisations put on a display or a stall or a competition. The biggest player on the organising side, besides George Chaney, was Mrs Lee-Smith the Hon.Treasurer. Then there was **YOUTH IN ACTION**, where the various youth clubs each put on a stunt before a large audience. One year the Scouts put on a 'rock climbing' display using the caretaker's scaffolding units in the corner of the hall! In 1973 we staged a big exhibition of OLD SAWTRY and, I think, from this evolved the Sawtry Historical Society. We also had all the usual events like evening class enrolment evenings, careers evenings, 'Meet the Teachers' evenings and of course concerts, plays and musicals.

Bookings of the college embraced an ever-wider section of the community. On most weekends there would be at least one big event, like a dance, a dinner, a conference or a wedding reception. All these events, quite apart from their main purpose, were valuable occasions in which people were communicating with each other. They came for one thing but, while there, they might well discover other things that were going on. And so the network of involvement grew apace.

One further piece of networking in 1975 was the agreement that we had a representative of the Community Association on the Governing Body. Thus the governors were able to recognise the 'clout' embodied in that Association. Recommendations could be put before the governors although the final decision-making powers remained with the governors themselves.

Open all hours... our winter plumage!

Christmastide at Sawtry Village College

For us, as a community college, this was always one of the busiest times of the year. There were the usual end of term events found in most schools, concerts, shows, and pupil parties. As we grew, each Year Group had its own party in a style suited to their passing tastes. Having a splendid hall and other big rooms and, most of all, a supportive staff, these were good times.

Many groups of the community homed in on the facilities for annual events of all kinds, dinners, dances and pantomimes, booking main 'slots' like weekends and Bank Holidays fifteen months ahead. But the Community Association itself reserved New Year's Eve for its own very popular Ball.

Thanks to the volunteer Swimming Club, the pool, once it was heated, often remained open in the winter as long as there was demand. Some years we even ran an unofficial opening for an hour on the morning of Christmas Day. Jack Cullup the indefatigable Caretaker was happy and his son Bernard would stand duty as Lifesaver.

Lastly, to cheer people up through this dark time of the year, from 1 December to 31 January, we brightened up the front of the college with a big string of coloured lights linked in the middle to the top of the flagpole.

05 **Events, events, events**

Life in Sawtry was an endless amalgam of events, school, adult, youth, community many of which were interrelated. To separate them all out would give an unreal picture of what went on. So, in this story, I have interspersed many things just as they happened and in the words that we used at that time.

Throughout these accounts I have quoted from various contemporary documents, such as Parents' Newsletters and the Community EVENTSHEETS.

Parents Newsletter • 24 October 1963

Only a month after we opened.

Swimming Pool

Although we are just about to face winter, it is very important that we should not delay thoughts on this subject until spring. If there is enthusiasm among parents for a pool then this is the moment to express it. I am preparing some detailed proposals which, with the approval of parents, I hope to put before the County in a fortnight's time. The question of a swimming pool is not a new one in Sawtry and I am glad to say that Mr Hall, Head of the Primary School, will be present at the county meeting so that we can, between us, explain the various schemes we have in mind.

Some community involvement did not get off to a good start. But below is an example of our taking things in hand and finding economical solutions.

Wardens Report to Governors • 5 May 1964

Fitzwilliam Hunt Farmers' New Year Draw

At this event some 225 cars came and some parked on and damaged the newly sown grass. The Architect had said that they should pay £78.19.0s for remedial work. But the county office had been very slow in sending out a bill. Meanwhile we had all put up with the mess. So we took action and arranged for our groundsman to do the work. Cost in overtime and seed: £10.

The Village College Hire Form

I discovered that the county had no hire form so, in this as in so many things, we started from scratch. In the preamble, we sought to set a positive helpful tone:

The Village College is a centre for educational, social and cultural activities, and the Governors welcome the use of the premises, subject to the Conditions in these Notes.

Parents Newsletter • 5 February 1964

James Blades Recital

...a concert by Mr James Blades demonstrating many interesting varieties of percussion instruments... mainly for children (free) but adults may come...

He was a local resident and the most famous percussionist of his time. Now we have, living locally, Evelyn Glennie. So again, we have people who make an impact!

Open Evening

… Mr Coward of the Addo Calculating Machine Co will demonstrate some modern methods in mathematics…

Sawtry ahead of the pack, even then.

Note to Staff • 22 May 1964

Spanish visitors

This is just a warning that we shall be having a top level visit from the Spanish equivalent of the Deputy Minister of Education. A party of 3 plus interpreter, liaison officer and Mr Currey, our Director of Education.

We were the showpiece of the county!

Wardens Report to Governors • 5 May 1964

School activities

Among the school activities of the term two highlights were the formation of a Motoring Club (with the purchase of a car for £10) and the US Air Force Alconbury running a First Aid course for Duke of Edinburgh Award pupils.

Governors Meeting • May 1964

Use of Playing Fields

The Governors considered that so long as the use of the field on Sundays did not take place during the time of the Church Services there was no objection.

Parents Newsletter • 16 September 1964

Swimming Pool

I am glad to report that the Barbecue last term raised £43.11s 2d. Ambitious plans are now well in hand for our bigger pool and, thanks to a grant from Huntingdon Rural District Council, we hope to start some of the work almost immediately. It is, however, most important for all children in the school to be encouraged to contribute regularly towards the fund. It is only by showing the County Authorities that we are willing to share the cost that we shall get the grants we would like. All organisations which hope to use the pool are, between them, asked to raise about £900.

Parents Newsletter • 11 January 1965

Film Society

Friday 5th Feb. Inaugural meeting of Sawtry Film Society…

We look forward to your attendance at this society, which will be providing very good value for money. Our first film: 'Seven Brides for Seven Brothers' begins at 7.30.

The nearest cinema was ten miles away, and of course not everyone had TV.

Lettings
Hunts Federation of Women's Institutes. The Warden said it would be difficult to control noise on this occasion since the meeting clashed with a meeting of the Youth Club…

American Day Camp
Held on the school playing field from 2–13 August… very well organised and had caused no difficulty whatever.

Note to me from a stressed teacher.
Surely for examination marking and reports and grade sheets nine working days is a bit steep! (Nonsense. Time enough – In fact 3 weeks - if you start marking straight away!!)

What do we pay? – a meditation on hire charges

All our events involved dealing with the wider community, and this interaction has its business side as well as its social side.

As soon as a local authority opens the school doors to allow use of the place by people other than pupils, it has to make decisions about charges for that use. While this may seem a small matter to those involved purely in school affairs, it matters a great deal to those who aspire to make use of those facilities. Many and various have been the schemes of hire charges devised by councils. All of them present something of a challenge to those who run village colleges. As I saw it, my brief as Warden was to encourage maximum use of the place with maximum community involvement. Am I a business manager or a social worker? An accountant's view might be that all use involves extra work, maintenance and deterioration and so merits a commensurate payment by the users. The third approach, which cannot be financially quantified, is for someone to decide what, overall, is the **community gain** by letting these events happen.

In my early years at Sawtry the county rule was that if a use was, broadly speaking, 'educational' it got in free or for very little money. There might be a small payment for caretaking/cleaning, paid by the county in respect of evening classes and youth club, plus something for heating/lighting in the winter months. An actual hire charge only came in when so-called 'outside groups' used the place and for them there were two levels of charging depending on whether their activity was deemed 'educational' or 'social/fund-raising'.

From a village college standpoint I felt that 'outside groups' was a misnomer, since, to us, they were all part of one community and our role was to facilitate community development. But community does not necessarily extend to having free run of the place, as seemed to be the case in the neighbouring county of Cambridgeshire. I found that people in our area were so pleased with the bright new facilities of the college that they were quite happy to pay something for what they got. And so all were happy. Groups like the (private) nursery school, the 'over sixties' afternoons and the Blood Donor sessions all got in more or less free because I had a feeling that the red tape attached to any categorising of these things would far outweigh the fees gained by the county!

Over the years, Huntingdon county policy came to recognise the benefits of increased community use both to them and us and, in the 1970s, they decided that at the end of each year they would rebate to us 50% of all lettings fees collected. Over £800 came back in the first year. The money was placed in the Governors' Reserve Fund to join other monies, which we were regularly collecting from all our fifty plus member groups. This was money relating particularly to the insurance cover that we provided. This windfall had a very positive effect on morale; we spent the money on new stage curtains and a fitted carpet for the Adult Common Room. It also encouraged us to seek even more lettings, which in turn brought in more money to the county.

In 1974, when we became part of the new county of Cambridgeshire, all this changed. At first we were instructed to go over to the old Cambridgeshire system of *'Affiliate and then come in free'*. This was firmly rejected by our Community Association, who handled these issues on behalf of the governors. They decided that they would prefer to continue to pay over the odds at the 'Hunts' rates, with the Association retaining most of the money so gained for internal improvements. Among those improvements was a key investment in a set of computers for school and community use. This, at a time when computers were almost non-existent in schools. (Yes, there was such a time.)

Unfortunately this situation was not to last, since financial stringencies at county level meant that Cambridgeshire felt obliged to cease their generous scheme and require all schools to pay charges direct to them. While this caused great distress in the colleges in the former county of Cambridgeshire we, who had always been used to paying up for much of what we got, did not mind too much. But of course we lost the direct income. Later, Cambridgeshire did give rebates, but only 5 or 10 per cent.

Gift of a Portrait

When, in December 1964, Huntingdonshire County was wound up, we were given, from their council chamber, a large portrait of Sir Charles Heathcote, who had been their first chairman in about 1870. Heathcote had lived at Conington Castle, and Conington Church is in the background of the picture. The portrait got a place of honour at the back of our hall. (No, he was not the Warden's grandfather.) On occasion, in Assembly, I was able to expand on the connection. For centuries Conington Castle had been the home of the Cotton family who were great collectors. In fact their library later became the foundation of the library in the British Museum where all his early works are labelled Cottonian Manuscripts. The most famous of those manuscripts was the Lindisfarne Gospels, one of the most precious books in the national collection. It is nice to think that it lay in our catchment area for centuries...

High Alumina Content Beams

I think it was summer 1965 when the 'HAC crisis' reached us. Nationally there had been a panic that many recently-constructed buildings had weak beams due to a faulty concrete mix. So, during the summer holidays, a complete new set of beams was inserted into the two-storey section of the school. The engineers did a splendid job so that there was no disruption at all. In fact you have to look closely, over the skylights in the 'Amphi', to find where the new beams are. This was a 'lesson' for us all.

Make it yourself

It is in my view a fundamental of village college philosophy that most of the initiative for community development must come from within the community. And this can start with the smallest things within the school itself.

To quote the Plowden Report:

'It should be the object of every school to do all in its power to add to the beauty of its equipment and environment in exactly the same way as a householder… will make such constant additions, improvements and adaptations as his means allow to the home and garden in which he lives.'

In Sawtry we sought to go one better, making the place not just more beautiful but also more serviceable.

Perhaps it was the underlying influence of the farming community, which surrounded us: people who, when they wanted some improvements, often got on and did it themselves. Their tremendous practical response in building the swimming pool set the tone. When we wanted a Livestock Unit for Rural Studies and county money was not forthcoming, we went out and bought an old 'Prefab' and kitted it out from our own resources. Later, when we needed it as a teaching space for metalwork, it was upgraded, again all on our own resources. Then we converted what had been designated a 'drying room' into a well-equipped photographic dark room. Schools never have enough storage space and the back of one room had its needlework cupboards extended by the Craft Department. And, as the ceiling was double height, they added stairs and a top room, for all the drama clothing and props. The school stage was a big, dark area and, as we were short of classrooms, by adding a console at one side and a stack of chairs, presto! We had given ourselves a TV viewing room.

Weekend dances needed access to toilets but school design meant that the only access to the 'Boys' was via the open-access classroom area. So, we arranged to steal a strip of space off the 'Girls', and run a short-cut passage to these facilities. Then there was the provision of a mezzanine room as a small study area for our budding Sixth Form. And underneath was the Adult Common Room bay that became the Community Association Bar. There was a trap door between the two but the students never got wise to this… or did they? Then, when the county gave us a year's supply of paper towels, to save money, and the only storage space was the boiler house (!) we built a loft in the boys changing rooms out of scaffolding poles and planks.

For many of the internal improvements the credit must go to the school Practical Studies Department. They converted the old cloaks area into the *'Amphi'* – a carpeted amphitheatre space where one could then gather a whole Year Group. Three sides were screened off and a ceiling fixture was arranged so that one could project slides or films. This was something now found in every classroom but then perhaps one of the first such arrangements in any school. The large heavy cloakroom seats, designed no doubt for sitting on while you removed your wellingtons, were recycled as very useful stage blocks. In their own department the 'Crafties' converted a seminar room into a mini lecture room, with tiered seating giving maximum viewing for demonstrations. Resource and display areas were all home-made and when they needed storage for their large collection of materials, for both school and adult projects… they built extra spaces outside. We were grossly over-provided with bicycle sheds – no-one cycles on the Great North Road - so they converted these into storage, mainly for our fleet of canoes, trailers and boats used by our school sailing club, and for large stocks of wood, for both school and adult use.

Some further examples: building canoes from scratch, making display cabinets, loudspeakers for the stage, bookshelves, floodlighting the playground for youth club evening sports, kiosk and seats for quadrangle, making an outdoor climbing wall, adding staircases, murals, - a complete one inch map of England and Wales - art room easels, weather station, making a mobile sound and vision unit - the *'Multi'* - and, biggest project of all: saving up for, and driving a large minibus: the *'Omni'*. The latter was to be later joined by a full size Sawtry 44 seater bus – to take whole classes here and there, frequently to the Lakes and once, in holiday time, to Sweden.

Activities every week
There are approximately 62 activities taking place at the College in an average week. About 1200 people use the facilities each week. This is over and above all the school use.

Organisations:

Sawtry Football Club
Branch Library
Youth Club
Scouts
Young Farmers Club
Glatton Drama Group
Tennis Club
Cricket Club
Judo Club
Swimming Club
Badminton Club
Photography Club
Discussion Group
Nursery School
Infant Welfare Clinic

Classes:

GCE English
GCE Maths
GCE Art
Woodwork
Mixed Crafts
Ballroom & Old Time Dancing
Dressmaking
Basic Dressmaking
Shorthand
Audio Typing
Learn to Swim
Improve your Swimming
Swimming for Adults
Parent Teacher Association
Silversmithing/Jewellery
Ladies Keep Fit
Ladies' Afternoon
Welding (3) at Ag.Centre
Golf

06 **Comprehensive prospects**

First intimations: 10/65

10/65 was the title of a government directive that went out in late 1965 to all LEAs. Henceforth all secondary schools were to be reorganised on Comprehensive lines and LEAs were instructed to draw up plans for government approval. Huntingdonshire, under Ian Currey, Director of Education, were proud of their education setup and keen to make a good job of the transition, though other counties dragged their feet for many years. The Huntingdonshire Plan was drafted and implemented within five years.

In the current view Comprehensives had to be large and so Sawtry presented them with a problem. People said that to provide the full range of courses, an 11-18 school must comprise at least six forms of entry at age 11, each form being a class of 30. (6FE). Total entry: 180 pupils. Sawtry, as a Secondary Modern, began as 2FE but soon became 3FE. With a full intake and local population growth that would soon enable it to provide a Comprehensive base of 4FE. But this was still too small a basis for an 11-18 school.

However, it did provide a perfectly reasonable basis for an 11-16 Comprehensive and this was the proposal eventually agreed for Sawtry. Catchment area pupils would all come to Sawtry for five years and then transfer to 11-18 schools for Sixth Form studies. Long term, with further population growth, Sawtry could become 11-18. But there was a world of difference between an administratively neat plan and the perception of that plan in the eyes of some parents. One is tempted to reflect on the dictum in George Orwell's Animal Farm: *'All Comprehensives are Equal. But some are more Equal than others.'*

The years to come were traumatic. Support for the new setup was not universal, although among those familiar with the school and its wider community role we had many friends. But some of the Primary School parents were most agitated. *'How could we possibly provide their little ones with the same education as that ex Grammar school up the road?'* The general educational arguments about balance of intake and access to resources cut little ice with them. A parent of an eleven year old has only one priority: be sure to get the best for their child. Ironically, it was an open forum of our (joint) PTA in 1970 that gave them the platform to air their grievances at a packed meeting. To our joy the biggest outcome was our supporters getting up a ***'Save Sawtry Comprehensive'*** petition. In four days parents, under Victor Powers' leadership, got 940 signatures. For our part we concentrated on building up what would be a firm Comprehensive foundation in readiness for our first 'Comprehensive' intake in 1970.

Governors Meeting • 31 January 1967

Comprehensive reorganisation

The Warden reported that the Governors of Orton Longueville Grammar School had recommended that (all) pupils from Sawtry Village College be transferred at the age of 11 years. This would mean that there would be NO pupils for secondary education at Sawtry. The Warden would shortly be attending a meeting to discuss this and would do everything he could to counter such a proposal.

At least we knew what we were up against! It was a good starting point for the traumas of the coming years.

07 **School out of doors**

To get back to the children. While classwork is the core of any education we also promoted strongly many aspects of work outside the classroom. These were particularly useful for children whose experience of the wider world had so far been rather limited. It is through such activities that pupils can expand their personalities and relate to others in many new ways.

In-school-time activities

Originally we timetabled these for the whole school on Friday afternoons. But the fact that they were held simultaneously meant that keen youngsters were limited for choice. And there was always the problem of 'the rump' - those who didn't go for any of the options. So, in common with most schools at that time, we reverted to normal lessons on Fridays and used time after school. The long lunch break was filled with such things as swimming, badminton, table tennis, chess, gymnastics, modern dance, film unit, cookery, Young Farmers, art, painting, paper sculpture, woodcarving, pottery, choir and all the usual sports team practices and matches. And library. Informally, many others would just be busy in classrooms or practical rooms. The fact that lunch soon needed two sittings meant that nobody need miss out through hunger! And of course most people, being bus pupils, stayed in school at lunch time. This was never a school where the midday mantra was *'everybody out'*. Provided you had good reason you could be in, and usefully active.

Letter from County Office • 3 March 1967

From the days when lessons beyond the classroom were considered unusual.

Educational Visits

...advance notice of educational visits is asked for from all primary and secondary schools in the county. Since some schools may not be aware of this we take the matter up with schools concerned as and when it arises... we hope to issue something in the nature of standing instructions later.

Outdoor Activities

OA week: the last week of summer term. This took extramural work a stage further. The trips themselves were nothing unusual; our claim for attention was in the fact that around 80% of pupils opted to participate for up to seven days residential. As I wrote in a Report at the time: *'It is not just a case of the keenest going out. We also take the shy, the diffident and the incompetent. These are generally the ones who benefit most'*. Activities in those early years included, first of all, many whole day trips from school itself. Then there was camping in the school grounds. Going further afield was the goal for many: Barge & Canoe cruises on Midlands canals, Youth Hostelling and walking in Wales, the Peak District & Isle of Man, Mountaineering in these areas plus Lake District and the Cairngorms. Conservation Corps work, Overseas trips to Austria, Luxembourg and Germany.

Residentials in school

Within our own establishment we were able to run residential courses using camp beds in the classrooms and staff kindly doing the cooking, using the facilities of

the Domestic Science room. Pupils then did the washing up. We had regular annual weekends in school for First Year pupils. Many pupils had never been away from home before, certainly not without their parents. As some wag once said: *'If kids get excited and don't sleep on first nights away, why go elsewhere and pay lots of money? Get over this stage at school!!'*

Apart from our own use of the college as a base, we were able to open up this idea to a wider market. For some years the Art Weeks, in the week after the end of the summer term, were open to pupils from all over the county and were well supported. Martin Shaw, our Art master, recruited fellow staff from other schools and intense activity and a high standard of work were interspersed with evenings of relaxation in discos and the swimming pool. Catering was in the hands of some of the usual school meals staff. And there were similar county sports weekends, again residential and given to intense activity under staff from across the county. Also youth activity weekends run by the county youth staff. Why did all this catch on? Because, as a village college, we would admit to few barriers against any desire for legitimate activity!

Letter to County • 29 January 1969

Use of county equipment for Residential weekends

As you know there is increasing interest in short term residential courses held on school premises eg Mr Lumley's athletics weekend, our Art week, and various youth courses are now well established.

One practical problem is the provision of bedding, and a great deal of chasing around is necessary. Last year, blankets came from Civil Defence but this source has now disappeared. I have already bought privately, for the Kings Cliffe Project, 28 frame beds. I also have some 20-30 of the older county camp beds for which we have our own foam mattresses...

It has been suggested that the new Grafham Water Centre has the accommodation required... and that we should go there. While it has the accommodation, that centre does not have the practical facilities that we have: art rooms, big changing rooms, swimming pool or sports fields.

MW Dybeck. Warden.

The result? We bought all our own stock and continued as before.

A Postcard • 1965

From the North Wales explorers to Mr Dybeck...

Dear Sir, We are having a smashing time. Today has been raining all day and I got soaked. Tomorrow we are going to climb Penyroleuwen. The hostel and food at Idwall is nice. It's hard work climbing rocks all day. Jillian.

The Kings Cliffe Project

This was a residential week planned to put into effect principles outlined in the Newsom Report (1963) *'to give pupils the experience of living and working together in a small community'*. We were able to set up our own residential centre by renting a redundant Youth Hostel at Kings Cliffe, some 15 miles north of Sawtry.

In 1966 we found that the YHA were giving up this Youth Hostel. We planned to take senior pupils there for a five-day experience looking after themselves under supervision and doing local geographical and other surveys. Costs were minimal but we had to collect together all the necessary furnishings and equipment. First trial weeks were a great success but, to be viable, we had to enlist other schools and so share the running costs. There was strong support from the Hunts Secondary Heads Association and we became the co-ordinating body for a consortium of schools who followed in our wake. In 1967 eight school groups visited and ran their own programmes. This could potentially rise to between 20 and 30 weeks a year.

The YHA wanted an outright sale and so the project was put before the county who, at that time, had no residential centre. They were not able to come up with the cost of buying the hostel (£6000) and so the project was terminated. However, the experience provided a useful model for their subsequent purchase of part of an old Primary school and Craft Centre, which became the Stibbington Residential Centre, which we, like others, then used. A 17 page report: *'Residential Weeks at Kings Cliffe'* was published.

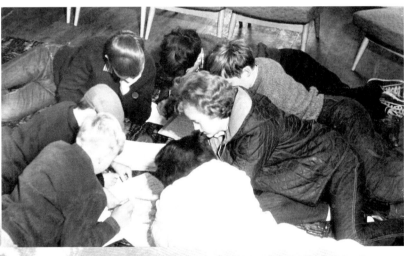

Studies at Kings Cliffe

Canoe Club

Although Sawtry was not on a river, we were aware that there were at least 40 miles of canoe-able waters within ten miles, and 200 miles within 20 miles. Most of this was in pleasant country and, under certain conditions, presented exciting challenges.

In the first seven years the club built wood & canvas/plastic boats and ran weekend excursions. In terms of 'man/miles' the record progressed from 1964: 180 m/m to 1969: 1245m/m.

More important than the total mileage was the fact that over 123 people had been out for the day and been introduced to a new sport. The club was not only for school pupils and on one trip they had three staff, Primary pupils from two schools, Secondary pupils from two Secondary Moderns and one Grammar School with ages ranging from First form to Sixth form.

Interest in the more advanced aspects of canoeing led to the formation of the Proteus Canoe Club, which, like the original club, had regular sessions in the Swimming Pool.

Later on the school club moved into the fibreglass age and, under the tutelage of Malcolm Coulson and Brian Parkin, made many boats in the School, bought a trailer and travelled far and wide, even to France and Sweden.

The Brathay Connection

In the 1950s I had been Chief Instructor at the Brathay Hall Centre in the Lake District. Brathay was founded as a charitable institution to provide outdoor courses in what we then called character training for young men aged 15 to 19 mostly in industrial employment. Brathay also had a wing, the Exploration Group, that ran expeditions in the Lake District and worldwide for apprentices and school pupils. Later, Brathay also developed a Field Study Centre, the first in the Lakes.

I retained my connection and Sawtry was able to use the place as a base for many of its own excursions. The Exploration Group huts were useful but groups also used the campsite. Staff and pupils joined in some Exploration Group expeditions and activities including film making with my company, Explorer Films.

One year the main Brathay Hall courses were able to help out; we had a particularly trying boy whom I had to suspend, a very rare occurrence at Sawtry. Our county offered 'Outward Bound' places every year and I was able to persuade them, and my friend, the Warden of Brathay, to take on Arthur for a month. But first I had to persuade his parents to let him go. This I did by calling on them with my 16mm projector and the 'Explorer' film on Brathay courses, which I had recently completed. For the boy this was not a 'reward' but a challenge, which he took well.

Alan Stevens was one who took geography field trips to Brathay liaising with their Field Centre staff. I recall one girl's excited writeup after studying some pond life: *'The water was full of little orgasms!'*

Thanks to our school bus and other transport help I recall that one summer we had almost 100 Sawtry students simultaneously in the Lakes; some at the Huts, some on the campsite and some in the nearby Youth Hostel.

08 **Our Swimming Pools**

The planning and construction of two indoor heated swimming pools can be noted as the first major project that involved a whole range of community agencies. In 1963 Sawtry Junior School was already working towards a small pool and this they intended to put inside one of the classrooms made redundant by the move of senior pupils to the Village College. At that time it was Hunts county policy to offer secondary schools five sevenths of the wherewithal to build a larger, but open-air, pool. Competence in swimming did not just improve fitness; water would become less of a safety hazard – an important consideration in fen country. Such was the interest in swimming that it seemed reasonable to aim for an indoor all-year-round facility which embraced both pools. At the time there was no *indoor* pool within 25 miles, including Peterborough, Huntingdon, Cambridge and Oundle. The nearest low budget indoor pool structure was 30 miles away in Norfolk. I visited it to get ideas. Ramsey Secondary Modern School already had an outdoor pool and this served as a model. The pool cover was a farm building design from Bristol:

appropriate enough since our Young Farmers were the ones who put it up, with the youth club fixing the translucent fibreglass cladding. Work was organised round two committees: the Fund Raising Committee and the Works Committee. Both drew in people from local schools and community with the Head of Sawtry Primary School leading the former. The latter was a practical group, recruited from the whole community. This met at weekends to work on site in all weathers. School pupils also did their bit, turning out in old clothes and painting the steelwork. We were fortunate in having, as technical adviser, Mr Bill Ferrar, Clerk of Works from nearby Oundle School, my old school. School parents from both Sawtry schools were able to play a full part in the work and this led naturally to a strong bond and the formation of a joint PTA with the Primary School.

Specification

The pool specification may be of interest. As a teaching pool it had to take up to 30 children under instruction. It had to have a shallow end (3ft) and be wide enough (30ft) to take plenty of beginners. A sloping bottom is useful to accommodate different pupil heights but a deep end (10ft) is essential for diving. The pool length (66ft) was regarded as the minimum for a proper pool and that made sense for swimmers doing lengths for racing and for fitness. A 10ft depth allowed us to have not only a spring board but also two fixed boards going somewhat higher. The large flat deep end was ideal for sub-aqua work. We also incorporated into the building the Primary school's 'Purley' pool (33 x 17 x 3ft) which further increased the teaching value of the space, being just right for small children, or handicapped groups for whom the water level could be lowered. The whole was enclosed in a 'Spanmac' steel and 'Filon' fibreglass structure and the translucent cover meant that one got best value from the sun. At first, heat was retained overnight with expanded polystyrene panels laid on the water for cover. Soon, thanks to local skills, the water circulation was linked to the school boilers. Thank you, Norman Hardy. The air was heated in the winter by a Calor gas blower heater. Including all the later community-funded additions the total overall cost was under £11,000 against a professional cost at that time of perhaps £60,000.

Letter from County PE Organiser • 16 January 1964

… a size of 66ft x 30ft is in fact a very modest size indeed, and there is no reason why this should not be covered in. If there is to be any diving there will have to be a deep end, and I know Mr Currey is personally extremely anxious that all swimming pools should be deep enough for diving.

Our fund raising and information campaign was greatly helped by a splendid 1/40 scale model of the pool complex made by Mr Walker, our Lab Technician. Placed in the centre of a Council Chamber it did wonders in showing that we were serious in our aims. And on display in school it helped all the pupils to visualise what would soon be a reality. *(What happened to it?)* When they arrived, pumps, filters, piping and steps also went on show to encourage interest and fund raising.

Plan showing the location of the Swimming Pools.

This plan includes the later developments: gallery, bigger filter plant, new changing rooms, office, toilets and disabled persons' changing room.

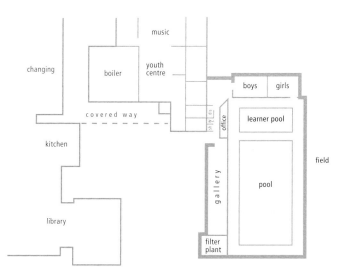

Pool use

The Sawtry pool soon became the venue for water events of all kinds. The American Air Force at Alconbury hired it, at a good fee, for air-sea rescue practice. But the alarm flares, which they used, caused a village upset when one lady's washing turned pink. The top swimmers of Oundle School came over for out-of-season practice as their pool was only an outdoor one. Fair exchange for the help we had had from Oundle not only with technical advice but also with some of their craftsmen doing weekend bricklaying.

Then there were the Galas. Many schools homed in on our pool for county events. The county Scouts also came for their competitions. The Proteus canoe club from Peterborough was established and had a regular booking. And of course our own canoeists used it a lot.

One day, Oliver Cock, the chief coach of the British Canoe Union came to demonstrate skills in front of the whole school, who were seated in the gallery. The RAF Brampton Sub-Aqua club came regularly. They liked the pool as it had a good deep end – three metres down over a good area. The Huntingdon Police Cadets had a regular weekly booking, as did the boys of Gaynes Hall Borstal. In return, they did much useful bricklaying when we needed extensions and improvements to the pool environment.

Training films for the Royal Life Saving Society were made there by Explorer Films using the skills of Keith Jackson and his Huntingdon Life Saving Club. The translucent roof made for excellent lighting conditions. In the underwater demonstration shots we were able to enlist the skills of one of the RAF Sub- Aqua Club: Peter Scoones, who later became David Attenborough's underwater photographer. I wonder if we gave him his first break?

Running the Pool
At a time when running costs are an accountant's biggest worry it is significant that Sawtry was able to keep costs well down by reliance on voluntary staffing and economical maintenance. All school swimming (classes went in every week) was covered by qualified teachers. Out-of-school use, which happened on most days, was in the hands of volunteer adults, plus qualified lifesavers, most of whom had learned their skills in this very pool. It is said that people stopped going on holidays in order to enjoy endless summer days in the pool! And some would say that occupation of this kind was a useful antidote to teenage vandalism! Educationally, the basic aim was to see that all pupils could swim. Soon this was 80%, with many pupils going on in their own time to acquire Water Safety skills. The county recognised the value of these skills (the Green Badge and the Red Badge) and, in cooperation with our Swimming Club, paid for one year's free membership. Over the years, club income, local fundraising and deals with the County over solar heating to save fuel bills led to a steady improvement in facilities: heating, better changing rooms, toilets, 'handicapped' facilities, including a hoist, insulation and a spectator gallery. By 1972 when expensive pools were springing up all over the place, Sawtry pool was still a big draw, with over 40,000 attendances a year. For the open club sessions the pool environment could safely accommodate up to 150 people in three 40-minute sessions.

Parents Newsletter • 18 May 1967

Can your child swim?
Eighty percent of the school can now swim, but I am anxious that the percentage should be even higher. Many of the remaining learners are not naturally keen on swimming, and I hope you will do all you can to encourage them to get the maximum amount of practice. Apart from the weekly lesson, they can come in every lunchtime for further practice.

... and if I was the one doing pool duty the kitchen kindly kept me a meal to eat later.

Inevitably, heavy use leads to deterioration of any structure. But, thanks to the support of County, District and Parish, major improvements were carried out on the pool and its building by the Huntingdon District Council. Their investment in it was backed by the Dual-Use agreement that assured good maintenance and a continued future for all users. The pool, on its original site, lasted 27 years, from 1965 to 1992.

Teaching swimming

In early days, when we were short of a PE teacher, I would find myself in charge of a class of swimmers. Every class had a lesson in the pool every week. As a well-qualified – but ancient – Lifesaver I was happy to stand in, though I had no formal PE training. My approach was what might be called 'mini-incremental'. Against a form list were ten tasks ranging from *1: I can go in the water, 2: I can put my head under water, 3: I can touch the bottom, 4: I can swim one width... to 10: I can swim a length.* Pupils did all but No10 in their own time, and a pupil not swimming that day would tick the list. Result: frantic activity and huge progress. Doing one's first length was a great occasion. The child would gently ease into the very-deep end and, under close supervision, strike away for the shallow end. Friends would encourage, cajole and clap…with a big cheer when the end was reached!

A similar incremental approach was used for the Royal Life Saving Society water skills training. The ten requirements were posted on big boards at the end of the pool so that swimmers could practice at any time, even at weekends. Then Peter Jones, as an Official Examiner, would test them. Soon we had far and away the largest number of competent swimmers in the county. And we were the smallest secondary school!

Swimming is not just about being good in the water. It is about all round confidence, and the 'spillover effect' into the rest of life is incalculable.

If I may indulge in relating one last water challenge – something that only came my way in the later years during some timetable crisis. Heads are often where the buck stops. This class all knew how to swim but were a bit too full of themselves. So I said *"How many of you would dare jump in from a great height?"* We had some scaffolding units and so I made up a one metre jump. All who 'dared' did it three times. Then I made it two metres. Nobody had to go on but most of them did. Then three metres, which was right up in the rafters of the pool. Most of them did it, and were that pleased!! For the record I note that the fixing stays for the scaffolding are still (in 2010) in place, in what is now the Sixth Form Room.

09 **Lots of everything**

No breakfast?

I am rather worried about the fact that quite a number of children come to school without having had any breakfast at all. This is not a very healthy state of affairs for a growing child and on a number of occasions children have felt unwell during the morning as a result of not eating any food. In some cases children make up for a lack of breakfast by eating quantities of crisps at break, and this is not a very good substitute. I urge you to make sure that children come to school adequately fed and ready for the day's activities. I realise that some of them may be reluctant to eat first thing in the morning. Or is it that they get up late? But I think their feelings on the matter are less important than yours or mine.

What's new?

Medical Alert

Dear Parents, In the Sawtry area it has been noticed that some cases of acute rheumatism are due to one particular type of bacteria which grow in the nose or throat.
... all children should be given a nose & throat swab... no cause for alarm...
G.Nisbet

Ladies Afternoon

Next Wednesday there will be the third of our afternoon meetings for Ladies, at 2.15 pm. The subject this time will be 'Choosing clothes and foundation garments.' Children under school age may be brought and left in our crèche.

Ladies Afternoons were one of our initiatives to interest sections of the community in meeting each other and discussing ideas. It was out of one such meeting that the first Nursery School began. The crèche for Ladies Afternoons was run by school pupils. Within a year we were also running, in the Adult Common Room, a weekly 'Open House' for retired people. *'Come along and have a cup of tea, a chat with friends and a read.'*

Accommodation

Two schoolmasters on my staff are both anxious to obtain sites for their caravan homes. I should be grateful to hear from any parents who can assist...

There was a serious housing shortage in the area. These two lived 'on site' for a while as I did not want to lose them.

Dental Inspection

The Dentist said that it had been a pleasure to come.

'Children pleasant. Teeth in good condition. Lovely clean mouths'.

Fifth Year Complaints
- *No free periods* • *Not enough English* • *Too much Art*
- *Too much Science* • *No time for Special Studies* • *Not enough Cookery time… and would like it to be in the morning.*

Our Union Jack?
Dear Mr Hall, I write to you in your capacity as Secretary of the Joint PTA to let you know officially that someone stole the (floodlit) flag on the night of the PTA Barbecue. Our usual practice is to charge hirers for misdemeanors of this kind but, seeing as I was the one who put the flag up, I'm not sure what I do this time. I am of course keenly looking for the culprit, and it might turn up.
Yours sincerely, Maurice Dybeck

It never did. Next time I'll haul it down at sunset!

Dear Miss Constable
I understand that there may have been some confusion over the bringing of your wheelchair into the College. I cannot image that this was intentional and I can assure you that you are as welcome as anyone else to come in and use our facilities. I gather that you did in fact come to the meeting and so there is no need for me to pursue the matter any further. MWD

Copy to Caretaker

Summer Floods
Severe flooding in July 1968 caused school closure and the postponement of Speech Day. Even houses in the upper part of the village were flooded. My son Nick canoed down Tinker's Lane.

Despite these warnings housing development continued in the low-lying parts of the village.

Sorry Christine was away on Thursday & Friday but due to the floods she was unable to get.

Sorry Colin did not come to school on Thursday and Friday, he good not get through the floods.

Taking up the story of Community Organisation from when George Chaney came on the scene.

Community Association
This Thursday we shall be holding the inaugural meeting of the Community Association… a representative body of the many organisations now using the college… to recommend how these premises are going to be used in the future.

Note to Governors • April 1970

You will recall that our present PTA representative is only (on the Governors) unofficially, and the County have never accepted this position. Perhaps this ought to be put right.

I also requested that we had a teacher Rep but Governors felt that this would be 'premature'. In fact, current rules 'expressly prohibited representation of this kind'. Plus ca change. (See page 165)

A Busy Place

From an Activities handout, 1969

You will notice that while the number of Evening Classes remained fairly static the real growth was in the number of clubs and organisations using the place. As well as the groups listed below, quite a few people county-wide found us to be a useful meeting place on occasion.

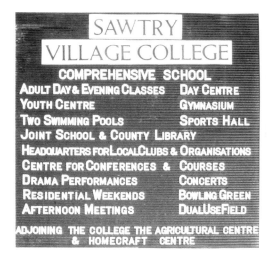

The entrance board, summarising all our roles

A busy week... but not untypical

Community Association Members 1976-77

Organisations:

Alconbury Weston Cricket Club
Army Cadet Force
Bell Ladies Athletic Club
Cambridgeshire Amateur Swimming Assoc
Cambridgeshire Fire & Rescue Service
Cambridgeshire Fire Service - Sawtry
Clarence H Beavers Lodge 124
Fitzwilliam Farmers
Fitzwilliam Hunt Branch of the Pony Club
Fitzwilliam Hunt Supporters Club
Gaynes Hall Swimming Club
Huntingdon & Peterborough Federation
of Women's Institutes
Hunts Ladies Luncheon Club for Cancer
Research
Hunts Public Services
Little Gidding Community Trust
Peterborough & District Winemakers' Club
Proteus Canoe Club
RAOB Salt Reach Lodge
Royal Life Saving Society
Sawtry & District Archaeological Society
Sawtry Badminton Club
Sawtry & District Bowling Club
Sawtry Bridge Club
Sawtry & District Cage Bird Society
Sawtry Cricket Club
Sawtry Ex-Servicemen's Social Club
Sawtry Feast Supper Club

Sawtry Film Making Club
Sawtry Football Club
Sawtry & District Gardening Club
Sawtry & District Golf Players Association
1st Sawtry Guides
Sawtry & District Hockey Club
Sawtry Judo Club
Sawtry Oaks (Football Club)
Sawtry Parish Church
Sawtry Parish Council
Sawtry Joint Parent/Teacher Association
Sawtry Photographic Club
Sawtry Pre-School Playgroup
Sawtry & District Royal British Legion
Sawtry School of Dancing
1st Sawtry Scouts
Sawtry Swimming Club
Sawtry Tennis Club
Sawtry Three Score WRVS Club
Sawtry Winemakers' Society
Sawtry & District Young Farmers' Club
Sawtry Youth Club
Sawtry Village College Evening Class Students
Sawtry Village College Parents' Association
Stilton Play Scene
Stilton United Football Club
West Cambridgeshire County Scout Council

Part two
Going Comprehensive

In September 1970 we began
our change to Comprehensive
status. The run-up had been,
to put it mildly, traumatic.
It is one thing to do well as a
Secondary Modern School or
to be a lively Community
College. It is quite another
matter to be launched into the
deep waters of Comprehensive
Education.

10 **Going Comprehensive 1970**

Policy and organisation, the educational requirements

A paper for staff January 1970.

It shows how we faced our particular challenge of evolving from a small Secondary Modern school into an 11-16 Comprehensive. This statement is intended as a general guide for all future planning. It represents what I hope is the most realistic of a number of alternatives bearing in mind (i) our unusually small size, (ii) our potential for growth over the next decade, and (iii) our unique connections as a village college.

Historical

The Village College opened in 1963 as a Secondary Modern school taking over secondary education from pupils in three All-Age schools. Selected children went to Orton Longueville Grammar school. Our staffing and curriculum were built up with the needs of the average pupil in mind. As demand grew it became possible to add courses leading to GCE O level in 10 subjects. However, after early experiments it was decided that it would be unfair to deploy a disproportionate amount of our resources on what was, after all, a 'Grammar School' exam. Fifth year work therefore concentrated on the then new CSE with the high fliers going for Grade Ones (GCE equivalent) Actual GCE work was reserved for the 6th Year. The results of this policy have been highly successful and a tribute to the teachers concerned.

Two streams?

As a two-form entry (streamed) school we have been very conscious of the fact that the A/B ability dividing line falls across the place on the scale where most pupils are found. Consequently transfers between A and B streams have often been hard to decide upon, with few children standing out from the rest at this level. Attempts at delaying selection for a year, starting with mixed ability, have been only partially successful: forms containing the full (Sec Mod) range of ability have been difficult to manage. The 1969 solution, possible because increased numbers now allow three forms, splits the ability range at a much lower and safer point, giving us two parallel forms of moderate range of ability (1X and 1Y) above the split and one below. At the top end of the school we now have over 50% of the intake staying on for a Fifth year and these have been taught successfully as a single form. It seems, therefore, that although fully mixed ability classes have not been completely acceptable, there has been considerable success with wide ranging classes where the lower ability groups are not included.

Key Characteristics

1 In so far as schools may be said to polarise towards the **egalitarian** or the meritocratic I think that this school has always tried to be egalitarian ie we try to consider all who come as of equal worth and equally deserving of the best we can offer. The child who is working flat out in 2C is as worthy of praise and recognition as any child in 4A. Education of this kind is not so much a matter of presenting them with facts and mastering techniques. It's a matter of discovering what are the real needs of each particular child and deciding how best those needs can be met.

2 This implies **personal attention** to the work of individual children; something that has always been possible with our comparatively small classes. I see no reason why our favourable staffing ratio should not continue for some time to come. One consequence of the personal attention that children get is that their individual achievement is probably greater than it would otherwise be.

3 I think it is important that we find ways of **allowing all pupils to excel**, or at least become creatively absorbed, in some activity or other. This in itself may not lead them very far but it can help their self-confidence sufficiently to make them happier in other subjects where once they floundered. In a small community it is much easier for the average child to do well - the kind of child who would pass unnoticed in a big school - provided opportunities are placed before them in the first place.

4 When it comes to **personal achievement** I would suggest that excessive comparison between pupils is unhelpful. Mark lists have their place but should not be public property. I hope we can introduce some scheme that recognises personal progress over a wide range of school activity. *(See later Achievement Award)*

5 On **rewards and punishments** we seem to have managed very well for seven years without any elaborate code. On most occasions the only necessary reward or punishment is the teacher's word, and this is as it should be. 'Ultimate Deterrents' have a very limited use, and even then, they don't always deter. If education has to be based on fear we shall not get very far.

6 Pupils' responsibilities. The old type prefect system is on the way out and we are attempting to replace it with something rather less authoritarian; something in which all senior pupils – according to their talents – can share. At the moment, because of the large numbers staying on, it has rather out-grown its size and lost its impetus. In future there will be a small and well-trained band of **Duty Assistants**, mainly 5th year, whose status will be emphasised. They will have clearly defined responsibilities assisting the staff on duty. I hope that all other senior pupils can be given responsibility in some corner or other. Lower down the school I am sure we give most pupils far too little responsibility. Many come here from Primary school where they have been entrusted with important tasks and allowed to make decisions, only to enter the big school where they are treated as just one of a class.

Future Form Organisation

Basically three stream but with the middle stream consisting of two largeish parallel forms

First Year Our first Comprehensive year. So those who are clearly A stream will go at once into 1A. The parallel 1B1 and 1B2 do work strictly comparable to 1A to allow transfers at half year or full year. The lowest quartile will form 1C but again with a chance of transfers.

Second Year As for First year but with an enlarged 2A. Again, A/B work must be kept reasonably parallel. The late developer must be regarded as normal, and the doors to the highest stream must be kept open as long as is practicable. Similarly it should be possible for someone to transfer without shame from 2A to 2B but do equally well in the long run.

Third & Fourth Years 3A is now geared towards an academic GCE in the Fifth year. During the third year the B & C forms will be asked to consider their future intentions. Late developers in 3B will have a last chance to join 3A or 4A. In year 4, most of the Bs will split into one class for CSE in all subjects and another in about six selected subjects. The C class may take CSE in one or two subjects. It is important for their self-esteem that they have the opportunity to sit for this exam. With ROSLA, all will be staying until age 15 anyway.

Fifth Year   5A takes GCE and can then go on to Orton for Sixth Form. Those in 5B who get CSE Grade Ones can also proceed to Orton. Those in 5B who get reasonable CSE grades may stay on at Sawtry to do GCE in 6A. Other pupils may stay on for a variety of reasons and we shall have to make provision for them. No A level work is contemplated at this stage.

Curriculum

Below are some general guidelines. The working out of the policy and organisation of the teaching is the responsibility of the three GROUP departments: Humanities, Sciences, Practical Studies.

(a) The curriculum of the past seven years, although designed for a Secondary Modern school, is in most instances, a very acceptable *foundation* for a comprehensive curriculum.

(b) However, it is not enough to graft a 'Grammar School' course on to the top of our current syllabus. This would be to misunderstand what Comprehensive education is all about and just replace one rigid system with another.

(c) We need to take into account the many recent changes in educational thought.

(d) Remembering that we shall in theory be including the potential genius in our intake, we ought to include plenty of 'strong meat' for the boy or girl who wants to get on. Conversely we must be on the lookout for those who fall by the wayside and be ready with individual help of a remedial nature. Programmed learning books, etc.

(e) With education for leisure becoming increasingly necessary, we are told, there ought to be some thought on what our responsibilities are in this respect.

(f) There may be whole spheres of activity not at present recorded in our school curriculum (e.g. Residential education) which we ought to 'write in' to what we do.

(g) In conventional subjects the national trend seems to be away from early specialisation. So I propose that we have a fairly common course to the end of the 3rd year with only the following variations: Begin French in 1st year but 1C French to be minimal. No French in 2C. 1st year all take General Science. Thereafter all forms take not more than two sciences. All study English, Maths, History, Geography, and RE to 5th year. Art, Music, Woodwork & Metalwork may be dropped in the 5th (4th?) year provided they are replaced with definite extra study in something else.

Buildings

Over £100,000 is due to be spent in the next few years but that will not be adequate. We must be clear about what we want, and when we don't always get it we must be prepared to adapt and improvise. I am hoping that the major extensions can be planned round the GROUP DEPARTMENT idea. Given the will and the imagination, good education need not be held up by inadequate buildings.

Where minor adaptations can be done as a school project so much the better, as long as they do not become, for pupils, a spectator sport, while teacher sweats his heart out.

Other extensions such as a Sports Hall and enlarged Youth Centre will be planned in such a way that they can also benefit the school. I have noted that there is a close correlation between government ROSLA designs and what we are wanting in both the Youth Centre and the Practical Studies suite!

Going Comprehensive in 1970

The politics behind the change

In 1970 all schools in Huntingdonshire began the transition to Comprehensive status, and this presented Sawtry with its biggest-ever challenge. Because we were the smallest secondary school in the county it was judged that we would not have the resources to provide specialised A level work. So those pupils wishing to continue to Sixth Form must move at age 16 to one of the larger 11-18 schools, based on Grammar schools. County councillors and some parents felt that a school without a Sixth Form was not a 'proper' Comprehensive, and that changing schools at 16 was unsatisfactory. In response, Huntingdonshire County Council decided to give parents in the Sawtry area the option of sending their children direct to the 11-18 school at Orton, at age 11. Free transport would be provided.

In defence of our position Sawtry Governors pointed out that such an open option could have a deleterious effect on the size and nature of the intake. Breaking all protocol I went to London and met some of the Men in the Ministry. The reception was cool and guarded. I was not even given a chance to remove my overcoat. But, I think it was worth it, judging by what they made clear to the county in a subsequent letter from the Minister: regarding *'...arrangements for transfer to larger schools where **the particular needs of individual pupils could not be fully met at Sawtry.** It was certainly not the intention that such arrangements should be such as to put in question the viability of Sawtry as an 11-16 Comprehensive unit.'*

Huntingdonshire County Council reacted to this by qualifying the choice option and asking all the 30 or so 'rebel parents' to state what was their 'particular need' that could not be met at Sawtry. In response to the government's letter their new Resolution stated *'that subject to exceptional cases of special need applications from parents for transfer to other schools be not approved.'* But most of the parents responded that as they had already been given an open option to go to Orton there was no requirement for them to state their 'special need'.

The damage had been done.

To rub things in the Orton prospectus made a point of emphasising in a separate paragraph that (all) pupils from the Sawtry area would be accepted and that they would be getting free transport.

The consequence was that the first 'Comprehensive' intake to Sawtry in 1970 was severely depleted. Of the estimated 103 eleven year olds in our catchment area only 53 came to Sawtry. (The previous year's 'Secondary Modern' intake had been 70) The Sawtry A stream had 19 girls and just three boys, two of whom were sons of teachers, one my own son. So I knew all about the parental viewpoint.

In future years councillors emphasised the revised position by stating that pupils could only opt for Orton 'if their needs could not be met' at Sawtry. Since our 11-16 courses were in all respects comparable to those elsewhere this condition was meaningless. This was realised by those who studied our courses and so the opt-outs in subsequent years began to decline. In spite of this, options to go elsewhere were still allowed.

The 'Free Transport' option was withdrawn in 1972, but not without protest and two court cases. This withdrawal caused some outrage against us. We were manipulating, the parents claimed, though the only manipulation at our end was to provide first class courses and facilities so that those who knew us well, the majority, could have no cause to think that they were being sold short. And the fact that we were actually running a Secondary Modern Sixth Form and doing some A levels – as part of our earlier status – helped to give parents confidence in our ability to teach at all levels. There were years of haggling about whether or not 'Orton opters' could take up spare places on the old 'Grammar school' transport, which still had to run for the older Years.

Then there was one other condition regarding entry to Orton: they were told they could only opt for Orton 'if places were available'. But the formula for defining available places varied from year to year so this was not a reliable indicator. One year, when we assumed that Orton was full, at 6FE, they surprised everyone, including the LEA, by reorganising their classes as 7FE, and so taking all comers.

All this time, Sawtry governors were campaigning for our status as an 11-16 Comprehensive to be changed so that we became 11-18, like the rest. But when, in 1975, our first Comprehensive year group reached the age of 16, the county refused to extend the limit, saying that Sixth Form status would only be granted *'when the time was ripe'.*

So, while the school had been steadily growing in size and facilities, thanks to a growing population, this brought the parental option issue again to the fore. Later, at Orton and elsewhere, because of declining rolls in the north, First year places were again available. On the bus issue, the fact that the county was now obliged to run a bus for our Comprehensive Sixth Formers going to Orton, meant that spare seats could usually again be available for 'rebel parents' from earlier years. So, despite our own growing catchment area population, and some ten years of growth, the school roll in my last three years showed a small decline. 1982: 667, 1983: 654, 1984: 644. The respective First year intakes were 1982:132, 1983:125, 1984:118. And because our numbers were going down, this was matched by our first-ever cut in staff. From 38.7 to 37.7

Publication of 'SEVEN'

On the threshold of the transition to Comprehensive education we produced this simple booklet as a marker of had been achieved in our years as a Village a Secondary Modern school. We were proud of all that had been achieved but those around aware of this achievement - the foundation on our rapidly-changing future based. Although it is the school achievements that are given prominence in that booklet we also stressed the importance of the village college context and the benefits brings to both school and

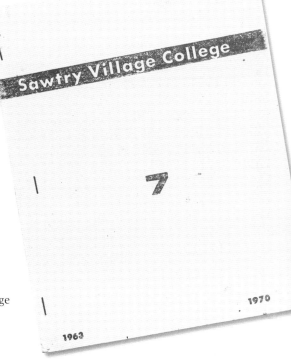

Reproduction facilities in 1970 were quite primitive and we could not afford proper printing. The booklet was typed at school and copied via the Roneo stencils – virtually the only reprographics system in use. Copies were given to all parents and associated bodies, and were available to all comers. There might still be a few copies around.

Most of the essentials from 'SEVEN' have been recounted earlier in this history but the following extract underlines the COMMUNITY dimension:

Interdependence

Special mention needs to be made of the fact that over 50% of the evening classes and events are **closely dependent on the services of the Village College staff.** *Most teachers come to work at a Village College because of the opportunities in this field and we have been fortunate in having such people to take a lead. There is also a social interdependence, which benefits many users. The foyer and the refreshment area are focal points to which all users come at some time during their evening visit. The chance to meet other people, to see other things happening, and to ask about and plan for the future are all factors that make coming to the college something more than just attending an event.*

… and in a Note of reassurance to Staff Applicants:

Class Sizes

The County has been very generous in terms of staffing and facilities and we have no classes of more than 30 pupils. Average class size is 21.

Youth & Community Work in the '70s
The Government's Milsom/Fairbairn Report

This is an extract from the County Working Party report of October 1969 on how they proposed to implement the above Report. It was the largest paragraph in the eight page report and it gave a nice boost to our morale.

'We were considerably impressed by the total situation existing at Sawtry Village College on the occasion of our visit. There was a wide variety of activity including formal learning situations, e.g. a German class, recreational activities e.g. swimming and dancing, and hobbies e.g. a winemaking group. Young and old were participating in these activities, but at the same time the Youth Centre, close by, was available for those young people who wished to enjoy the particular social atmosphere it provided and quite clearly they choose to spend time in other activities as well as in the centre. It is appreciated that a village college is intended to provide this kind of situation and also that the particular geographic location of this college facilitates this development. But this has been achieved at Sawtry without extensive leadership provision. Furthermore we received considerable evidence of voluntary services and self-help developed in the community through the efforts of the village college including the youth centre.'

11 **Publication of Comp-one,1971**

With so many people asking questions about whether, as a small school without a Sixth Form, we could be accepted as a 'proper Comprehensive' we felt it important to mark the end of our first Comprehensive year with a statement of what had been achieved. Comp-One therefore concentrates almost entirely on the school work. In terms of intake it was, of course, only the First Year that was Comprehensive, and that year was somewhat depleted.

Comp-One describes the fully Comprehensive courses that were put on for this First Year intake. The main aspects of the curriculum are explained in some detail to parents and prospective parents. Communication of this nature was something that was not common in those days. Equally important were reports on the expansion of courses in all the other years, even though still 'Secondary Modern' in intake, and our considerable successes there are indicated.

And special mention is made of the wide range of activities available both in and out of school. Distribution of Comp-One began with all the present parents and for them it took the place of the Speech Day speech by the Head. In fact by 1970 we had moved away from formal speech days and replaced them with an Open Day event when all could see for themselves what was going on and many more school people could put their efforts on show.

Besides 'Comp-One' we used our periodic **EVENTSHEET** to keep people in touch with the wide variety of activities that continued throughout these school developments

Eventsheet One • March 1971

Secretarial Service

For members of the Sawtry Village College Community Association a secretarial service has been established to assist organisations in membership. This should be particularly valuable to secretaries who require duplicated notices etc. Details from... etc

Eventsheet Three • September 1971

Swimming Pool Extensions

Once again the swimming club has been able to finance improvements to our pool and very soon we shall have a proper entrance foyer, covered access to the shower and toilets, and a large spectator gallery. All the foundation work was done by the boys of Gaynes Hall, who also added the lighting and heating to the girls' changing room. A parent, Mr Thompson, has done all the actual building. We are most grateful to all who have helped.

Gaynes Hall was the local Borstal and this was their return for their weekly use of the pool for swimming. Some years earlier they had walled up all the sides of the building. Originally we had just moveable screen infills made in the Woodwork Room. The spectator gallery was really large. For school galas it could hold the whole school.

The new spectator gallery

Small is Beautiful

In size, Sawtry Comprehensive School, at 300, is unique. All the other Comprehensive schools in the county are at least three times as big, having between 800 and 1,600 pupils each.

If there had ever been any doubt about the viability of this school it was because of its small size. Twenty years ago it was assumed that a Comprehensive school must inevitably be a large school. The arguments to support this were usually based on the fact that a certain number of pupils were needed to sustain a wide range of courses. Recent experience has shown that the needs of the vast majority of pupils can be met in much smaller schools, and an article in TRENDS, the official quarterly journal of the Department of Education and Science, underlines this view. The article describes in detail a successful Three Form Entry 11-18 Comprehensive school, and it is interesting to note that the planned curriculum at Sawtry provides considerably more than they do. From the results of research in a considerable number of small schools they conclude:

Persons in smaller institutions are absent less often, are more punctual, more productive and more interested in the affairs of the organisation, find their work more meaningful, participate more often, and function in positions of responsibility more frequently and in a wider range of activities. Higher percentages of students in small schools reported that it was easy to make friends, and that they liked all their acquaintances.

They also say that smaller schools have a higher staying-on rate into Sixth Forms, and this is borne out by our experience. In fact, even at this early stage, our Sixth Form staying-on rate is higher than the best of those quoted.

On activities, they say:

Individually, small schools participated more in both inter-school and community activities, and they were more versatile and less specialised. They also participated in more extra-mural activities inside school.

They also point out something that we have found to be very true:

The pressures which small schools are shown to exert more successfully than large ones help to contribute to a sense of competence, since whether weak, strong, inept, skilful, young or experienced, each pupil is really important. Many activities cannot continue without his participation, and the increased sense of responsibility, which this situation generates, is likely to produce greater and earlier maturity.

A small school has disadvantages. It cannot produce great numbers of examination certificates. It is less likely to offer 'minority' subjects. It has a smaller pool of talent from which to draw the one or two who hit the headlines. In spite of this, the above report and our own experience show that when you divide a school's facilities by the number of pupils, the **facilities per pupil** in the small school are at least as good as in the larger schools. It is at this personal level that we know our strength lies.

A panel from the Booklet: 'COMP ONE'
Making a virtue of our smallness.

Parents Newsletter • July 1971

Open Day

The response to Open Day this year was quite overwhelming and we had over 500 people here. Nevertheless everyone managed to get in and by all reports, the evening was much appreciated. Copies of COMP-ONE the full report of our first year as a Comprehensive school, will continue to be available so please ask if you would like a copy.

Sa-Ha-We Sawtry Harvest Weekend, 1971

An example of community co-operation as recounted by the Rector, Rev Hugh Swan

This event arose out of the need for major repairs and redecorations at the Parish Church. We needed about £1200... and it was decided to run a special four-day Harvest Festival in Autumn 1971. The council appealed for the help of the village as a whole. The aim was, on the one hand, to make use of the talents of everyone who volunteered and on the other, to cater for a wide variety of tastes so that we had sports events, swimming events, a sponsored walk, a film show, an exhibition and a concert of music and readings. All this in addition to the usual Harvest Services and Supper.

There were two 'centres of gravity': the Parish Church but also the Village College... Without the village college facilities and the generous and wholehearted assistance of its staff it would have been impossible to attempt a venture on this scale. We have learned a great deal about church-college-community partnership. THW Swan.

Toad of Toad Hall, December 1971

My Report to the Governors.

Up to now we have tended to avoid the 'showpiece' type of production in the belief that it is not relevant to the mainstream of school work and generally involves relatively few people. However, our staffing and resources are now sufficient to allow such a production to take place without detriment to normal work. In fact, it was such a success and so many people were involved that I am sure it had a beneficial effect upon the whole school. Over a quarter of the school took part. Virtually the whole staff was involved in some way or other and a particular tribute is due to Miss Clark who initiated the idea.

And, remarkably, the community production of HMS Pinafore followed only four months later.

Toad of Toad Hall

12 Publication of 'College for All', 1972

This, our third, and last, annual booklet brings reporting back into the total village college scene featuring both school and community. Like the other reports, *'First Seven Years'* and *'Comp One'* , its first aim was to assure parents, and prospective parents, that we were successfully fulfilling our role as a Comprehensive school despite being only one third of the size of all the other schools, and lacking what they would regard as a Sixth Form.

By giving, this time, equal emphasis to school and community we are 'playing a card' which the other places do not hold: the fact that pupils are being taught in an environment far less cloistered and with wider opportunities than elsewhere. As in *'Comp-One'* we also take the initiative in proclaiming the advantages of a small school: the increased chance of being noticed, and of getting into sports teams. We also point out our close links with the six Primary schools through the joint PTA and staff contacts.

Underlying all this is what we see as the overall convenience to a community of having, in its midst, a college that not only provides an education suited to all its children but also one that meets many of the educational, recreational and social demands of adults. Hence the title: **College for ALL**.

Sadly, in the eyes of some people, we had not yet reached that happy state.

Sawtry Village College
Comprehensive School

COLLEGE FOR ALL

ANNUAL REPORT 1971:2

Extracts from 'College for All'

Some 1971 exam results

Note that all these successes relate to pupils in the 'Secondary Modern' years of the school.

A level Art: Carol Branson, after only one year of study. Our first A level.

O levels gained by the following pupils: Andrew Adams, Jane Ayres, Cheryl Bullivant, Christopher Day, Sheena Donaldson, Brian Gummer, Sheila Heyes, Sheila Johnson, Michael Mason, Carol Branson, David Mundell, Denise Murch, Alison Naylor, Julia Robson, Trudie Teat, Nigel Toulmin, Pamela Whittaker, Barbara Wilson.

CSE Grade Ones by: Justin Beaumont, Paul Cox, Michael Mason, David Mundell, Zena Bowtle, Barbara Dunkley, Sheila Heyes, Sheila Johnson, Valerie Miles, Denise Murch, Trudie Teat, Barbara Wilson.

Also successes by many others in CSE, in RSA Typing & Office Practice, and in the NAMCW Child Care Examination.

Foyer Exhibitions

These were one more aspect of our emphasis on Publicity.

With over 2000 people passing through the college every week we have a great opportunity to present to them a 'shop window' of things of interest. Apart from schoolwork, which is always on show in the corridors, we have had the following exhibitions:

September	Industrial Training Opportunities – by the Training Board
October	Sawtry Old and New.
November	Road & Home Safety – by Police & Fire Service
December	Children's Christmas Books – by Foyles Ltd.
January	School Activities
February	Fabrics for Spring – by Gordon Thoday Ltd.
March	Careers Exhibition – by Youth Employment Service
April	County Archives – by County Archivist
May	Crafts etc – early entries for the Sawtry Show
June	Engineering – by Gaynes Hall Borstal boys

Sawtry Old and New

This exhibition was part of Sa-Ha-We and included Parish Baptismal registers going back to the 16th century, the Enclosure Map of 1809, many early photographs, instruments from the original Sawtry Temperance Band. There were household relics including a three wheeled pram, a 10ft baker's paddle, local fossils, Roman & Mediaeval coins, pottery, rubbings of the Moyne Brass, the first school log book and plans of the first school of 1876 and the new infants school to be opened in 1973. The centrepieces were the large banner of the original Friendly Society and the 18th Century Toll Board off the Great North Road. Later, the Toll Board became a permanent exhibit in the Library.

Achievement award

The launch of an Award in 1972 that would encourage all-round development. In a Parents Newsletter this is how we put it to the parents. Achievement Awards became the main 'prize' that we gave out annually. Every year fifty of more of these Awards were given out on Open Day. These, rather than 'top-of-the-form' certificates, indicated where approval lay.

I would like to remind you of the whole range of opportunities that lie on our doorstep. One of my reasons for doing this is to guide you into encouraging your son or daughter to take our Achievement Award.

To win the Award a pupil must do well in classwork, practical work, sport, hobbies and service to the community. The scoring is so arranged that the hard-working pupil who does his best in many things has an equal chance against one whose talent only lies in one direction. This is in line with our aim as a Comprehensive school to encourage all children equally and to reward merit of all kinds.

Classwork – Good classwork comes first and any reward depends on this. Reference is made to the Grades that are given five times a year and noted in the Work Diary.

Practical Studies – A great range of opportunities exist in ordinary lessons and pupils may decide to submit their best work for assessment.

Fitness – This recognises team games, swimming badges, canoeing and out of school activity ranging from camping to table tennis.

Hobbies – Either school clubs or home activities such as keeping animals, stamps, etc.

Service – We provide plenty of opportunities such as library monitor, register monitor or fifth form supervision duties. Also work that helps other people such as learning First Aid or helping at an old people's party.

Since achievement depends upon a desire to achieve, we do not press this Award. It is up to the pupil to ask for a record card and start collecting points.

The comprehensive struggle, some more details

Extracts from my Report to Governors 9 Feb 1972.
This was two years after the transition had begun and although, curriculum-wise, much was happening in Sawtry, there were still considerable worries about the intake.

In sharp contrast to our achievements is the continued unsatisfactory nature of our position in the county Comprehensive system. The large number of parents who still opt for the former Grammar schools is the prime indication of this...

A most serious blow to people's confidence could be the curtailment of our recently-started A level work. In the competitive situation in which we have been placed, as the only school NOT offering A level... we cannot afford not to develop them.

In the long term the problem boils down to the familiar one of intake...with two large ex-Grammar schools on each side, both in well-appointed new buildings, the choice is heavily loaded against us.

Sawtry was nearing capacity and its own main extensions, although under construction, were far from ready. But among those who did choose us we have many loyal but worried parents.

Letter from a Sawtry parent to the Director of Education

I am a parent of a 13 year old pupil at Sawtry Village College. I entered him in September 1970 on the assumption that he was coming to a Comprehensive school. Now I have no complaint about the general level of facilities offered. But these alone do not make a Comprehensive school. An essential ingredient – particularly for an intelligent boy – is the stimulus of equally intelligent contemporaries.

Thanks to the total lack of restraint in allowing parents to go to former Grammar schools he has practically no friends of his ability in his year group... Each year that you allow the intake to be severely depleted in this way you make it harder for parents to send, or keep, their children here.

Surely you owe a duty to those who loyally support the place in the expectation of a Comprehensive education and the hope of development into an 11-18 school with a genuinely equal status in the county.

Until this happens the outlook is bleak.

My interest, as Head, in our successful transition to Comprehensive status was not only educational; it was highly personal. I was also a parent, and my son, Nick, was to become one of the first batch of 'comprehensive' pupils to enter Sawtry Village College at age 11.

Christmas Eve 1972

A reminder that it was not all roses.
A phone call to my home at 4.35pm
Mrs 'J' rang.
She stated that I ought to know that there had been incidents last night involving children from 'your college' who had set upon children who went to school 'elsewhere'.
(Her own child 'H', it transpired)

This had come about because of the way I had, in 1970, somehow set them apart from the others. I replied that if there had been incidents last night between any children then she should go to the parents concerned.

She repeated...

... that any split in the village was entirely my fault, claiming that in 1970 I said that if the college did not get a proper Comprehensive intake it 'would close'

... that I had used my influence with councillors in 1970 and since to see that 'this situation' (not specified) had arisen.

... that I should now use my influence again with them to get this wretched decision over the withdrawal of (free) transport (to Orton) reversed. If nothing was done there might be more incidents, and perhaps even knifings.

I had no chance to make any further interjections. She became increasingly heated and it was difficult to follow her meaning.

It built up to a great climax at which she rang off.

Happy Christmas.

Part three
An Established Institution

Despite many ups and downs I think that one could regard the years after 1972 as ones where the College felt firmly established and in a position to develop in a variety of ways appropriate to its status as a Comprehensive Village College. In the transition to Comprehensive status we were four years ahead of (former) Cambridgeshire, to which, from 1974, we now belonged. And, as an independently-founded community college, we were aware that (new) Cambridgeshire were looking closely at how we had evolved. When they once said to me "Welcome to the enlarged Cambs!" I retorted "Welcome to the greater Hunts!"

In Part Three, I have gone away from a strictly chronological story and instead grouped events by themes. Thanks to my 'hoarding', much of this text is quoted from contemporary sources.

13 **General philosophy**

Eventsheet 11 • June 1973

Tenth Anniversary of College Foundation
This is probably what people now call a 'Position Statement'.

What We Do

We at Sawtry are very proud of the way we do things.
We believe we are in the forefront of education and of community development.
We believe in the importance of people of all ages.
We see them not as age groups or categories but as People.
People who need each other, who can help each other.
People who can give.

A quote from 'College for All'

Have you heard of Sawtry Village College?

It is a small place on the edge of a small county. But, through its staff and its activities it is surprisingly widely known. With its 70 or 80 weekly meetings or events there must be up to 2000 people who make use of the college each week.

This, apart from our school pupils. People come from the county, the city and far beyond.

Sawtry staff are involved far and wide beyond the village. Last year the presidents of both the county NUT and NAS were Sawtry staff. Staff serve on National committees and on local councils. A Sawtry resident is President of the county WI and a leading member of our Community Association.

The name of the college is to be seen in the front of over 400,000 geography books (later, almost one million) all over the world including American editions and Danish and German translations. College staff and pupils have played leading roles in the principal training films used in this country for Hillcraft and Water Safety. Films in the latter series, including RLSS Lifesaving, have been made in the college pool and pupils have starred in a whole series of Canoecraft films.

For my part I also managed to 'fly the flag' in one or two fields outside Sawtry. In my desire to foster the concept of community schools I was on the Community Schools Committee of the Secondary Heads Association, the committee of the Community Education Association, the East Anglian Committee of the Centre for the Study of Comprehensive Schools, and the Community Education Association's International Committee, attending conferences in Australia, New Zealand and USA, taking a Village College display and film to each. I was on the government Advisory Committee for Outdoor Education, and the Executive of the Commonwealth Youth Exchange Council. I was Secretary and later Chairman of the Young Explorers' Trust and a Trustee of Brathay Hall. Locally, I have been a Governor of the County Agricultural Centre, on the Huntingdon Rural District Council and, of all things, the Sawtry Internal Drainage Board! *(And, they ask, 'When was he at school?' Answer: check the records!!)*

Just bragging

Shortly after our amalgamation with Cambridgeshire (1974) and at a Heads' conference I was approached by a senior Adviser from Cambridge HQ staff:

'We have been so impressed by what we have found out goes on at Sawtry. Quite a few of our colleges could learn a lot from you'

The Academic Ethos

The following notes were prepared in 1974 for the Local Education office in reply to a prospective parent who complained that because the school was not developing out of a Grammar School it could not have an appropriate academic ethos.

It is our duty to educate all pupils according to their age, ability and aptitude. An academic education would be inappropriate for our less academic pupils – we must aim to provide all things to all people. But this includes being academic for 'the academics'.

The following are indicators of the academic ethos that we try to create for our most able pupils. In studying them, in relation to claims made by 'other places', two points need to be remembered.

1. Just because a thing happens in a school does not mean that it reaches all pupils.

2. We are born of Secondary Modern parents. The Comprehensive infant is not yet five years old and he suffered considerable malnutrition in his early years.

1 Work Standards

All pupils are expected to produce work of a standard appropriate to their ability.

2 Homework

They do homework in three subjects per night. Time allowed increases from half an hour per subject in the first year to an hour in years Four and Five. Academic pupils who finish set work in less than the allotted time are expected to fill in with general reading.

3 Extended Study

Pupils are encouraged to pursue their studies beyond the basic essentials through private study and the use of the library. We have over 11,000 books in the school and county libraries available to them.

4 Streaming

Pupils are streamed from the time they come here. The top stream is selected on academic ability by personal reference to Primary school work. We have strong links with all our contributory schools through regular heads meetings and staff meetings, visits and, of course, the joint Primary/Secondary PTA.

It is sometimes said that an academic ethos cannot develop in mixed ability classes. We agree with this to the extent that our top 30% ability group have, since 1970, been separately taught for academic subjects. This has been done with three forms in the year, in spite of the fact that, in 1970, we were still officially only 2FE *(a two-form entry school)*. This is a measure of our desire to give these able pupils the education they are entitled to. Now that we are 3FE we have gone one better and pupils in the first two years are in four classes with the top 25% receiving a thoroughly academic education.

5 Common Curriculum with Academic Approach

Though the content of all subjects in the early years is similar irrespective of stream there is, nevertheless, a strong academic emphasis in the presentation of this work to the A stream. The reason for keeping other streams roughly in step and not allowing the A stream to zoom off on an entirely separate course is so that late developers can transfer at any time, and vice versa.

6 Time Spent on Academic Work

The proportion of time spent on various groups of subjects is shown on the attached timetable analysis of A stream work. *(But not in this book)* However, it would be wrong to regard subjects as 'academic' or 'non-academic' since so much depends on how they are taught. What, for example, is Music? Our Practical Studies course includes a 'think' basis that is as rigorous as any classical subject. In fact it has been praised as one of the best in the country, largely on that account.

7 Public Recognition of Academic Merit

Academic ability is turned to public good in many ways. Last summer an 18th Century comedy was presented to the public by staff and pupils. On Open Day, the French Dept. put on a series of slides and recordings made by a senior girl for use in teaching junior pupils. Last week a First year group put on, in Assembly, a playlet on Greek myths with pupils' own verses. School corridors always contain examples of good academic work, and not just pots and paintings. Poems and other literary efforts are given the compliment of publication not in a school magazine, but in 1500 copies of our Community EVENTSHEET which goes to all our Community Association (ie college users) five times a year.

8 Speaking Competition

A speaking competition is held annually. This is an indication of the value we place on verbal communication: the need to make points concisely and attractively to get across a point of view. The value of this work is being increasingly recognised in CSE/GCE. The way in which many 'academics' are poor communicators points to the need to include this work in an academic education.

9 Examination Results

Exam results are an obvious indicator of academic ethos. See the very full report produced for HMI in February indicating our growth in GCE and CSE. But an examination of pass rates, good as they are, and entry figures is of course no proof of success unless one is aware of the entry policy and teaching philosophy behind them. However, even in that part of the school which is still, entry-wise, 'Secondary Modern', pupils are passing up to nine O levels taken from a range of 15 subjects. Although these pupils are small groups these results are an indication that an academic ethos already exists.

10 Graduate Staff

Though possession of a degree does not in itself make anyone a better teacher it is generally taken to confer in some way a measure of academic ethos. We have 12 teachers with degrees or equivalent. This is about 50% of the staff. The national proportion of graduates in all secondary schools is about 35%.

11 Influence as a Village College

Our role as a village college can contribute to our academic ethos. Pupils can see that academic learning is also valued by adults who come back in the evenings to take O levels. Older pupils can join these classes where it fits with their courses. eg Fourth Year boys come to evening electronics classes. Our 'Winter Lectures' - four lectures by distinguished experts including two professors - are open to all.

12 Travel and Field Study

Our extensive programme of expeditions, mostly in the holidays, includes plenty of intellectual stimulus. Surveying a glacier is, at its best, a pretty intellectual exercise, as is the accompanying physical geography. This year, Fourth year pupils are being offered a day trip to France, an exchange holiday in Germany, and ornithology in Shetland. These are but a few of the major trips offered. To equal this achievement one would expect a school three times our size to put on three times as many trips.

13 A Friendly Atmosphere

The staff do not simply encourage academic ideals; they also find that these ideals are accepted. It does not always follow. This acceptance is largely based upon an open friendly classroom atmosphere. We believe that ultimately people work best under encouragement rather than under stress.

14 A level Work

The tremendous desire to establish A level work is also, surely, indicative of academic ethos. We have succeeded in getting a 'Secondary Modern' pupil to pass three A levels. Others, ex Secondary Modern, have gone on from here and taken A levels at Technical College and gone on to university.

15 Staying-on Rates

Staying-on rates are generally taken to indicate a pupil's sympathy with the academic ethos of his school. Before ROSLA, our Fifth form staying-on rate was always high, around 50% of the intake. This occurred in spite of the fact that, unlike the bigger schools, we did not offer a big range of 'fancy' courses. Just good basic academic stuff.

16 The Sixth Form

Pupils have stayed on for Sixth Form work for the past seven years and numbers have varied between four and twelve. This year *(1974)* numbers have risen to a remarkable 18, which represents almost a quarter of the Secondary Modern intake. While their ability range is wide they nearly all, according to their lights, are sufficiently influenced by our academic ethos to want to stay on and gain certificates.

Conclusion

The above points describe the academic ethos, which I hope exists within this comprehensive school. But this does not describe the ethos of the school as a whole. One could equally well describe its *caring* ethos or its *adventurous* ethos. Or its *encouragement-of-achievement* at all levels. These matter to all pupils and they help the intelligent child just as much as any academic ethos.

My debt to Oundle

From a memoir that I wrote for the Oundle Old Pupils' magazine, my old school.

It is my impression that most Oundelians of my day graduated into science, business, the City, or The Empire, as it still was, and not many chose education as their career. Some exceptions, I recall, included two contemporary Sandersonians who went on to spend much of their lives as beaks back in their beloved Oundle. (Gordon Lindsay Jones and Martin Brooks)

My path was different. Oundle had taught me more than book learning. I have to thank them for a curriculum which, even in wartime, offered much to stimulate interest in creativity, leadership, and a love of the outdoors. So, though my CV lacked a top class degree, I felt I had enough skills to launch into the wider world of education and – wait for it – plump for one of those bright new Secondary Modern Schools. And it was Dudley Heesom, Oundle's History Sixth Master who first suggested the idea!

And so it was that, in 1963, with a Cambridge Geography Degree, an Oxford Dip Ed, and at the age of 33, I became Head of a brand new school in Sawtry, only ten miles from Oundle. We had a pupil catchment area of 90 square miles with 21 villages including the Giddings and Stilton. In the following 20 years the population would more than quadruple. Home-owning commuters would soon replace farmers as the dominant species.

No Oundelian can fail to feel the influence of Sanderson and, taking on a new school gave me enviable opportunities to apply some of his ideals in a state school setting. 'Look for the good in every student' was my starting point. 'Work things out for yourself' was another maxim which, in those days of far less dictation 'from above', allowed one the freedom to develop a curriculum suited to the needs of that small but fast-growing rural community. And Sanderson's idea that every boy should have creative practical experience found a place in Sawtry. In fact this work got us published by HMI as one of ten schools with a model Practical Studies Department. Sanderson's love of the outdoors also found echoes in much of our extra-curricular activity. Outdoor Activities Week happened every summer.

My school was a Village College, which meant that co-equal with the school was work with the adult community: evening, day and weekend courses, and youth work. We had the support of innumerable local community groups, for whom the College became their chosen base. Although we were not, at that time, part of Cambridgeshire, where village colleges began, we were, within ten years, able to vie with the best of them in numbers of community benefiting from our many facilities.

As for improvisation, let me tell of an early and very fruitful link with Oundle. In 1964, we planned to build a covered heated indoor swimming pool. For technical advice, design and support I was able to enlist Oundle's Clerk of Works, Bill Ferrar. I knew of his school work, finding pragmatic solutions to accommodation problems, like adding extra classrooms in the Cloisters. He did us proud and within a year we had the only covered pool within 25 miles! We even had the Oundle school swimmers doing out of season training in the Sawtry pool! The pool was also the venue for a series of films we made for the Royal Life Saving Society with Peter Scoones, David Attenborough's underwater cameraman, making a memorable contribution.

Another link, though not many present may have realised it, was in two of my Speech Day personalities. Both Lord Hemingford, OO, and Lord Renton, OO, did the honours on different occasions. And I like to think that it was probably the moral support of these two local worthies that helped us in the difficult transition to full Comprehensive status in the 1970s.

The current debate about closer liaison between state and public schools makes me chuckle. The rather arrogant suggestion that benefits would all be one way is, I suggest, rather wide of the mark. True, the hurdles can be daunting but state schools can, in many ways, open a few windows. For us, sports fixtures and concert exchanges were a start. Now, (2009) despite Oundle's high reputation in computer technology, we, or rather my successors, share ideas and aspirations in applying new approaches to individualised learning. In fact, Sawtry has again leapt forward in being one of the first schools to have very widespread use of classroom laptops. Thanks to commercial partnerships, students and staff can work online at school or at home; true 'anytime anywhere learning' they tell me. (So I wonder why they go to school!)

Lastly, there's a highly personal link between Sawtry and Oundle and it relates to the coming of girls to Oundle. We, of course, had been co-ed since the beginning of time and from the earliest days I had a very keen and supportive group of parents. In 1982 I entered two new pupils, not yet from a local address, but Tuvalu! Yes, they would be starting late in September but there was a small matter of the Queen visiting. And as Dad was, I think, the retiring High Commissioner of that remote island, they felt that they had a good excuse to stay for the party. Mum was soon a very active member of our PTA and all worked out very well. Then Mum got a new job: Housemistress of the first girls' house at Oundle! Perhaps some 'Sawtry ways' found their way into Oundle's new setup!!

Maurice Dybeck. Sanderson House 1948

The Practicalities of Community Use
My exchange with the Minister of Education

This was part of the address I gave at the Annual Dinner of our Community Association, always one of the big events of the year.

In 1977, at the National Federation of Community Associations' AGM in Stevenage, I was fortunate enough to hear the Minister of Education, Mrs Shirley Williams... talking on *Community Associations in liaison with Local Authorities*. Despite the boring title her talk was to do with things that matter a lot to the clubs and societies that make up any community association. At its lowest level the issues were about: *Where can we hold our meetings? Can we use the local school? Will it cost £105 if we book New Year's Eve? (That happened somewhere.) Can anyone help us get planning permission to convert a building for our playgroup? Can we get a grant for our sports club or our swimming pool heating?*

Shirley Williams lifted the whole meeting above these mundane problems and gave what I felt was a very encouraging picture for the future. True, there are vast problems as anyone having to pay the full cost of running their own centre will know. It's even worse for those who are paying to build new centres or extend existing ones. It's a colossal struggle for hard-working volunteers to raise money, only to be overtaken by inflation, or some impossible regulations about so-called standards of construction.

After her talk, I pointed out to Mrs Williams that at Sawtry we had solved many of the major accommodation problems by linking community association activities to the school premises. As we all know, it's crazy to build your own centre, nice though it might be, if there are suitable rooms available in the local school. In reply Mrs Williams said that nationally over the next 9 years (1977-1986) there would be a 20% drop in school population, and this was going to mean available space in schools in most parts of the country. Now in some places I guess that this idea of others moving in will be greeted with some reluctance – a second-best to having your own centre. People don't want to go back to school. And some schools are not too happy about having adults around in the daytime. But at Sawtry I hope the position is very different. Although we are far from dropping in numbers and having empty classrooms we are, thanks to our village college status, able to provide suitable space for the benefit of the local community. And it now looks as if the pattern which we have established could become a general pattern throughout the country.

This is not just a matter of vacant rooms let out to the Public by the Local Authority. We at Sawtry have encouraged participation by the users so that they control the use, set the standards, make the rules and charge the fees. With this participation goes the opportunity to contribute to the common good, both in providing extra services, like our excellent catering organisations which, under Mrs Lee-Smith and Mr Tuplin, have really established themselves this year, and the social events like tonight and the Sawtry Show in the summer. We're back to the old story that those who are prepared to club together and do something positive make far more progress than those who sit back and wait for someone else to provide facilities and grants

I'm not pessimistic about the future - whatever cuts are made from above - since we at Sawtry possess the biggest asset of all: people. As long as we have the freedom to use our limited financial resources in what seems the best possible way, then we shall continue to give good service to the community.

Compartmentalism 1978
Request from window cleaners: *'Can you tell us where the Youth Club ends and where the village college begins?'* There's no answer to that!

Promoting Village Colleges
1977 was the year of the Queen's Jubilee but it also seemed a good time to celebrate more widely the virtues of village colleges. So, through the Association of College Wardens a consortium was formed and, under my general direction, we produced, with a professional team *'Cambridgeshire Communities'* – a 30 minute film which was widely welcomed. Later I was able to 'tout' the film at Community conferences in Australia, New Zealand and the USA. Thanks to the county Resource Department we produced a travelling exhibition: *'What About Village Colleges?'* on some 42 A1 cards. This I also took round the world in the Summer and Christmas holidays of 1979. 'Cambridgeshire Communities' was welcomed by the British Council who bought copies for their libraries worldwide. I was aware of them going to Zambia, Sierra Leone and Nepal. The message, as they saw it in those countries, was that the Village College concept was one that was particularly apposite for use in countries with limited resources. An annotated DVD of that film is included with this book.

An Academic study of Village Colleges

The Village College Way
an Approach to Community Education

For the whole of 1980 I was given leave to study at the Cambridge University Institute of Education leaving the college in the capable hands of Peter Jones. My subject was *The significance of the Village College movement and its relation to present day needs*. The moment was timely since1979 had been the year in which most of the (old) Cambridgeshire Village Colleges completed their (11-16) transition to Comprehensive status, and were therefore, for the first time, regarded as schools for the whole of their local community. My study ended up in this book.

The Village Colleges Conference
1980 was also the 50th anniversary year of the foundation of Village Colleges and one of my roles was to coordinate, for Cambridgeshire, an international celebratory conference, in which Sawtry was, of course, to play a leading part. As a background paper for the Conference, the College Wardens agreed to produce a booklet of basic facts covering all the 22 village and community colleges in Cambridgeshire. The booklet: *'Village Colleges Today'* is a mine of information covering school and community numbers, takeup of classes and youth work and the special characteristics of each area. From a Sawtry viewpoint it was interesting, and gratifying, to see how we compared with all the other establishments. A summary of the key findings in relation to Sawtry is printed on page 103.

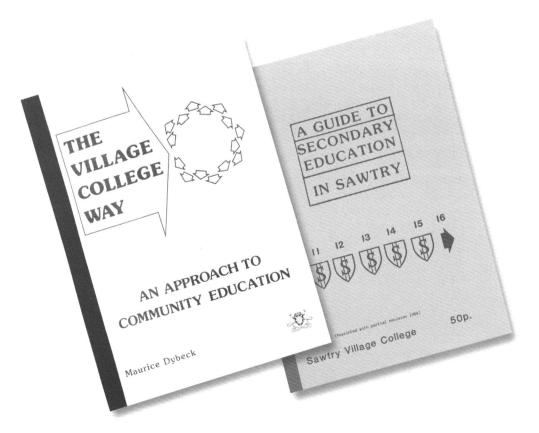

A Guide to Secondary Education in Sawtry

The Guide 1980

The 1980s were a time when there was increased interest in the content of education among parents, the public and government. Schools were soon to be required to describe themselves in various formulaic ways: league tables, basic facts, open evenings. We decided to anticipate these changes, go one better and produce a fifty page description of the courses we ran, the history of the school and its role within the village college. With, now, no immediate prospect of a Sixth Form we decided to use these requirements to go on the offensive and describe what we saw were the many advantages that lay in our status as an 11-16 school.

The **Guide** was a useful summary of where we had got to in the 18 years since our foundation as a small Secondary Modern school and now a Comprehensive with over 500 pupils. Here is the first page:

Introduction to the Guide

Schools have changed so much in the last 25 years that many people not professionally involved in education are understandably bewildered by what is going on. They may be amazed and delighted to see all the facilities and the opportunities that were not available in their own childhood. But they may also be uneasy and sometimes critical, suspecting that all this variety might have been achieved at the expense of basic learning of the three Rs.

It is almost certain that today's school organisation will be totally different to that of their younger days. They would have attended a Grammar School or a Secondary Modern School or an Elementary School of some kind. Today, almost 90% of the nation's children are in Comprehensive Schools and the percentage is increasing annually.

As a Comprehensive School of over ten years standing, Sawtry Village College seeks to embrace the ideals of both Grammar School and Secondary Modern. It has a responsibility for the education of all the children in the community. It must ascertain what are the prime needs of all children, whatever their ability, and then educate them in a manner appropriate to their ability.

This booklet could be subtitled 'A Guide for the Thinking Parent', although it is written not only for our parents but for all adults who are interested in the way we do things at Sawtry. Many parents are, of course, quite content to send their children to school and just let the teachers get on with their professional job. We respect and appreciate the trust which such parents put in us. Nevertheless, whether we like it or not, education is a process in which teachers are only one of many influences, and if parents and teachers educate in isolation from each other and in ignorance of each other's ways, we may all end up doing a less efficient job.

This booklet is the longest statement of aims and practices ever produced by Sawtry. Others were 'The First 7 Years' 1970, 'Comp One' 1971, 'College for All' 1972. Even so, it can only look at the surface of all the planning and thought that goes into running a school. Subject Syllabuses, which are the briefest summaries of what work is planned, run to over 100 pages. Staff Notes on school administration are 60 pages. A school half-year examination involves setting, writing and marking some eight thousand scripts. In any week something like 1300 lessons are taught, and about six thousand individual homeworks assessed. This booklet is therefore selective and in it we have tried to pick out the things that parents are most likely to ask about. If, as a result of reading it, you feel you have a greater understanding of what we are about and can better understand what your son or daughter is up to, then our objective will have been achieved. If your reading stimulates you into comment may we remind you that we have a Parents' Association whose prime interest is intelligent partnership in education. Intelligent supportive involvement by parents is therefore practicable and welcomed.

A few copies of this Guide might still be available.

Publication of Government's 'The School Curriculum' 1981

All schools were 'invited' to study this document and make comment. If this was to be our future guideline it seemed that we were at least 75% On Course, as I noted in this Report to our Governors. Our first response to the growing debate was this 'Position Statement'.

Report to Governors • May 1981

Curriculum

This month the seventh major government publication on the school curriculum is about to descend upon us. A number of these documents are conflicting in their advice and it is sometimes difficult for a practising teacher to be sure what is really intended. Many of the contentions in these publications are strongly challenged in the educational press and among teachers. To challenge is not to be reactionary – for few would deny that it is always worth re-examining carefully what we teach and why – and then sifting out the irrelevant, and building on the significant. Personally I feel that much of teachers' scepticism towards the new schemes stems from a suspicion of the motives of those who propose them. While it is true that the country is in a bad way it does not follow that you should blame the education system, as some do, and turn it upside down. Much of what we teach is of proven worth, and a careful reading of the 'new' schemes shows that much of what we do at Sawtry is recommended. At Sawtry, our results over the years – in terms of examination success and pupil progress – show that we are reasonably 'on course' and we shall continue to stand by our beliefs in steering that course.

Report to Governors • 5 May 1982

Governors' Visits

Mr D Williams reported on a most enjoyable visit. He had been most impressed by all he had seen. Mr Horrell reported that he had spent an unhappy afternoon at the College and had made a number of criticisms, which the Warden replied to. No further comment!

Letter from the British Council

... to express thanks for your warm hospitality to the Colombian Study Group. Everyone was most impressed by what they observed, not only the competent and effective way in which activities were being carried out, but also by the warm and congenial atmosphere which prevailed in the college from the elderly people right down to the youngest children...

So many visits of this kind, though a distraction, made it seem as if our influence was spreading wider than we realised.

14 **Activities**

A record community week

The number of special events hit an all-time high in the third week of
November 1972. The list below speaks for itself about the degree of our
involvement with the community.

- Youth Employment Committee
- School Drama Rehearsal
- Community Association Catering Meeting
- Stilton Drama Rehearsal
- Playgroup Committee Meeting
- WI Old Tyme Dance
- Parish Council Meeting
- Film Society
- Sawtry Winemakers' AGM
- Pony Club Meeting
- CSE Advisory Group Meeting
- NUT Council Meeting
- Royal Life Saving Society Meeting
- Child Health Clinic
- Sawtry Football Club Dinner Dance
- British Legion Bingo
- Peterborough Youth Service Canoeing Course
- 21st Birthday Party
- Teachers' Day Course (Drama)
- Swimming Club AGM
- County Women's Hockey Association Match
- Youth Club Football Match

On top of all this there were all the usual school fixtures, plus about
100 other regular events, evening classes here and at the Homecraft and
Agricultural Centres.

Joint PTA Meeting • January 1974

'Producing for Schools Television'
An illustrated talk by Peggie Broadhead, Producer of 'People of Many Lands'
probably the BBC's longest-running and furthest-reaching TV series.

I was very glad to introduce Peggie to Sawtry. We first met when I was a keen
young geography teacher in Birmingham and she filmed one of my classes. I had
worked with her on a few projects and she helped me in many of my films,
including, in 1979, 'Cambridgeshire Communities': the film accompanying this
book.

Sawtry Lectures 1974/5

A chance to hear distinguished lecturers on aspects of **The World About Us**

23 October	**Climbing Everest** *Mr George Lowe, one of the leading members of the first ascent in 1953*
27 November	**Discovery Of Africa's Past** *Professor Merrick Posnansky, Professor of Archaeology, University of Ghana*
14 March	**Britain's Weather** *Professor Gordon Manley, Former Professor of Geography, London University and Professor of Environmental Studies at Lancaster*
19 February	**Conservation In Action** *Mr Ray Collier, Conservation Officer, Lincolnshire Trust for Nature Conservation*

In guest lecturers, Sawtry *'Aimed High'*.

George Lowe, was one of the team of School Inspectors who visited us in 1974.

Prof Posnansky I had first met on a Brathay Uganda Expedition.

Prof Manley I had known since University days and

Ray Collier was a fellow member of the Brathay Exploration Group.

Proposed Archaeological Society, December 1975

This is just one example of the grassroots growth that was going on all around us. Our role, via the Community Association, was not to 'own' these groups, but simply to give them the encouragement to grow in their own way.

Mr T Woods, formerly of Roughs Farm, has recently presented the College with a number of items of Roman and Iron Age pottery from a site close to the village, which has never been completely excavated. Some of these are now on display in the glass cabinets in the College. It is felt that a number of people may be interested in forming a local Archaeological Society to continue the exploration of this site in cooperation with the Peterborough Museum authorities. Any person interested… etc.

Archaeological finds on display in the College

SAWTRY
VILLAGE COLLEGE

EVENTSHEET

17

DECEMBER 1974

NOTHING ON ?

Believe it or not one occasionally hears of people who say "nothing ever happens around here." I can only assume that such people live inside a soundproof concrete cube. Just to remind you all, here are just a few of the things you could take part in this winter.

If you are feeling energetic you could play football, or badminton, or join Judo. Or you could swim (the pool re-opens in January) or canoe. Those at school have a much larger range of sport open to them both in and out of hours, including walking in the Lake District.

If you want to exercise your brains we probably have one of the largest ranges of evening classes to be found in a village anywhere. This is inspite of severe financial cuts. In school the change to Comprehensive now covers ages 11-16 and a full range of courses is provided. 25% of our pupils have stayed on into our SIXTH FORM and they are benefitting from the opportunities to do courses suited to their particular needs.

Those in our community who wish to excell with their hands should find plenty to do. Our evening practical courses are very well supported, as are the popular Homecraft Centre Courses in the daytime and in evenings.

If you want to join a club or society these range from Young Farmers to Winemakers. Culture is offered by the Leisure and Arts Society and a glance at our foyer notice board will generally tell you of plenty of musical or drama presentations in the area. Do-it-yourself drama ? Join the Stilton Scene !   Films ? Join the Film Society. Talking of Drama don't forget "CHRISTMAS CAROL."

Most of us like a night out and in Sawtry you can chose according to your taste and affiliations between Disco and Ball, and there are plenty of "in betweens" as well. Our November 5th Folk and Fireworks seemed to please everyone judging by the attend- ances.

Finally for those who want to explore a little deeper into discovering in The World About Us, there are the SAWTRY LECTURES. Details of events taking place at the College are given well in advance in this Eventsheet. Further details can be obtained from the blue annual brochure or from the organisation concerned. By the way if you live in Sawtry and do not receive this Eventsheet direct please let us know.

NEW PARENTS:

Parents of all 11 year old children receive at this time of the year a letter from the County about the transfer to secondary school. All parents in the College catchment area (i.e. with children at the seven local primary schools) will be invited to the College on Wednesday, 7th May, 1975. However, if any of them have queries or would like to see round earlier than then, I shall be very glad to see them.

M.W. DYBECK,
Warden

Archaeological Rescue Dig, June 1979

Emergency! The site of the mediaeval priory by Archer's Wood is to be ploughed up almost immediately. We have permission to excavate it right up until the time it is levelled... Working parties on site each evening from about 6 pm and at the weekend... We need as many people as possible...

This site was the former manor of Sawtry St Judith and, under the leadership of Harry Milford and others, the Society did great work on the site in question. Many people helped the Archaeological Society in this work. The site was legally unprotected and was about to be ploughed up, but not without strong protests from Sawtry. Afterwards we kept a semi-permanent display of the many discovered artefacts in the 'Amphi', using display cabinets acquired from a Huntingdon draper's shop.

Parents Newsletter • 27 October 1972

Fiona Dybeck

I would not normally bring personal matters into a school newsletter but on this occasion I feel I must since many of you knew my late wife, Fiona. You have recently, by your words and actions, expressed your feelings and I can only say how grateful I am. She took a deep interest in school and community and her concern for welfare of people showed itself in many ways. To so many people she was truly one of the 'Sawtry Family'. Like all families we have our times of trial. But the stronger the family the easier it is to bear up. In this strength we are greatly blessed.
MW Dybeck.

Cancer came to Fiona in 1967 and she bore it and the treatments bravely for the next five years, continuing with family responsibilities and community interests. These included an active interest in Sawtry Parish Council in which she was Vice-Chairman. When she died our three children were aged 16 Brita, 13 Nicholas and 9 Rachel.

In October 1973 I married Marjorie Thomson, taking her away from a Deputy Headship in one of Scotland's largest Comprehensives! Soon she too was making waves in the community. In November, the PTA Folk & Fireworks included a 'Scottish Thistle' firework in her honour. Marjorie became clerk to the Sawtry Parish Council and, thanks to this and other work for WRVS, her links were not only marital! And, long before we finally left Sawtry for the North, she founded CARESCO and then proceeded to write a book about it, to which our local MP, John Major, kindly contributed the Foreword.

A note to Foyles Education Ltd • 26 November 1974

Bookswap

Order No 017/5/113. Dear Sirs, Please find enclosed Ancient Egypt. Would you please replace with Ancient Rome, as ordered. Yours faithfully, CE Laxton. Secretary

Chris Laxton was to become by far the longest-serving member of the College community. First appointed to the office staff in 1970 she soon became my right hand in administration and continued in this role with my successor, Jim Stewart, and is still in office after 40 years of service. 'Rome' was never built in a day.

Clangers

... a little light relief for readers

Clanger 1 I was new and it was a time when politically correct job titles were coming in. I had a long and friendly talk with the, er *Attendance Officer* who was at pains to point out that he was now an *Education Welfare Officer*. In comes a colleague. *'So may I introduce to you the, er* (what did he call himself?) *the Attendance Officer'.*

Clanger 2 From the earliest days we had a few shelves reserved for the County Library, and they had their own makeshift counter. To me it seemed logical to join forces and let them share the use of the proper issue counter built for us. And it saved space. Fait accompli! They did not like this at all! Independence, please. But we ended good friends some years later.

Clanger 3 One Speech Day I praised the work of a very bumptious but efficient helper at the swimming pool. I said something like: *'He's a great chap and we all love him. But I wish he was as cool as the water!'* He promptly resigned.

Clanger 4 The police called. *'We understand that you have a revolver?'* 'Yes.' *'And how many rounds of ammunition?'* 'About 50.' *'You realise that it is a serious offence to possess a weapon without the necessary licence?'* The fact that the revolver in question was a blank starting pistol that I had inherited from Mr Hall did not apparently lessen the seriousness of my position. I used it every year on sports days and it made a splendid noise. But when I used it, indoors, for the swimming sports it was too much of a good thing, unless you had ear plugs. So, to avoid arrest and the annual police checkup, I surrendered my arms. School discipline did not suffer.

Clanger 5 It was in the days when self-stick hessian wallpaper was all the rage and I had bought some in order to make a display panel outside the office. With pins you could then put up the latest posters. Come the day for school redecorations and I thought if I took it down the decorators would do a better job. One big haul... and down it came... complete with half the wall plaster.

Clanger 6 They say my coat got buried in the concrete foundations of the pool. Not true but how about this? I was 'testing' the restored spring board by jumping up and down on the end... and misjudged my biggest jump. Splash! Quick retreat home and into a dry suit. Nobody knew?

Clanger 7 It was what I hoped would be a deep discussion with a senior education officer about Vision and Policy. *'But Dybeck, this is all very well, but you need to apply yourself to addressing the REAL issues!'* By which he meant budgets and staffing. Vision could wait.

Clanger 8 Phone call: *'A large piece of panel off your outdoor climbing wall has blown off in the wind and dented my car.'* Fortunately the owner knew me well and we settled amicably.

Clanger 9 This member of staff had been neglecting quite a few duties and I had a frank talk, which I hoped would do the trick. Next day there was a letter of resignation on my desk. Perhaps it was just as well.

Clanger 10 In 1977 the roof sheeting blew off. Great swathes of sheet steel slapped in the wind against the classroom windows. The county emergency services were beaten to the scene by the press, sans permission, who proceeded to click away at our distress. Anxious that the public would not see this as some sort of nail in our coffin *(times were fraught just then)* I demanded his film, got it, and stripped it out of the cassette. I was within my rights as the policeman next to him knew!

Clanger 11 This one is a clanger in reverse – not mine. I had been invited to a rather belligerent gathering of prospective parents so I could 'justify' my school, and I did my best. But one retort floored me. *'We don't want our young to be educated alongside a lot of farm children!'* I think my farmer Governors would have exploded at that one.

Clanger 12 In our 1977 extensions the Domestic Science room was to be stripped and turned into a staff room. I asked: *'What about the wall cupboard units?'* *'Scrap!'* So I sought to 'Womble' them for use in our diy Sixth Form room. My tool: a jemmy. Result: five forehead stitches! Rescued again – by my Deputy.

Clanger 13 We were getting a new science lab complete with a traditional style heavy teak Demonstration Table on a dais which effectively sealed off the teacher (demonstrator?) from the rest of the class. So I sliced a large section out of the centre part to allow the more direct form of communication which our style of teaching required. I was not popular with the County Science 'Adviser'.

Clanger 14 After a long and friendly talk with a keen parent I suggested he might like to get more involved by coming to PTA meetings. His reply: *'I'm on the committee!'*

Clanger 15 *(At least they thought it was)* In school Assembly I once said *'I don't want this to be a good school'*. All heads looked up in surprise… until I added *'I want it to be a VERY good school!'*

Clanger 16 It was one of my only two 'nuisance calls' by former pupils. As the former call had been a mysterious brick through the window – unsolved – I was going to act quickly this time. I gave chase and they did not think I would follow them across the ploughed field opposite. But cross country running skills come in useful. I got him and shouted back *'get the police'* to Marjorie. I held him in a Half Nelson for most of the next 20 minutes until they arrived. All in the day's work.

Clanger 17 I don't recall the actual incident but I had, as often, been sending missives to the county making suggested improvements in their setup. This time, they sent me a standard *'Thank you for your Helpful Suggestion'* Plus a plastic coaster *'Chairman's Award'*. I think they were taking the Mickey…

Clanger 18 In a rather fraught interview with a parent about their child's misdemeanour (…and I think this parent must have been learning transactional therapy or something). *'Mr Dybeck, during that exchange you didn't look at me once!'* Time to go.

15 **Information for Parents**

As stated in Parts 1 & 2, we regarded parents as an important but nevertheless just one part of the surrounding community. So, besides the main link via regular Parents Newsletters, parents also heard from us via the EVENTSHEET and the Annual Brochure. In early days the joint Primary/Secondary PTA had been another means by which we kept in touch, not only with our own parents but also with those of children who we expected would join us at age eleven. Then of course we had links to many parents via membership of our various associated organisations. Overlaps like this helped to reinforce our role within the community. So what follows is a mixture of domestic politics and day-to-day practicalities

Notes to parents • 1981

NOTES TO PARENTS was the document produced each year for parents of children just entering the school.

Being in a Village College
Any pupil who attends school at a village college becomes aware that education is not something only for children. The evidence of adult education is all around them and advantage may be taken of the Adult rooms, the County Library and the Youth Centre premises. The swimming pool, built as a community effort, is available all the year round. As a pupil grows up he is encouraged to take an increasing share in the community activities that surround him. With sharing comes responsibility and, hopefully, a community spirit. A village college is designed to give country people facilities as good as those in the towns. Over the past eighteen years we have been so successful in providing for further education and leisure that few would claim there are any disadvantages attached to living in a rural area. In fact the general facilities offered here often surpass those found in the towns. With the rapid growth of the Comprehensive school these facilities will improve even further to the benefit of the community and all the pupils in the school.

Letter to parents • February 1973

No Mixed Ability Classes?
We have today made considerable changes in some of the forms in the First, Second and Third Years. The aim of these changes is to put pupils of similar ability together in the same form. As you may know, 'Mixed Ability' teaching is practised nowadays in quite a number of schools. However, we believe that its effectiveness in the context of a secondary school has yet to be proved. For this reason we have never gone in for completely mixed ability classes covering the full ability range, preferring a compromise somewhere between rigid streaming and fully mixed ability. You can rest assured that we have taken this step because we believe it will give all pupils the most effective teaching and allow them to get the greatest benefit from their school work. I must emphasise that these changes do not mean that people are being moved 'up' or 'down'. It is simply that we want everyone to be in the group in which they will work best. MW Dybeck, Warden

Mixed Ability became all the rage when Comprehensive education came in. We were always sceptical and became one of the first schools in the county to abandon it despite urgings from 'Advisers'. How many today do Mixed Ability?

Parent Governor • October 1974

You may have heard in the press that all school governing bodies are in future to have on them, a Parent. In Sawtry we have been somewhat ahead of the legislation in that the governors have had a PTA representative for the past nine years... You are now entitled to elect another parent...

So, for a while, we got two... until we were rumbled.

Parents' Association • 1975

At their last meeting they agreed that the following list of SUGGESTIONS should go out to all parents.

Ways of helping your child at school

Parents and teachers are partners in the upbringing of children. Our joint task is to help a child grow up from the dependence of childhood to the independence of adulthood. At each stage we must be careful to give him the right amount of help. Too little will leave him poorly equipped for life. Too much could leave him without a mind of his own or the strength to face the challenges of adult life.

General encouragement

1. The greatest help any parent can give is to show interest in a child's work and progress at school. Not an excessive interest, which continually breaks into the world of work and play that each child is creating about himself, but a friendly encouragement 'from the touchline'. Talk to them and encourage them to tell you about their work and progress.

2. *Please see that all pupils have the time and the right conditions for homework. If you can encourage them by supplying suitable books then so much the better.*

3. See that your child has all the equipment expected of him: pen, pencil, ruler, crayons etc and something suitable to carry them in. Also see that all items are marked with the pupil's name.

4. *Pupils are often asked to bring small items to school for their work. These might range from newspaper cuttings to jam jars. Schoolwork is all the more interesting and beneficial if these items are brought.*

5. See that your child is suitably dressed for school. Our range of acceptable clothing is deliberately wide to keep down cost and to encourage some independence. Therefore choice of clothing around the borderline of what is acceptable is something where we need your help and co-operation.

6. *Please see that the school is aware of any home factors that may affect behaviour or work at school eg a bereavement.*

7. We hope it won't happen but if your child is involved in any trouble at school please do not 'take sides' until all the facts are known. Our principal aims are to see that all children know right from wrong and that they can live happily in a community.

8. *Please encourage your child to take part in the visits and residential trips that are put on for his benefit. They are a valuable part of education and always good value for money.*

9. As ratepayers and electors you have a say in how education is administered. See that your views are known by councillors and taken into account when developments are planned.

Practical help

There are many ways in which parents can help the school in general. And thus indirectly help their own child.

10. Fund Raising. Supporting fund raising events eg Jumble sales, Sponsored Swims, Draws.

11. Donations of books to the library; either new books or suitable books for which you have no further use.

12. Donations of old magazines and illustration material for cutting up for projects.

13. Donations of materials of all kinds. School finances do not go far these days and many items which might be scrap to other people can be most valuable to us. eg offcuts of wood and material, scrap paper, equipment of all kinds.

14. Donations to improve the appearance of the place eg outdoor seats, trees, plants, materials for decorations, display panels, picture frames.

15. Offers of help in practical projects. Our swimming pool was largely built by voluntary help of this kind.

16. Offers of help in the library. Cataloguing of books. Arranging and display.

17. Regular help with flowers to go around the school. Giving and/or arranging.

18. Taking pupils home after sports fixtures.

19. Help on school visits – even to Morocco. Usually we can cover all supervision but may need assistance with transport.

20. Talks to pupils. Not easy when people are at work during the school day. But we have quite a few 'visiting lecturers' who speak to classes about their work or interests. How about you?

21. Publicity. As parents, you know better than others, the work we do. Therefore please help in spreading the good name of the school among local people.

If you wish to help please fill in the slip below…

That Sixth Form?

It should be noted that although we took our first Comprehensive intake in 1970, it would be five years before that intake reached GCE level. In 1973/4, the pupils taking A levels were ones belonging to the former Secondary Modern setup. By the time our 'Comprehensive' pupils reached age 16 we were required to operate under a different setup; ie as an 11-16 Comprehensive without a Sixth Form. The fact that we could easily and naturally have evolved into a school with a Comprehensive Sixth Form was not taken into account. In fact a local Member of Parliament told me that unless a school could offer 100 pupils age 16+ it could not have a Sixth Form! So where does one ever start? The only future promise that we obtained was when the County Education Committee, in 1974, approved a Sawtry Sixth Form *'…to be started when the conditions were right'*.

As an aside I recall one Head of an ex-Grammar Comprehensive declaring proudly on a speech day three years after the start of the transition that his exam entries were *'as good as ever'*. How many of his audience realised that he was simply talking about the 'grammar rump' that was still extant in his upper school? Our complaint was that local parents saw this remark as evidence that they were 'better' than us.

1974/5 was the year when our first 'Comprehensive' intake was entering their GCE year and, although small in number, we were confident that they would put up a good show. They did. Equally pleasing had been the attainments of pupils from earlier 'Secondary Modern' years. So, the standards had already been set and we took every opportunity to point out their successes. In the coming years it was very gratifying to note how many of our pupils were to do equally well in higher education. However, academic success was but one aspect of our role as a comprehensive village college, as I hope this account demonstrates.

Parents Newsletter • 24 March 1975

Sixth Form?
College Parents Association Meeting… to discuss Sixth Form provision.

All parents, particularly those with children who may one day take A levels are urged to attend. The parents' committee intends to be most active in promoting the welfare of pupils in this area. Contrary to press reports this is not a 'battle'. It is a reasoned campaign to achieve the most logical development in a rural area.

Unlike the Joint PTA, which successfully brought together Primary and Secondary schools but had its ups and downs, this extra body was formed largely to promote the development of a Sixth Form in the college and to fund-raise.

Despite the vigorous promotion of our case to retain/extend Sixth Form work, this was turned down by the county. Below is the full text of my letter to parents in June 1975.

Sixth Form at Sawtry
As you know, Mr Horrell, the Chairman of the County Council and Mr Cunningham, the Chief Education Officer, came to the College last Monday to explain the Education Committee's decision with regard to A level courses at Sawtry.

Briefly the decision is that A level courses may not begin in 1975 or 1976. However, the position will be reviewed in Autumn 1976 though this must not be taken to mean that approval would then necessarily be given. The opinion was expressed that it might be 1980…before courses were allowed.

I know that many people will be disappointed… and that many people are feeling confused by comments in the press and elsewhere. It may, therefore, be helpful if I summarise the whole position.

1. When the former county planned Comprehensive reorganisation in 1967, it was planned, as far as possible, with 11-18 schools. If an 11-16 school had to co-exist with an 11-18 school it was felt that this should only be an interim arrangement. It was recognised that the 11-18 school would be a strong counter-attraction. It was even accepted by the Hunts Education Committee that if the 11-16 school *could not meet the needs of any pupils* they should be allowed to go to an 11-18 school. It is important to note that this provision was only intended for those *whose needs could not be met* at Sawtry. In the event, the Education Committee stated in June 1970 (just as we were about to go Comprehensive in Year One) that Sawtry, as an 11-16 school, COULD meet the needs of all pupils.

In fact our courses matched those offered elsewhere both in range and in standard. Our exam successes fully justify the faith placed in us by parents and by the Education Committee, and the recent HMI Report makes it quite clear that the College is doing its job as a Comprehensive School.

2. In January 1974 the Education Committee resolved that the College be allowed to develop A level courses (a) when there are sufficient pupils to create a viable group, (b) when the College has sufficient staff and resources and (c) when there would be no under-use of resources elsewhere.

3. Each year the Governors have put forward a case that those conditions HAVE BEEN MET and each year the case has been rejected. This year the newly-formed Parents Association joined in the campaign to hasten Sixth Form development

4. In passing, I think I ought to put paid to the myth of the 'illegal Sixth Form'. Until September 1975 any pupil who stayed on after age 16 was in the 'Secondary Modern' sector of the school. In common with many other Secondary Modern schools we developed courses appropriate to our pupils and these included sixth year courses in CSE and GCE. In 1971 these courses included some A level work. Although this work was done without additional staff it was hoped that it would provide the basis for the formal development of Sixth Form work when the Comprehensive wave reached the top in September 1975. This hope was made clear to parents when they joined the school and again when they made choices of courses for the upper school. However, because it was felt to be costly in resources to offer A level to 'Secondary Modern' pupils, new A level work was not allowed to start in 1972. Non-A level work continued, and this year we have a Sixth Form of 18 pupils. As a 'Secondary Modern Sixth' this form is in no sense illegal. It amazes and saddens me that people not associated with the College should be so agitated about a development which was nothing less than the fruit of our success with our most able 'Secondary Modern' pupils.

5. The position in September 1975 is different. Now that the Reorganisation is complete we must follow the new pattern. Pupils wishing to continue education after age 16 may do so in a variety of ways:

(a) Those wishing to proceed to any A level work may transfer to an 11-18 Comprehensive school at Orton or Huntingdon, or to the Technical Colleges at either Peterborough or Huntingdon. Free transport will be provided by the Authority to the most appropriate of these places.

(b) A similar provision applies to those wishing to do commercial or technical courses at the Technical Colleges.

(c) Pupils wishing to do repeat O levels or repeat CSEs may stay at Sawtry and do a further year in the 'Fifth form'.

6. I am most anxious to ensure that no pupil who can benefit from further education is put off by the fact that he or she cannot continue at Sawtry. Many parents and pupils have expressed a strong wish to continue their education within the College and their support is heartening. But the most important thing for them is that they do not 'drop out' of education. I am in touch with the Principals of all the neighbouring establishments and my staff will see that pupils are transferred satisfactorily where this is appropriate.
MW Dybeck, Warden.

Despite the county rebuff, the parents and governors continued to press annually for 11-18 status

Sixth Form Developments

At one time it was felt that one needed a comprehensive school of 2000 in order to support a Sixth Form of viable size. Then it was found that small schools had many counter advantages… Small is Beautiful became the cry. But now we have the pressure of the economic crisis, and the result is that it is no longer enough to prove success. You must be viable not only now, but in the severer times of the years ahead… It is, therefore, unlikely that we shall start Sixth Form work until we are Six-Form Entry, ie not until 1981 at the earliest.

Sixth Form Now. A 1976 campaign document to promote Sixth Form at Sawtry

```
┌─────────────────────────────┐
│   A  SIXTH FORM NOW    !     │
└─────────────────────────────┘
```

A Sixth Form is not only educationally desirable :

It will also COST LESS ❋ than the present interim
plan (- to bus all sixteen plus pupils ten miles away.)

Remember , in 1974 the Education Committee approved a
Sixth Form ... "to be started when the conditions were
right "

THE CONDITIONS ARE NOW RIGHT :-

```
┌───────────────────────────────────────────────────────────────┐
│ 1.  There is a "Firm Base" of 110-140 pupils in years 1 to 4.  │
│ 2.  Despite declines elsewhere intakes remain at 140-160 ,     │
│          plus new housing.                                     │
│ 3.  We have already produced highly succesful 'A' level        │
│          results from "Secondary Modern" pupils.(School        │
│          was then 300. In Sept 1977 it will be 600)            │
│ 4.  In 1970 people felt we were too small, even for "O" level. │
│          Yet we produced excellent 'C' level results.          │
│          (In spite of considerable losses to other schools)    │
│          Surely we can do the same for 'A' level ?             │
│ 5.  We have seven years of Comprehensive experience.           │
│ 6.  All other pupils in the area have their own Sixth Forms,   │
│          or Sixth Form Colleges.                               │
└───────────────────────────────────────────────────────────────┘
```

TO HOLD BACK UNTIL WE ARE FULLY VIABLE IS TO WAIT FOR EVER :-

```
┌───────────────────────────────────────────────────────────────┐
│ ALL growth includes a development period.                     │
│        (-- Were you 18 the day you were born ? )              │
│ ALL Sixth Forms start small.                                  │
│        (--Did your school do 'A' levels in small classes?)    │
└───────────────────────────────────────────────────────────────┘
```

❋ IT WILL COST LESS THAN NOW :-

Here's how

About 25% of the pupils are likely to need Sixth Form education
          i.e. about 30 aged 16, and 20 aged 17. Total 50.

	Cost if educated elsewhere	Cost if educated here	Difference?
Teachers:	4.5	4.5	SAME
Capitation	50 x County all'ce	50 x County all'ce	SAME
Accommodation :	Space for 50	Space for 50	SAME
Transport	Av'ge daily trip- 11 miles	Average trip - 4 miles	Saves about £3,500

Lost Property 1976

One occasionally hears of pupils losing things. Here is the other side of the picture. *This week I auctioned 30 unwanted items, which seemed to belong to nobody. Good duffel coats, pullovers and towels went for prices mostly between 1p and 10p. A few items were 'saved' at the last moment when people belatedly recognised their own property. Would you please help to impress upon pupils that they should look after their property and not leave it lying around. Sheer carelessness is the cause of most losses. All pupils have a personal locker. They also have their own peg. But because of the very heavy community use of the college, their peg is for daytime use only.*

Caretaker Derek kindly looked after lost property and we (ie the Craft Dept) were able to fit him out with a 'den' just outside the gym. Caretakers love a den. From there he returned items, in exchange for a fine, which he put to charity. The charity did quite well. Keeping lockers and keys up to date was quite a headache but it worked, thanks to the patience and ingenuity of Malcolm Coulson.

Eventsheet 28 • December 1977

RF Hoefkens

Those who have been associated with Sawtry Village College for some time will be sorry to hear of the death of Alderman RF Hoefkens. He was a good friend and a keen supporter of the College from its foundation in 1963. At that time he was Chairman of the Hunts Education Committee, a post he held for many years.

I think it would be true to say that in partnership with Ian Currey, Director of Education for 25 years, he was able to ensure that the standard of the education service in Huntingdonshire was one of the highest in England. I believe it was largely his interest in the village college idea, which led to this place being so designated. We were fortunate to have him as our first Chairman of Governors and then Vice-Chairman for almost a decade.

He was a keen supporter of the Community Association and was our first individual member and a regular attender at our council meetings. His interest in the school led to the donation of annual prizes and, through his generosity, we continue to have, annually, a Speaking Festival and a Modern Languages Competition. At one time, when he was challenged in County Council about Education in Hunts costing a lot of money, his defence was not to make cuts but to see that all the money was well spent. All who knew the Hoefkens Era would know that it was well spent. And so also was his life.

We mourn him, but we rejoice in his achievements. MWD

Jim Green

As I recall, Jim died cycling to work on a particularly stormy morning. Earlier in 1977 Jim had been awarded a Queen's Jubilee Silver Medal.

It is difficult to put into words a tribute to Mr Jim Green – not only the Youth Leader of Sawtry Youth Centre but also an inspiration to any young or old people who knew him. If there is any consolation at this time it must be to know that during his life Jim gave enthusiasm and leadership to so many. There is hardly any facet of village life that will not be sadly lacking now. But Jim must have known that through his hard work sufficient people will ensure that the quality of Sawtry life will continue. Our deepest condolences go to Mrs Green and Jim's family. Roger Hemming, Community Tutor.

Parents Newsletter • 10 February 1978

2nd Year's Sponsored Spell-in

Last term's spell-in did not hit the headlines though for two reasons it ought to have done. Firstly, it gave all our 2nd Year pupils a new and interesting incentive to improve their spelling. (... and this, long before the Government stepped in with their required 'improvements') *Secondly, the event raised the magnificent sum of £180, which the pupils put towards old people's needs. It will help our school old folks' party go well, covering all its costs. It is intended that it should also benefit other events such as the Sawtry Feast Supper for old people.*

Governors Meeting Minute • February 1980

Design Council Award

Following the award by the Design Council to Mr Parkin for his method of teaching design in the school, and Mr Parkin's lecture at the Design Centre in London, members of the Design Council Committee are visiting the school on 27 February.

Parents Newsletter • 12 May 1980

School Meals

For years we hung on to the 'civilised' system of family service at tables of eight with a set menu, and we were the last school to do so. But now we have to bow to this major change: ...we will have a new system for purchasing food at lunchtime. Each item will be separately priced and there will be a variety of choice. Pupils will be able to make their own selection and to chose without any restriction... An advantage of the new system is that children who do not want a full lunch need not have one. A disadvantage is the opportunity it offers for children to choose a totally unbalanced diet.

Prophetic! Come back, Jamie!

School Rock Concert

Andrew Clifton who regularly produced LEAVES, the school literary magazine, was also very active in promoting young musicians:

On Friday 21 Jan, as an alternative to the usual school disco, there will be an opportunity for pupils to dance to live music. 'Mithrandir', who represented the school in last year's TSB Rock School Competition, 'Butterfly Stew' ,the Fifth Year group who played at the Upper School Christmas party, and 'Blue Mist', of the Third Year, will all be playing. 'Mithrandir' have just released their second Single: 'Dreamers of Fortune' (New Leaf SVC 570) available locally...

Computer laboratory

Brenda Elshaw was one who played a leading part in this early development.

From the start of this term we shall have a computer laboratory fully equipped with sufficient BBC Acorn computers to enable any class, at up to 3 to a machine, to do work involving computers. I need hardly underline the importance of such a development as something of a break-through. It is now an activity in which a whole class can participate. To my knowledge we are the first school to have made this break-through with modern equipment. Our thanks to a number of staff, past and present, whose experience and enthusiasm have made this possible. At the same time it's thanks to the parents and the community for helping to raise the money to make all this possible.

Computers were so new at this time that when the architect added a special – small, unwindowed – room to the new maths block he mis-spelled it COMPUTOR room.

Community stalwarts

Looking back over the first 25 years, and into the following 25, here are some of the names of people first appointed to the college staff in early days who went on to make their mark in various ways in the community at large: Peter Jones, Dick Tuplin, Pam Tuplin/Pettifor, George Chaney, John Gillis, Brian Parkin, Alan Billson, John Atkinson. And, if I added all those who followed this example, there would be a great many others.

Behind the scenes was Jack Cullup, our caretaker. His interest in all aspects of College Community life and his concern to see that everyone had good service went far beyond the call of duty.

16 **Numbers and results**

Report to Governors • September 1973

The first 'Comprehensive' intakes.

Pupil Numbers	1970	1971	1972	1973
First Year intake	53	63	69	104
School Roll	241	282	309	374
% going 'elsewhere'	43%	40%	22%	6%

The creaming to other schools has now dropped to an insignificant number. This is all the more encouraging when one realises it has happened in spite of the continued opportunity to attend 11-18 Grammar-based schools to the north and south.

Loss of pupil intake

The lighter coloured shading in these five columns indicates the proportion of catchment area pupils who did not come to Sawtry.

In 1969, under the old 'eleven plus' the ablest 20% of pupils went to Grammar Schools and 5% went to Orton Secondary Modern

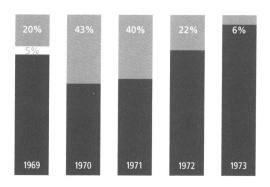

College growth 1963 to 1974

This shows that after early years of slow growth things were beginning to 'take off'.

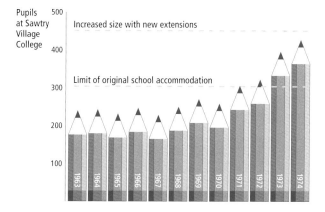

Could pupils get good results at Sawtry?

This was the big question that exercised many minds when we went Comprehensive, and it was important that we took every opportunity to advertise our ability. The following case study shows that, far from losing out, pupils coming to Sawtry did at least as well as elsewhere and, arguably, even better.

Good exam results in relation to intake
In this graph, the columns represent the total number of pupils living in the Sawtry catchment area.

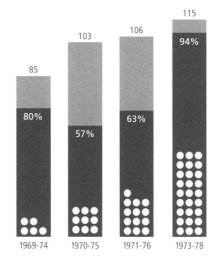

Column One -1969 when we were still Secondary Modern. About 20 pupils would have been selected for Grammar School and most, but not all, would get 4 or more good O levels. In that year group, five years on, five of our pupils, 'eleven plus failures', gained good O levels. Indicated at base of column.

Column Two -1970 our first 'Comprehensive' year. But 43% of this year group (48 pupils) went to Orton or elsewhere. Five years later only 19 of the 48 going elsewhere got good O levels. In Sawtry, nine pupils got good O levels. i.e. 17% of our full intake. So, even without those 19 achievers elsewhere we were getting acceptable results.

Column Three -1971 We still lost 40% of our intake to Orton. But five years later 13 Sawtry pupils achieved good results. So again, even if we ignore the Orton results, we had almost 21% of the Sawtry intake achieving good results. This was the national norm.

Column Four -1973 We got 94% of the expected intake. And five years on, over 25% of Sawtry pupils got good exam results.

Parents Newsletter • November 1973

Sawtry A Level Exam successes

The pilot scheme which we began with Sixth Form pupils in 1971 led to the following successes last July.

Nigel Toulmin *(an ex-Secondary Modern pupil)* is to be congratulated on achieving A levels in English, History and Geography. Andrew Adams passed Geography and Alison Naylor, French.

Teachers of the above were English: Mrs Stuart; History: Mrs Cambridge; and French: Mrs Ilott. My geography class, which met weekly in my study, also included an 'illegal' adult, Mrs Beryl Bartter, who also passed. And I should give credit to my geographer colleague at Uppingham School, Tony Land, who prescribed all the right books.

School Inspection

We had only one full inspection in my time by Her Majesty's Inspectors, later called OFSTED and other designations. This was in March 1974 and it went very well. When they first got in touch they were quite thrown when I said that I hoped that they were coming to inspect a Village College and not just a school. But they did not work that way and the only concession I got was that on one day they sent round their Adult Education Inspector to have a look at the Evening Classes. The concept of an all-embracing institution was quite foreign to these gentlemen. Nevertheless they gave us a very favourable report to which we were able to refer, but only in general terms. In those days HMI reports were confidential. But the officer from the County Education office told the governors it was 'glowing'! (Tell that to our 'rebel parents'!)

Moving on from Sawtry

With no proper Sixth Form of our own after 1974 we had to ensure that pupils wishing to continue studying had a fair deal. To many, the choice was Orton Longueville and it is good to note that, despite having to make this transition at 16, many of them were able to excel and show up well against those who had been in that school since age 11. At university level we could report that our 1971 'Comprehensive' intake of 64 pupils produced eight graduates, double the national average. This, despite the creaming caused by the iniquitous 'Parental Choice'.

Pupils leaving us had the option of other 11-18 schools where they often made a name for themselves, and us. We also had strong links with the Technical Colleges in Huntingdon and Peterborough to which many other pupils went for various advanced courses. The Huntingdon links began in the days when they would take 14 and 15 year olds for a day a week from school – an arrangement that helped us to widen our offer of courses in the technical field. And we had similar arrangements with our adjoining County Agricultural Education Centre and its associated Homecraft Centre. Our own school bus was a great asset when it came to transporting those pupils for their Huntingdon Tech. courses.

Report to Governors • February 1975

Despite our success in so many fields, keeping our end up amongst the 'big boys' was a constant struggle. While we had strong support from all who knew us well there remained a minority who felt that we could never be as good as some other places. Here I was reporting to the governors on two elements of school life which feature most often in the minds of outsiders.

Examination results

In 1968-70, before we went Comprehensive, when the whole question of our viability was being discussed, it was claimed that, while we might do well with average children, the school was not big enough to provide the range of examination subjects for 'Grammar School' children.

In fact Sawtry was already quite as capable as other schools of educating intelligent children as indicated in the following case history.

Case History: Five girls of almost identical ability left Primary School in 1967. Three went to Grammar School where one got 9 O levels, another got 7 O levels and the third got one O level. One girl went to the neighbouring Secondary Modern, which later amalgamated with the Grammar school. She got no O levels. The fifth girl, an 'eleven plus failure', came to Sawtry. She gained 9 O levels.

By 1970, when we went Comprehensive, it was our claim that courses offered at Sawtry would cover the needs of all abilities. Now, five years later, those students are confidently entering for the full range of O levels. It should be remembered that all these entrants come from a year group which lost over 35% of its number to Orton through parental choice...

Discipline

It is very difficult for anyone outside the school community to assess the standard of its discipline. Every school has its gum chewers, its untidy ruffians, its bullies and its truants. For viewers from outside who choose to seek out these miscreants it is perfectly easy for them to give the school any label they choose.

It is significant that the 1974 HMI Report on us says not a word about discipline. It concentrates, as we do, on stressing the good relationships that exist between staff and pupils. Good relationships, like good health, do not show up to passers-by. The indications are often trivial, unspectacular and rather personal. Bad relationships are indicated by graffiti on walls, broken windows and unchecked rudeness. At Sawtry there is no 'writing' on any walls, toilets included. I can recall less than six broken windows, accidents included, in our 12 years. I could count on one hand the times the dining room has been noisy enough to be called to order. Truancy is so low that the few offenders are all well-known and suitably dealt with. We have had only one break-in in 12 years, and that was two pupils who merely desired each other's company in private. School dress has been deliberately liberal in order to encourage economy and dress sense within prescribed limits. Those who step outside those limits are dealt with. The school has never found it necessary to have a 'detention'. 'Lines' are a rarity. In the last five years caning has only been used on 15 occasions. Compare that with elsewhere. And never has there been a published sheet of School Rules. Breaches of discipline are normally dealt with by deprivation of privileges or extra work.

We study closely the background of all our 'problem' children and it is noticeable how often a disturbed child is from a disturbed family. In such cases sympathy and understanding are more appropriate than anger and punishment. It is very rare for a pupil to be excluded from school life more than briefly. The one or two who have been suspended are invariably those with psychological or medical troubles.

If a school is to be Comprehensive then it must be Comprehensive, ie non-selective, in social as well as academic matters.

We see our task as trying to educate mentally and socially all who live in our catchment area. We have high standards, but we claim no right to cast off those who fall below these standards. It is probably worth adding that it was rare to see a pupil turned out of class and standing in the corridor.

Not sure where I picked up this quote but it seemed apposite:

'In proportion that the laws were good fewer sanctions were needed.'
'They learn from their EXPERIENCE'
Williams 1774

Parents Newsletter • 20 July 1981

More Degree Successes

Christine Wynne – Oxford University. Kevin Randall – Reading University, and now going for a Doctorate. Nick Dybeck, in Civil Engineering at Trent Polytechnic. Also Alison Naylor.

Parents Newsletter • 4 June 1981

Head Girl of King's!

If there still remain any people who think that our children may be at a disadvantage through having to change schools at 16 here's some interesting news. Last week I had a phone call from a delighted parent who told me that her daughter Hazel Farrington, a former Sawtry pupil, had just been appointed Head Girl of King's School, Peterborough. And let me remind you that the first big year of transfers to Orton Sixth Form managed to produce, from our ex-pupils, their Head Girl and Deputy Head Boy. We are thinking of taking orders from any other schools interested in our products!

Report to Governors • 7 March 1984

Exam results

Of the six secondary schools in the area Sawtry was only topped by one other school. And in the statistic for success with lower abilities the Sawtry norm was best of all and twice as good as the county average!

FACE THE FACTS	Nationally	At Sawtry	
	1980	1980	1981
Percentage of leavers with FIVE or more O level (A-C) or Grade 1 CSE	9.4%	19.5%	25.2%
Percentage with ONE or more ditto	35.8%	48.3%	60.3%
Percentage of leavers with NO ditto (Low is good)	12.2%	7.6%	3.4%

Letter from Orton Longueville School • 1978

I wonder what they were after?

I understand that you would be willing for a group of Fourth year children to visit your College... The (27) children are studying Sociology... and would like a chance to see a different educational establishment in operation...

Fan Mail

Dear Mr Dybeck,
I like are lecon with you next week will you show us a film.
Love from Joy. 1D

School Leavers Survey

Governors were asking where pupils went after leaving us so Alan Billson, Senior
Master, did this most useful survey of the 1979 leavers
I have added the similar surveys for later years.

	1979	1980	1981	1982
School elsewhere for A levels	7	7	12	9
School elsewhere for O levels	5			
Tech College for A levels	6	23	40	8
Tech College for O levels	4			
Tech College Vocational	13			46
Engineering/Garage apprenticeship	10	5	6	2
Building apprenticeship	1	3	2	9
Agricultural apprenticeship (at Ag Centre)	4	3	1	
General Eng/Garage/Boat building	9	6	2	2
Clerical/professional (Accounts/Banks)	5			
Clerical/general	5	3	3	1
HRC Animal Tech.	4	2		
Farming	6	4	3	
Cook/Hotel work	5	5	2	2
Ballet dancing	1			
General labouring	7	1		
Sales assistant	4	6	9	3
Hairdressing	1	2	2	1
Unemployed	2	9	5	4
Youth Opportunities Schemes		5	12	8
Industry		4	6	
Factories		5	2	
Plumbing		2		
Dept Environment		1	1	
Sports Centre		1		
Warehouse		1		
Housewife		1	1	
Left area		5	3	4
Unknown		10	6	13
HM Forces			2	2
Temporary work			7	
Upholstery & Carpets			2	
TOTALS	**102**	**118**	**119**	**124**

Some Sports Reports

PE staff, especially Ian Tait, sent in regular sports reports to boost morale. These I would regularly read out in school Assemblies.

Sawtry Top of Two Leagues! Oct 1972

Their win against Lincoln Road School took the college football XI to the top of the Peterborough Schools Under15 Football League for the first time in their history. It also made possible a unique double, as the college under 12 XI have been top of the Hunts school league for some weeks. For a small school it is indeed a remarkable achievement to have both regular teams leading their league competitions. Well done!

Undefeated Netball Champions Dec 1976

Congratulations to Miss Farnsworth and the First Year Netball Team on a very successful Autumn Term. Undefeated in all their matches, they have won the South Hunts under 12 Netball League, beating the teams from Ramsey, St Peters, St Ivo, Hinchingbrooke, Ernulf and Longsands and scoring a total of 77 goals. Only 15 goals were scored against them. All the other schools have First Years at least double our size. All the team members have, throughout the term, worked extremely hard to achieve their success. The team – Wendy Hoskins, Susan Hart, Elisabeth Burton, Debbie Wilson, Ann Buckingham, Margaret Hall and Diane Johnson. They say 'Small is Beautiful'. It is also successful!

Eventsheet • 31 July 1978

Note that by publishing sports prowess in the EVENTSHEET we were making school successes more widely known.

School Sports report

Athletics *The recent Mid Hunts Area Championships at St Ivo Recreation Centre saw the Village College achieve 12 first places, 4 seconds and 5 thirds. As a result, the following athletes were selected to represent the area in the County Finals: Wendy Hoskins, Charlene Farrington, Joy Drake, Alison Gillis, Hazel Farrington, David Jones, Paul Quinn, Neil Atter, Terry Wing, Paul Newell, Keith Billson, Richard Brooks, and Richard Haynes. This is one of the highest totals of representation in the college's history. Wendy Hoskins will also be representing Cambridgeshire in the Six Counties Championships at Spalding.*

Swimming *Recent pass totals in the Royal Life Saving Society's examinations are: Green Badge: 53, Red Badge: 10, Bronze Medallion: 7. This last award is for Susan Towler, Colin Brooks, Barry Gray, Gerry Ricketts, Conn Heery, Sean Jeffrey, Mark Lloyd. This makes them qualified Lifesavers.*

Cricket *The College teams in various age groups have already undertaken 25 fixtures. The Senior Team has been most successful – they are still undefeated after seven games. Individually Mark Cox (Second Year) and Barry Holt (Third Year) have batting averages in the high 50s and 30s respectively, while some of the most successful bowlers have been Simon O'Sullivan & Richard Haynes (Fifth Year) and Simon Moulds (Second Year).*

Parents Newsletter • 23 June 1981

Congratulations

Congratulations to the Third Year netball team who successfully defended their unbeaten record to retain the **South Hunts League Title** *for the fifth year running. Wendy Hoskins (Capt), Anne Buckingham, Elisabeth Burton, Margaret Hall, Sue Hart, Diane Johnson and Debbie Wilson have played together as the same team throughout their five years at Sawtry. This is an achievement in itself and during this time they have never lost a league match to any of the schools in this area.*

How did we rate against other Village/Community Colleges?

In 1980, as part of the contribution towards the 50th Anniversary of Village Colleges Conference, all college principals were asked to send in key statistics about their work. The survey **Village Colleges Today** covered 21 institutions including some urban community colleges. Most of the schools were 11-16 in pupil age range except for Impington and Sawston (11-18) and two that were 9-13.

	Sawtry	Average	Biggest
Catchment area (Sq miles)	63	44	63
School Roll	630	788	1180
Contributory Primaries	6	5	10
No of FE Classes	36	48	77
Youth Service Numbers	989	367	989
No of Voluntary Groups	54	24	54
Total membership	5000	1100	5000

17 **Opportunities, mostly for Pupils**

Soundbite

Stated against a picture of our pools

*What other school has, on its premises, **two** covered heated swimming pools? But then what other school has 96% swimmers?*

Climbing Wall

A hill too far?

A new feature of the college landscape is the 35ft 'mountain' which is being built for training purposes. Its construction has been largely possible thanks to the generous donation of materials. (By the Scout leader, Mervyn Donne) This feature will first be used on our big County Venture Scout Weekend. It will then provide a good training ground for the school Iceland Expedition and, later on, all interested in 'rock' climbing. Unlike many artificial walls this one is not almost vertical and therefore not so exhausting to climb. Climbs will include 'slab', an 'arrete', and a 'chimney'. Needless to say it is strictly out of bounds to all except people under instruction.

This feature achieved national fame with a centre page spread in the Times Educational Supplement, but the LEA were not so thrilled. To them it was a structure, and not in their plans. I argued that it was within my brief to build it since, technically, it was not a fixture: just *an item of PE Equipment.* I lost this one.

Bird Show

This autumn's Cage Bird Show was very popular and there was a great deal of interest shown towards forming a Cage Bird club or society for the Sawtry district. There was also a show for bantams only at the Autumn Fair and this was extremely well supported. So it was decided to try and organise a society to cover both. Anyone interested….contact Mr J.Messenger….

Over the next two years the Community Association was very supportive of John Messenger and his colleague Andrew Swales, who later went on to found the Hamerton Wildlife Centre as a permanent attraction. Both were former pupils of the college.

College Expedition to Iceland

Thanks to the 'Adopt a Glacier' scheme of the Young Explorers' Trust, we were able to latch on to a project to do a really useful geographical survey in a remote part of Iceland. Dick Tuplin had discovered that we might get support from the Winston Churchill Memorial Trust and this helped to make the expedition viable. Four staff and six 4th and 5th year pupils spent a snowy and challenging August camping in Iceland at the foot of a glacier and returned with an original plane table survey

of its snout. Pupils all contributed to the 33 page Report on this memorable experience.

This was something that very few schools of our size and status had ever attempted.

Parents Newsletter • 21 October 1975

Next Year's Expeditions
The response to Mr Tuplin's letter about the various expeditions has been quite phenomenal. Over 50% of the school want to take part in trips, many of which will be run out of term time.

Here is the full text of the letter, which offered to our pupils seven big trips in just one school year:

1st and 2nd Years
1 A visit to the Lake District, *staying in a Youth Hostel during July.*
   1st Years: Tuesday 29 June returning on Sunday 4 July.
   2nd Years: Sunday 4 July returning Friday 9 July.
Activities will include fell walking, visits to places of interest, a farm visit, canoeing, and pony trekking.
Cost £16

2 A weekend in school. *Last year's pilot scheme proved very successful and we hope to continue with a similar weekend in 1976. Activities included roller skating, orienteering, swimming, map reading and a visit to Woburn Wildlife Park.*
Cost £3.50

3rd Years
1 A visit to the Lake District *from Friday 9 July to Thursday 15 July.*
Activities will be organised along adventure lines and we will have additional help from an Army Youth Team.
Cost £16

2 A day visit to Calais. *This will involve two nights at the Canterbury Youth Hostel and a day hovercraft trip from Dover.*
Cost £10

4th Years

1 *A camping trip to France,* *staying near Rouen, during the summer holiday. From Wednesday 21 July to Wed 28 July.*
Cost £30

2 An expedition to Morocco. *At the end of the Spring Term and continuing into the Easter holiday. We hope to do some mapping in the High Atlas Mountains on the edge of the Sahara Desert. As for our Iceland Expedition, Grant-aid will be sought to hopefully keep the cost down to £75 per pupil.*

3 *If sufficient pupils are interested it may be possible to arrange visits such as last year's one to the* **Calf of Man Observatory***.*
Cost about £20.

5th Years

As the 5th Year are now legally allowed to leave school on 1st June, no special visits will be arranged for them. However we are willing to consider applications to join 4th Year trips.

This last note seemed to signal what became 'the beginning of the end' for many schools seeking to end the Fifth Year summer term in an interesting way.

Speaking Competition March 1975

This is now more of a festival than a competition. Heats took place in form periods in the entrant's classroom and on the last afternoon of term we gave our speakers an opportunity to show their skills to amuse or educate, in front of a large school audience. Who said oratory was dead? Prizes were donated by our Governor RF Hoefkens.

Sawtry Visual 1975

This was a multi-room Festival with a great many projects on show, all using the media of sound and vision and all pre-recorded in various forms.

Items shown included: film and slides of Iceland with pupils' commentary, slides of school trips, slides of Art and all aspects of work in the Practical Studies Dept., recorded TV interviews by pupils, recorded French items with slides drawn by pupils. On the spot interviews with Sir David Renton, a commuter, and people in Trafalgar Square, all made during a London visit, plus photographs, 'A Christmas Carol' slides and comments, TV interview on 'Editing a film' plus 16mm film. Humanities work display. Photographs taken by and of pupils. Poster competition.

Parents Newsletter • 23 April 1975

Army Cadets

I am pleased to announce that, thanks to the initiative of a college parent, a branch of the Army Cadets has now been formed. This is clearly of great interest to many boys and is a useful basis for many worthwhile activities. Those wishing to join should contact Mr WA Paterson... or simply come along on parade night. Minimum age 13. The Unit meets every Friday night 7-9 pm in the Youth Centre. Activities include camps, sport, shooting and expeditions.

Eventsheet • June 1975

This, at a time when NO schools had computers of their own...

Computer Link

From next September the college will have computer terminal facilities for senior pupils for one half day a week. This has been arranged in co-operation with Huntingdon Technical College whose generosity is gratefully acknowledged.

Help for Handicapped Child 1975

A small sister of one of our pupils who is unable to use her arms and legs has recently been helped by the college. Doctors said that help could be given to her by using a special slide. The school Practical Studies Department have made this slide and pupils in the first three years have contributed the £15 needed for materials.

Film Making at Sawtry June 1975

Sawtry pupil John Messenger is the 'star' in a Road Safety film recently made here for the County Road Safety Committee, entitled: 'Safe on a Moped' and destined for national distribution. Almost complete is 'Looking at Glaciers', a classroom geography film mostly made last summer during the college Iceland Expedition.

Films had been made at Sawtry for many years under the Explorer Films label: a whole series of official training films: 'Lifesaving', for the Royal Life Saving Society, and a 'Canoecraft' series for the British Canoe Union. Pupils also starred in the 'Hillcraft' series in the Lake District.

Later, there was to be 'Cambridgeshire Communities' describing the work of village colleges, made in association with a consortium of Cambridgeshire colleges. A version of the latter, concentrating on the Sawtry elements has now been made in DVD for the college and is included in this book.

Sponsored Swim June 1975

An amazing total of over twelve thousand lengths was swum in the college pool in our sponsored swim last month. This is over 150 miles. Over 100 pupils took part - a quarter of the school - and 63 of them swam over a mile, 38 swam over two miles and nine swam over three miles! A total of £330 was raised.

Morris Men 1975

I find a note telling me that Rod Fitzpatrick, Head of Science, is recruiting for a team of Morris Men.

He got them! All senior boys. And they became quite a local star turn.

Eventsheet 22 • March 1976

That Big Map

The college has always had what must be one of the few complete One Inch maps of all England and Wales on its staircase. This went up 12 years ago and has stood up extremely well to the passing traffic. Never a single smudge or scrawl on it in all those years! But it is now a little faded. It has just been completely renewed with the very last printing of the old scale map. The new scale map - 1:50,000 - will be too big for our staircase. Early next term there will be a small map exhibition next to this permanent wall map.

When the original map came down it was still in fair condition. So I re-fixed it all on the ceiling of the Geography Room, 'Look up for England!'

Residential Weekends in School 1977

Owing to the popularity of these weekends, there will have to be three weekends this year: First Years: Jan 21 or Feb 5. Second Years: March 4.

Marburg Exchanges Feb 1977

A party from Marburg (Germany) will be arriving in Sawtry on 18 April and stopping for a few days… The Sawtry Marburg Exchange Committee will be their hosts and we hope everyone will help to make their stay a memorable one.

George Chaney had a lot to do with the establishment of this link and it led to regular visits in both directions by Sawtry students (school and adult). Marburg became the official 'twin' for Huntingdon while Sawtry Parish Council developed links with another German district: Weimar.

(Not THE Weimar!)

Wombling Saturday 1977

Sat July 16. Collection lorry to be at the Green at 11am. Participants to be given a raffle ticket for every bag of rubbish collected.

Huge amounts were collected!

Parents Newsletter • 7 October 1977

Revue

The staff and a supporting cast will present a Revue at 7.30pm on Thursday 17 November. On the Friday night there will be a slightly revised version of the Revue followed by a Buffet Dance with Licensed Bar. Proceeds from both these events will go towards school funds.

Now, speculate on the difference in the content of these two Revues!!!

Parents Newsletter • 22 May 1978

Traffic Education

More and more young people are taking to the road as soon as they are 16. No training whatsoever is required by law, and the results of this are obvious by the standards of driving seen on the roads, and by the tragic accident statistics. We are trying to do something about this. We have our CSE subject: Traffic Education, in which we are helped by the Police and the Road Safety Dept. We have just run a successful Moped Training Course, and on Open Evening there will be an exhibition and demonstration of the work involved. The school has bought its own motor-bike for training purposes. We still owe £120 for this. Will you please buy a raffle ticket to help this worthwhile cause?

Remember the car we bought for ten pounds in 1964?

What's New? 1978

It's funny the things that Press and TV pounce upon. Recently a local school was hailed as doing the latest thing by having a course for girls in Child Care, with mums bringing babies into school. We have run such a course, leading to a national examination, for seven years.

Last week we also heard about what the press called some School's Open Day a 'New Look' Speech Day. We gave our Speech Day its very popular New Look four years ago.

As I write this, the press ring up to ask if we had 'anything' happening at the college between now and Christmas.

Anything?

Young Explorers' Trust Conference

Anyone wanting to do some armchair travelling to exciting and dramatic parts of the world would have done well to drop in last Saturday or Sunday. The Young Explorers' Trust – a national body, of which I was Chairman, set up to aid schools and young groups planning expeditions – had here the inaugural meeting of its **Norway Unit**. *Participants included John Vessey, who took Eton College to the Lofotens, and Ray Ward, a British Schools Exploring Society leader. Schools represented came from as far apart as Edinburgh, Derbyshire, Birmingham and Sussex. But it was not all Norway. In another room staff from Oundle and Impington Village College were poring over satellite pictures of the Sudan, planning for a Brathay expedition. One practical outcome of the conference was offering the school as an overnight stop for the Edinburgh school on its way to Austria via Luton airport. Did anyone ever say that Sawtry was a backwater?*

The *YET* often came here for conferences and I recall that one year some leaders came the night before and attended a Dinner at the college. I took great pleasure in introducing one of them: his name was Shackleton. Now, they believed we were genuine explorers! And, yes, he was related!

Swapshop 1978

Mrs Cheer, secretary of the Playgroup Committee… announces the Swapshop for childrens clothing etc… to provide a community service for the maximum possible use of equipment and clothing.

I think this was the fore-runner of New to You which was later run by CARESCO

Drama in Sawtry Church 1979

My congratulations go to all the First and Second Year pupils. Under the leadership of Mrs Anderson they took part in a Presentation of music, dance, poetry, prose and drama on the Christmas theme. Mr Swan, the Rector, kindly allowed this to take place in the very appropriate setting of the parish church. It says much for the discipline of the school that, despite the half-mile walk each way through the cold and drizzle everyone behaved wonderfully. The pupils' performances were of a high standard and reflect great credit upon themselves and their teachers. It was wonderful to end the term on such a high spot.

Residential Weekend

Parent's letter re a First Year weekend in School, 1979

Dear Mr Tuplin, Many thanks to you and all the staff concerned with the weekend. Martin thoroughly enjoyed it and I am sure the experience gained by the children will be most beneficial to their future development.

Sawtry Weather Station

Some of you may have noticed that this has been given a face-lift, and that there is increased activity among our pupil observers. This is because our Science Dept is working in conjunction with Ministry of Agriculture scientists on a research project aimed at finding an answer to the problem of the Wheat Bulb Fly which has been causing East Anglian farmers considerable problems.

The New Computer Oct 1979

As you know the Parents' Association recently raised over £500 which helped us to buy a PET computer. This is now installed and in full use. While not wishing to brag we now have, once again, what is probably the best computer setup in the county. We lost the lead a few weeks ago but that has now been restored.

Christmas Events 1979

*Parents and families are invited to two events. First a Revue: '**A Turkey in a Pear Tree**' compiled and produced by Mr Whitehead involving quite a few members of staff in unusual roles. Secondly, Mr Houghton is producing '**An Evening of Music and Drama**' with the pupils.*

Parents Newsletter • 15 February 1980

Cancer Scanner

Thanks to Mr Short, our Caretaker, we have been able to donate £20 towards Addenbrooke's Cancer Scanner Appeal. This money was collected by Mr Short from pupils in return for claiming lost property.

Parents Newsletter • 8 May 1981

Beat the Bounds

Over 70 people took part in the Sawtry Beat-the-Bounds this year despite ominous weather. 37 people of all ages from 7 to 70 completed the 15 mile course and gained a ceramic badge stating 'I Beat the Bounds'. All sponsor money will go towards Sawtry Feast Week Disabled Persons' Fund.

Parents Newsletter • 2 September 1981

Help with beds – Thanks

Many thanks to those who helped us to once again make up a good set of foam mattresses for use on in-school residential courses. This includes the anonymous donor who left material in my room. The beds were used for a very successful Social Service/WRVS residential week here in late July.

Parents Newsletter • 14 June 1982

Sponsored Marathon Walk

School and Youth Centre are combining for a 20 mile sponsored walk to raise funds for re-equipping Maths dept. computers and improvements to the Youth Centre. The target for the walk is £3,000. Full police co-operation has been obtained. Please note the date has been changed because of the World Cup.

104 took part and 92 gallant people completed the whole 20 mile route.

Parents Newsletter • 17 November 1982

Parents meet the Queen and the Pope

There can't be many schools that can claim this headline… The parents of Rachel and Richard Davidson work on the lonely island of Tuvalu. "Please can I have time off to meet the Queen?" (for a royal visit.) is hardly a request that a headmaster could refuse… So, if they are now learning more Geography than Maths I am sure it will all balance out when they get back.

In another family. Rachel Scott's father is a representative of the Anglican Society of St Francis and his meeting with the Pope marked one more small step towards Christian Unity.

Internal note 1982
re problems following a Former Students' Disco.
To MWD from PTJ: Fire extinguisher missing from the hall. 'Paul K.' returned an empty extinguisher which he 'found' in his car boot on Sunday morning.

Radio Cambridge   1983
Our college weather station is about to take on a wider usefulness. Following the one hour 'Down Your Way' broadcast on Sawtry last term the producer, seeing our Met. Station on the front lawn, asked if we would like to provide regular reports. Mr Stevens is now arranging for these to be collected for broadcasting and each month we hope that pupils will be able to do a 3-4 minute report on the air.

Parents Newsletter • 3 May 1983

National Gnome Week
No, we are not taking part in that event, but the occasion prompts me to appeal for help in tracing the owners of a collection of Gnomes, complete with windmill, who appeared round our pond some months ago. They are now safe and warm in the boiler house but soon we shall throw them out. Anyone for Gnome?

Whatever next?

18 **Youth & Community**

Youth Work

Youth Club Report to Governors • 1973

Who says they spend all their time playing ping pong?
This is just part of one of the regular reports from Jim Green, the Club Leader.

Our Community Work

In conjunction with the college Social Studies group we did the following:

1 *Surveyed the area to find senior citizens who were unable to attend clubs etc.*
2 *Raised enough money to give them a Christmas Party.*
3 *Ran a party on 4 Dec. for seventy senior citizens with film show, bingo, & community singing.*
4 *Refreshments served by college staff and pupils.*
5 *145 parcels of tea & sugar distributed to people in our outlying villages together with cards designed & printed in the college. Many letters of thanks have been received.*
6 *We went carol singing raising money for Peterborough MENCAP*
7 *Thirty parcels of sweets were given to the children of the Nursery school.*

Feast Supper for senior citizens

This is part of a report from Roger Hemming, our Community Tutor about the first of our annual **Youth in Action** concerts.

Youth in Action

The idea of a concert by the area's youth was floated by Mick Jungic, the voluntary leader at Folksworth village youth club… It did not prove too difficult to persuade Derek Wren, a local experienced actor… to become producer. I introduced Derek to the club leaders, Scout leaders, Guiders, Brownie Brown Owls and Cub Akelas, and our Army Cadet Lieutenant. There followed four/five months of rehearsal (but) it was not until the performers came together on the Village College stage… that the wealth of talent became apparent. The college's 44-seater bus was indispensable for the final three rehearsals. Both performance nights were sellouts with over 700 audience and 150 performers. Over £300 was raised for the UNICEF charity.

Crime Rate

The police have reported to us that we have one of the lowest juvenile crime rates in the area. Les Green. Youth Club Leader

(Tiresome people!)

Youth Service Review

Dear Mr T, A lot of work went into the questionnaire response which was sent in. I take it that, in return for all this work, you will, as a matter of courtesy, send us a copy of the Report. (They never did) *To ask for contributors and then expect them to pay to see the results is hardly likely to attract people to respond in the future. MW Dybeck, Warden*

By 1984, despite downturns in many other centres, Sawtry youth work was thriving and the overall 'takeup' covering all youth activities, Scouts, Cadets etc., was well above the national average. Looking at the provision on offer in the 1984 Brochure there were, in our area, a Scout Group, a Venture Unit, Four Cub Packs, Four Guide Companies, and Ten Brownie Packs.

Youth clubs outside Sawtry were not so numerous as in the past, with only Alconbury Juniors and Gidding having their own clubs. The position is underlined in this note in that Brochure:

'… though we have leaders to run a club in Stilton, there is no space available to meet in, while in Alconbury (senior), Folksworth and Holme there is space but no leaders.' Peter Davies, Community Tutor

Evening and Day Classes

With the 20 year growth in population and school facilities we were able to offer an expanded growth in classes for all ages. We began in 1963 with 19 evening classes and 222 enrolments. By 1970, before the big growth, there were 21 classes but 340 enrolments. But by 1981 there were over 800 enrolments, growing in 1984 to around 1200, with 80 classes. The earlier figures exclude the Agricultural & Homecraft Centres.

The biggest expansion was in the age range of clients with many shorter classes for youngsters doing swimming or ballet and coming in at all hours of the evening and weekends. The 1983 'Saturday School' offered courses mostly for children in Tap Dancing, Ballet, Music Movement, Mini Rugby and Badminton. There were also all-day Saturday classes in subjects ranging from Spinning and Weaving to Micro-computers. The 1983 brochure advertises 17 all-day courses at weekends.

In the later years there was much turmoil in the county over the administration and costing of community classes. The pressure to 'pay their way' meant that all classes had not only to reach a required size; they must also return in fee income something estimated at 125% of their running cost. In many centres this led to a decline in takeup. But in Sawtry we managed to thrive.

This index from the 1984 Brochure indicates the enormous range of opportunities available through Sawtry Village College.

Adult Literacy	Fabric Printing	Overseas Visits
Agriculture	Farming	Painting
Archaeology	First Aid	PTA
Art	Flower Arranging	Parish Council
Army Cadets	Football	Physically Handicapped
Badminton	French	Playgroup
Ballet Dancing	Gardening	Photography
Batik	Geography	Pony Club
Blacksmithing	German	Pottery
Blood Donors	Golf	School
Bowling	Grafham Centre	Scouts
Bridge	Guides	Senior Citizens
British Legion	Health & Beauty	Shorthand
Brownies	Hiring College	Soft Furnishing
Burwell Courses	Hockey Club	Spanish
Canoeing	Homecraft	Swimming
Cage Birds	Jewellery Making	Table tennis
Carpentry	Judo	Tennis
Catering	Keep Fit	Twenty Club
Church Clubs	Lace Making	Typing
Communication Skills	Ladies Athletics	Upholstery
Community Association	Latin American Dancing	Weight Training
Cookery Courses	Lectures	Welding
Crafts	Leisure Crafts	Winemakers
Cricket	Lettings	Women's Institute
Crochet	Library	Woodwork
Cub Scouts	Lifesaving	Yoga
Dancing	Lino Printing	Young Farmers
Discussions	Literacy	Youth Clubs
Drama	Macrame	
Dressmaking	Mathematics	
Electronics	Meetings	
Electrical Repairs	Metalwork	
Embroidery	Motor Maintenance	
English	Music	
Exhibitions	Needlework	

Community Association

As will have been seen in Parts One and Two the activities of the Community Association weave themselves through so much of what goes on at the college. But here I will bring together some of their many activities. Some are so big, like the Bar, that they merit their own place later. This section also includes some general community office matters.

Report on College Usage Summer 1972
I would say that some 100,000 people have passed through this college in the year since last September. The only un-booked Friday or Saturday evenings in the next 15 months are 4 this autumn and 8 next spring. Member organisations are invited to bid now for these dates so that we can arrange a balanced programme. GEJ Chaney, Community Tutor

Catering - School Kitchens
The Community Association Catering Sub Committee is (1972) going into the question of Event Catering at the college. Suggestions are welcome before their next meeting...

One concession already negotiated is that it will no longer be necessary for organisations to apply separately to Huntingdon for use of the school kitchen. The normal college booking form can be used and accounts for hire will be sent out with the other charges. The School Meals staff member on duty should be paid direct in the same way as the Caretaker.

Betty Endicott (right) and Joan Lee-Smith, Community Association Catering.

While the Catering Committee aim to provide a service of benefit to all users, it needs to be remembered that they are still bound by the rules of the School Meals Service regarding use of specialised equipment. Nevertheless there are exciting possibilities that a really useful and profitable scheme can be worked out eventually.

The scheme became 'really useful' when a leading member of the School Meals staff, Betty Endicott, came on the Community Association and became our Honorary Catering Manager. Not that we then broke the county rules; simply that they had sufficient trust in us to, shall we say, 'extend the boundaries'.

Community Association AGM • January 1973

From the Secretary's Report

This network of community relationships provides an invaluable area of educational opportunity and experience for pupils at the Comprehensive School of all ages, and a framework in which they can engage in dialogue and association with adults, helping to bridge the generation gap. This is particularly valuable in view of the raising of the school leaving age. GEJ Chaney.

Eventsheet 18 • March 1975

Extract from Community Association Council Minutes 29 Jan 1975
Plans to add a further room at the back of the hall.
Extended Community Facilities

Mr Quinn (Architect) presented his outline proposals, drawn up at the request of the Community Association. Costs were estimated at between £6700 and £10,000 depending on the standard of furnishings. It was… agreed that the project should go ahead subject to money being available… 28 for, 2 against.

There are many hurdles yet to be crossed but you will see that things are moving. This project could bring great financial benefit to the Association and soon provide further facilities for member organisations.

This is an indication of the vision and confidence within the Community Association. But it turned out to be 'a bridge too far' in the economic climate of those times. See sketches of when it was next discussed in 1979, below. The project was, I think, revived in 1985 and the drawings are still on file.

Exhibition of Hangings

Relax, nothing mediaeval. These are contemporary Works of Art! This was something sponsored and underwritten by the Community Association, and there were a number of resulting sales.

The exhibition (June 1975) was a great success and attracted a lot of interest. Many visitors dropped in to see these works of art by nationally famous artists in batik, macrame, and tapestry. All school pupils were given a questionnaire to stimulate interest. The hangings were valuable (£3500 in all) and some were delicate, yet their presence in the corridors of a busy school was respected.

Eventsheet 14 • April 1974

Evidence of the Community Association in a 'watchdog' role

At the last Executive Meeting it was pointed out that some newcomers to the area were having difficulty in joining certain organisations using the college. Anyone having difficulties are invited to get in touch…

Report to Community Association AGM • January 1976

At a time when many institutions performing a similar function in society are finding it difficult to maintain the momentum the public interest and the support that is necessary for continued social, educational and economic development of the community, it is interesting to note that our Association and its member organisations continue to flourish, despite the setbacks.

… comments from visitors to the area from far and wide over the past year have indicated that this situation is quite unique, and something that members of our Association have a right to feel justifiably proud of. GEJ Chaney, Secretary

George, ever fulsome but dead right!

Eventsheet 24 • October 1976

Huntingdon Hydrotherapy Pool

This much-needed pool at Spring Common Special School is being built by Gaynes Hall Borstal Trainees and volunteers using funds largely raised by the local community. Mr Moore of the Clarence H Beavers Lodge (RAF Alconbury) is involved and asks for 'any donations from our various groups to help against inflation.'

The 'Beavers' were stalwart members of our Community Association. All black and probably keen to have their celebrations away from 'home ground'. But Sawtry locals were always very welcome at their dances.

Eventsheet 26 • April 1977

This is part of what I wrote on the retirement of our Community Tutor, George Chaney and it underlines the unique and ground-breaking role of our Community Association. National Association take note!

Our Association

Most community associations in this country are independent of schools. As a result they have to struggle for premises and for a voice in public affairs. At Sawtry the attachment to the school gives our Association strength coupled with considerable independence. It has been a difficult process to balance the needs of all the users but it is very much to George's credit that he has not only succeeded in doing this; he has also guided and assisted the local community in taking an active and responsible part in the running of their affairs.

County Note to Schools • 1977

An example of how attempts to categorise use can produce bizarre rulings:

Queen's Jubilee

The County Education Authority has agreed that organisations running celebrations in schools on 7th June should take place at a concessionary rate provided they are entirely for Celebratory Purposes. There will be slightly higher rates if the organisations arranging the event are doing this for Fund Raising or Charitable Purposes.

Community Association • 16 June 1977

Insurance Cover

The Rev THW Swan observed that... *the unlimited liability shouldered by hirers... was seen to be very unsatisfactory. (This)... placed the hirer in an invidious position. Agreed that the conditions of letting and insurance cover be thoroughly investigated.*

This was an example of where the Community Association could 'take on' the county on behalf of all its member users. In fact our own insurance scheme, an extension of that of the county, was sufficient to assure most users. But evidently not Hugh!

Report to the Community Association • Sept 1978

On attending the AGM of the National Federation of Community Associations.

Getting things Done

The best thing perhaps that came out of my visit was to convince me yet again how progressive we are at Sawtry Village College – many things tentatively talked about by other community associations have been going on for years, here. We could help others a great deal... Roger Hemming, Community Tutor

Community Association Meeting • June 1979

Foyer Development

This proposal, from the Community Association, first brought up in 1975, was for some much-needed extra meeting space at the rear of the hall.

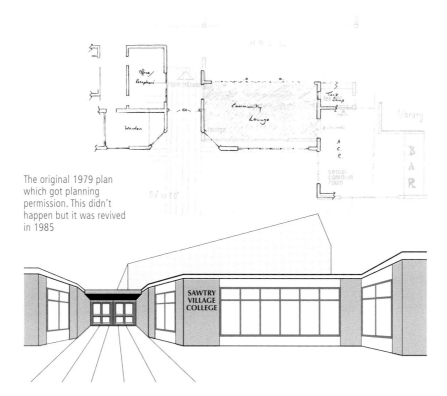

The original 1979 plan which got planning permission. This didn't happen but it was revived in 1985

Community Association Minutes • 21 June 1979

Banking facilities

A meeting had been arranged with Barclays Bank… two members of the Parish Council would also attend.

This was our Association taking a wider interest in local needs and working with others. The lack of a bank in Sawtry had been a worry for years. It still is.

Eventsheet 38 • March 1980

So it's not only the school pupils who resort to verse. This from a loyal community member introducing the Sawtry Friendship Club.

To all good Sawtry folk over 55
Sometimes called the 'has-beens' but very much alive
Here's one way to beat that blues day
Meet us in the Adult Common Room every Tuesday
At 2 pm we meet and chat
Listen and learn, do this and that
With the aid of slides we travel the world
As habits and customs are unfurled
Bingo addicts are not 'verboten'
And raffles certainly are not forgotten.
Outings to Bedford and Broads in May
Perhaps the seaside on some future day
So! No need for you to go round the bend
Just 30 pence to join and 20 pence to attend
We've a jolly nice college and a jolly fine pub
And now we have Sawtry Friendship Club
So don't delay whilst you remember
Ring Ramsey 830193 and become a member!

Signed KGB

Community Association Meeting • 8 April 1981

Stilton Players

A letter was read asking for assurances that a booking they had made would not be infringed by a School Production again. The Secretary assured the group that a future recurrence was most unlikely.

Parents Newsletter • 11 April 1981

The Atkinsons

This term we say goodbye to Mrs Atkinson who, besides teaching here part-time for many years, started the Sawtry Playgroup. We wish her and her family well. John Atkinson, a full time staff member left for promotion elsewhere having been not only an active member of the science staff but also Manager of the Community Association bar facility since it began in 1976.

Report to Governors • April 1981

Community Usage

It is not unusual for some 350 people from 15 or so different groups to be in the village college at once. Peter Davies, Community Tutor

Community Association Meeting • 7 December 1981

American Visitor

Mr Dybeck asked that a visitor from America, Mr Tom Bernard, Past President of the International Community Education Association, be invited to the AGM.

I first met Tom when I went to the International Conferences in Australia and New Zealand in 1979. Then again in USA when I attended the American Conference. These wider links helped both us and them to get to know each others' ways. I then got Tom to talk to some classes. No easy escape!

Community Association AGM • January 1984

Part of Secretary's Report

Nineteen Eight Four, in George Orwell's book, was a frightening year. Decisions were made for people. There was little freedom. Big Brother was watching you and listening everywhere. Our 1984 is not like that. Our Association and others like it across the county have many times refused to be told what to do. It may well be time to stand up and be counted. 1984 is the year when the County Council will review the whole of Community Education. Let us all ensure that those on the Review Body really know what goes on. It is time for us all to let the County Council know how important Community Education is to all of us. It would be all too easy for the County to save money by closing schools at 4.0 pm. Is it Orwell's 1984 or ours? The choice is yours. Peter Davies, Secretary

From 'The Trader' • 6 June 1984

Still in the Front Line?

'Salvoes in two directions were fired at the administration of Sawtry Village College last week and both allege an autocratic attitude by Warden Maurice Dybeck.

On one flank, a veteran community worker (George Chaney, no less, now retired) *is upset over an item in the college newsletter suggesting that the Dual-Purpose field,* (see page 133) *open to general public use, is now being restricted to group use only.*

On the other, local licensees say bars for outside functions held at the college are a closed shop. Others should be given the chance to tender for them.'

Parents Newsletter • 20 July 1984

Computer Printout

You may be interested to know that this Newsletter is the first one to be produced completely on our computers. The final print-out was done entirely automatically, on the special typewriter in the Community Office.

Do you remember life without computers? Rather like querying life without sellotape, or ball point pens.

19 **Premises**

So much activity, both in school and with the community depends upon the availability of suitable space. In theory there should always be plenty of available space in any school. After all, school classes only happen for about seven hours a day and in 38 weeks of the year. The problem is juggling with all the various requirements and being fair to all parties. The claims for exclusive 'ownership' of space which is only used for a fraction of the day or week, need to be set against community requirements that can be slotted in without harm to anyone. At the same time it is not unreasonable to expect those who 'come in on the act' to make some contribution towards those premises. The first example is an interesting case in point, though it is one in which I did not come out on top!

Medical Matters

The ante-natal clinic met at the college regularly for most of the first 20 years. The Blood Donors also came regularly. We welcomed these groups, believing it to be part of our role to help them. But they never paid a penny of benefit to us. Perhaps that was as it should be? We did not want to drive them away or put up the cost of their services unnecessarily. Or create bureaucracy over payments. But where else would they get free accommodation? I pressed the Health Authorities on this matter but to no avail. Not even thanks ever came back.

Sawtry Child Health Clinic

This was something that Henry Morris felt should be in every village college. The clinic met monthly in the Youth Centre but it seems there had been problems.

My letter to the County Medical Officer of Health, 10 Oct 1972

Dear Sir,

I have just read today's 'Peterborough Advertiser' front page lead story on the Sawtry Clinic. It is difficult from such a report to judge the real extent of the problem but if it is one of accommodation then may I suggest that we meet and discuss the matter?

As you know, we, as a village college, are anxious to help as far as we can in any community problem. Our approach is to see that buildings and facilities are used to the full, to the maximum benefit of the local community. We find also that there can be considerable social benefits from meeting in a place that is, or will be, familiar to users in other contexts. eg County Library, Nursery School, Youth Centre or Swimming Pool.

From our end two possible solutions spring to mind:

1. You may wish to extend the number of sessions. (Currently monthly) There is no problem here in accommodating a weekly clinic. Also we could suggest ways and means of providing more privacy, if this is desired.

2. You may wish for more room. Our building expansion programme could offer some hope here. However, joint use can only give maximum benefit if there is a joint contribution as is exemplified in our recent dual use/dual investment with Parish Council, Rural District Council and County Council in an additional sports field. So perhaps you could think in terms of a capital contribution towards an annexe that would be yours when you need it, with offices always yours, but with the hall space available for community use at other times.

I believe that such a scheme would enable you to put up a clinic when otherwise it would be uneconomic, ie if the Health Dept could put up say 50% of the cost, then other agencies in the village, working through our Community Association, might possibly put up the rest. Non-clinic use would probably be such things as play group - urgently needed - an old people's centre, or an annexe to the new Library building. There are considerable precedents for this type of development in many parts of the country.
Yours sincerely, MW Dybeck, Warden.

The building expansion never happened but, by December, we had doubled the time available for his clinics!

Eventsheet 9 • December 1972

Sawtry Clinic

We have been able to offer the use of the Youth Centre for double the time. In future the Child Health Clinic will open twice a month.

From the County Medical Officer

I am sorry I did not keep my reply. But I think it would have been in my 'usual vein'.

Sawtry 'well baby' clinic 17 April 1973

Dear Mr Dybeck, I was concerned to hear from both the Health Visitor and the Doctor... that (last week) they found the premises most unsatisfactory. The premises were far from warm, which you will appreciate is necessary where babies are undressing, and there were dirty Coca Cola bottles littered about, cigarette butts, and an unsavoury stale atmosphere. I should be grateful if you could help to ensure that the premises are cleaner and warmer in the future. Yours sincerely, G Nisbet

Eventsheet 21 • December 1975

Health Visitor

The College has been able to provide the Health Visitor for the Sawtry District with an office in the Youth Centre. Mrs Abbott will be based there on Mondays, Wednesdays & Fridays from 9am to 5pm...

Playgroup

A committee has been formed (1973) to explore the possibility of forming a playgroup in the area. If you are interested please contact...

This development was prompted by the fact that Mrs Nash was giving up the Nursery School, which she had run for many years in the Youth Centre. Such was the growing demand for pre-school groups that parents of young ones had to think out their next move. We could still offer some space, but they needed more. At first a second play group met in the adjoining Homecraft Centre. Later, we helped them to acquire the old Telephone Exchange in Fen Lane, and its later extension to which they then all moved.

The years of building growth 1972-1979

It is remarkable to reflect that while our first nine years of existence saw steady growth in all our activities, and in the school population, there was no new building until late 1972.

Our first extension 1972

This was prompted by the tranche of money coming to all secondary schools as a result of the raising of the compulsory school leaving age from 15 to 16. (ROSLA) With both school and community needs in mind we chose to put this on to the Youth Centre thereby extending the overall usefulness of the whole building.

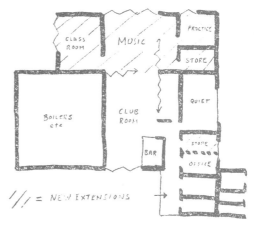

Growth at last
The 1972 ROSLA (Music Suite) extension to the Youth Centre

Eventsheet 7 • June 1972

Expansion of Youth & Adult Facilities?

No provision is made in the new extensions for extra room for the community. If the community want extra room they must find ways of obtaining it. At the Community Association Council on 22 May it was agreed that extra room was in fact urgently needed and that money for this should be raised.Requests for grants were made to the appropriate authorities. It was proposed that the community's share of the cost should be met through a **Development Levy.** *This would be shared by all users. The proposal was approved by the College Governors and a scheme is now being worked out.*

This is an example of where we were trying to go one better. It never happened because the County said that it had to be voluntary and that defeated its purpose.

Expansion of Premises 1973

A threefold pupil growth during the first 20 years meant that much of the time we were bursting at the seams and living with mobile classrooms until each new growth was eventually authorised. Many people liked mobiles, but reaching them always meant outdoor trips. At one time I think we had at least seven mobiles on site.

The first permanent expansion took place in 1973, increasing the official school capacity from 300 to 450. This growth was the result of two factors: local housing developments and the raising of the school leaving age from 15 to 16. To cope with the latter, all schools that needed it were given extra space and in our case it was decided to graft this on to the Youth Centre (see above) with special rooms for music and our small Sixth Form

But the major new construction was of the Practical Studies block, embracing not just the usual Woodwork and Metalwork but also Art, Domestic Science and Needlecraft. All this, under one roof, became organised as a far-seeing integrated department, which was to achieve national recognition.

With the move into Comprehensive education other room changes enabled us to develop, in the old practical rooms, a Mathematics suite of rooms and another suite to cover all the Sciences. Further extensions in 1977 brought us the big library - see below - a sports hall and a large new block on the field below the quadrangle for languages, history, geography & maths/computers. That block was given a further expansion in 1980.

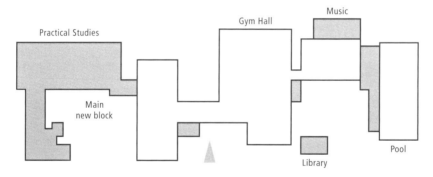

1973 expansions from 300 to 450 places

By early 1973 our main new buildings were coming on very well... The plan above shows the extent of our expansion. Light blue parts are all new building.

Apart from the Practical Studies Block and the Music Suite on the Youth Centre there was (a) an addition to the school kitchens – most people had school dinners. (b) an extension to the offices. The County Library expanded, temporarily, into its own mobile room next to our library and our Pool Committee organised toilets, reception and a gallery on the Swimming Pool.

Practical Studies Block

Opposite, is a detail of the main extension: the Practical Studies Block, or as it soon became renamed: the **Sawtry Craft Centre**. This was very much 'Open Plan' to which the staff were able to make considerable 'improvements' to facilitate their approach to school work.

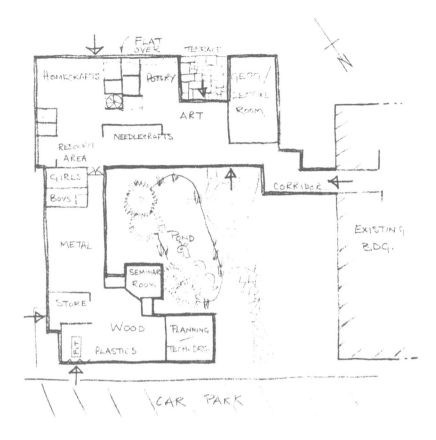

Not only was the school getting bigger; (300 – 450) there was also growth and success in many other fields, small and large, as these very varied reports indicate.

Letter to Eastern Electricity Board • 26 April 1974

Up the Pole?

Dear Sirs, I notice that for some time there has been a pole of yours lying by the entrance to this college. This pole would be very useful to us. If it is now surplus to your requirements perhaps you would let me know. We could shift it and would be prepared to pay a reasonable sum for it. Yours sincerely, MW Dybeck, Warden

That pole became the foundation of our outside diy climbing wall.

Parents Newsletter • February 1975

Recent acquisitions

We have just bought a video tape colour recorder and this will greatly extend the opportunities for use of schools TV broadcasts. We also have a new colour TV set. Lest you think this sounds extravagant I should point out that our current TV set was bought second hand with school fund money - not on the Rates - eight years ago. It still goes well but now takes second place. We have also obtained a television camera, tripod and dolly. Our Drama Room is being equipped with a set of portable studio lighting, largely through our own efforts, and this has already been used for one Play with staff and pupils. Another acquisition has been a $4^{1}/_{2}$ inch reflecting telescope which again opens up many possibilities.

Governors Meeting • 19 May 1976

Discovery of a construction fault in the 'New Block'.

Roof repairs

The Practical Studies block now contains 72 temporary supporting pillars (Accro Props) and the chairman expressed concern about safety... Mr Davey said that the County Architect had given a written undertaking that they were safe. The contractors have asked the school to move out on 1st July for repairs. Term ended on 16 July. I noted that the contractors did not in fact move in until 24 July. But the job was done by September.

Further School expansion 450 - 600 in 1977

New teaching block and Library

The Library was now to be a fully-integrated school and county library; a 'first', as reported below. The teaching block, in a pleasing 'Post Modern' red brick, accommodated all the mathematics and the history/geography rooms. The part marked 'staff' never happened, which was just as well. It was 'over the top' in more ways than one. But its deletion, and the need to relocate the staff room in a converted classroom meant that our promised growth to 600 places was cut to 570. And so we also lost 30 places-worth of capital grant.

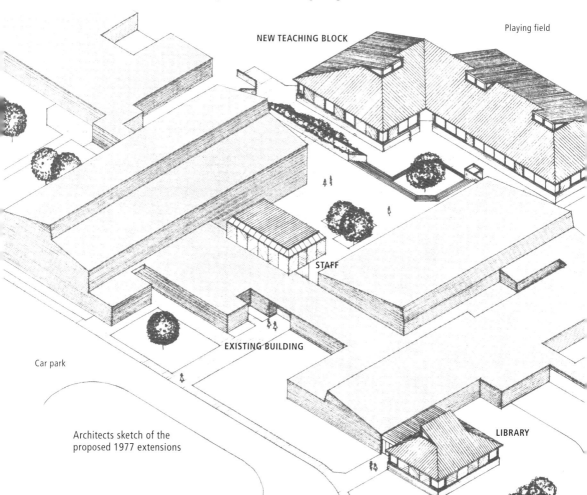

Architects sketch of the proposed 1977 extensions

New Extensions

Last term ended with the confident forecast that we should be in our new building at the start of term. In the event no rooms were ready and it was not possible to open school until the second day… In the last nine days before the school was due to open the builders only worked for four days.

Strong criticism was expressed at the unauthorised appearance of a hut (destined to store materials for Adult Education and Practical Studies classes)…

Minutes of Sawtry Parish Council 22 June 1976

Mr Dybeck explained that the shed had been bought as the only economical means of storing wood for and articles made by Adult Evening Classes, which would otherwise have to be closed down.

Further Extensions 1979

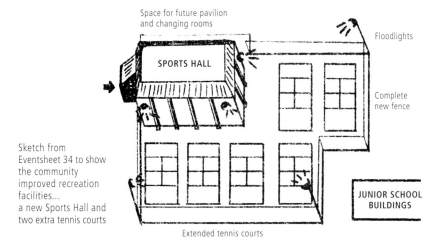

Space for future pavilion and changing rooms

Floodlights

SPORTS HALL

Complete new fence

Sketch from Eventsheet 34 to show the community improved recreation facilities... a new Sports Hall and two extra tennis courts

JUNIOR SCHOOL BUILDINGS

Extended tennis courts

School numbers were growing so fast that by 1979 we needed to expand from 600 to 750. This time it would be a straight-forward extension of the lower red brick block, with dedicated space for Languages, Remedial, and more Maths. And there would be a Sports Hall. The only consequent loss was of playing field space, which was to have serious consequences in the years ahead. Although this was, strictly, a school extension, the community would greatly benefit from that Sports Hall.

The growth of school numbers ahead of the new extensions was causing some space problems. Some of these were solved by once again using mobile classrooms. For other classes I note that we had, for the first time in our history, to encroach into rooms given to us for youth and community. For a while the Adult Common Room became a classroom, and so did the Quiet Room in the Youth Centre. I was uneasy about spoiling the décor of the latter with a blackboard but we got round it with a discreet set of curtains. The long-suffering Dave Houghton managed quite well in it and later, in recompense, he got his own set of Remedial rooms in the new block.

Expansion next door

CARESCO Sawtry and District **CA**re and **RES**our**C**e **O**rganisation

In 1983, for Senior Citizens, we had just the Wednesday Club. Now this has extended to a Welfare Club every Thursday and, on Tuesdays, the Over Sixties Club meets.

These developments have largely been the responsibility of CARESCO, which is now well-established and an important welfare force in the village and district… The college has been behind many of their operations and help ranges from negotiated use of the old Homecraft Centre as a base, to driving tuition and a share in one of our minibuses, which was fitted with a lift. An additional store cupboard for craftwork has been built in the disabled persons' toilet.

The custodianship of the double mobile classroom, which housed the former Homecraft Centre, has passed into college hands. Half of it is the Youth Training Services' Community Printshop with 8 trainees and 1.5 staff. It is flourishing, winning national awards and is much in demand among community groups all over Cambridgeshire. Like so many Sawtry developments I believe that this is another 'First'.

CARESCO was pioneered by Marjorie Dybeck and, after I had retired, all of CARESCO expanded into its own premises in that former Homecraft Centre.

Activities at the CARESCO centre

20 **Response to Challenges**

In this section I have blocked together a number of issues and projects which illustrate how we approached some of the many and various challenges that came our way. In most cases you will not find anything like them in most other schools. Whether this indicates that we were pioneers, pig-headed or just plain stupid is for others to decide.

The 1974 National Fuel Crisis

How local action enabled us to stay open when all other colleges closed!

In Spring 1974 the whole country was facing an economic crisis. An instruction went out from the county that all community activities must cease. Our Community Association, although appreciating the need to economise, argued that closing down community premises, while saving the county fuel bill, might not be as patriotic as it sounded if one took the overall view. If, say, 20 gallons of fuel are saved by not opening the college, this may mean that 200 people have to stay at home and, between them, use far more than 20 gallons of fuel in extra heating to keep warm or brew up. So, the Association pressed the county to say whether the ban was based on patriotic duty, unavailability of fuel, or the escalation of the price of the fuel. They said it was the third reason.

At this the Executive of the Community Association held an emergency meeting and decided that they should offer to *buy fuel* from their own funds and recover the cost from members using the college. So, once a rate had been agreed, the county allowed the college to buy its own load of fuel for the school boilers. Users paid £1 an hour levy to cover the cost. And since the county were not now supplying the fuel they could not themselves charge for heating. So the payment difference was not great.

Moral: Never take NO for an answer if you feel there are sufficient people wanting YES, and prepared to pay for it.

Dual-Use field

As a community school in a fast-growing village, we were aware of the constantly increasing need for recreation facilities not only for pupils but also for local sports teams. In particular the thriving village football club shared its field on Gidding Road with cows and was threatened with eviction in favour of housing. The amount of land available to us, as a school, was limited by the size of the school roll. But, thanks to a statutory planning notice that came to us as neighbours, I became aware that some fairly 'dead' land on the south edge of our playing field was about to be developed. The only building on it was an ancient tumbledown cottage long vacated. Ultimately, but not immediately, we would be glad of that land for sports fields. So I alerted the District and Parish Councils who, I thought, would share our interest in recreation space. In Sept 1972 we had a joint meeting. They would buy it, and put it in order as a sports field, if we would administer it for school use in school hours. For the rest of the time, it would be available for community sports events. All parties signed a 15 year agreement which entrenched their respective rights of use.

So was born the *Dual-Use Field*, which gave us enough space for a second cricket field and, on each side of the wicket, two football pitches, one of which was a full size 'adult' pitch for the local club. Included in the area of land acquired was a square piece adjoining the Green End Road. This was too small for school sports but just right for a Bowling Green. We had been trying, for some years, to find such a venue. The Green took three years to develop, with County Council and Community Association support as is recounted below.

It was the logic of Dual-Use, the persistence of Community Tutor George Chaney and the support of the District Council that led to later similar co-operative developments at the Swimming pool.

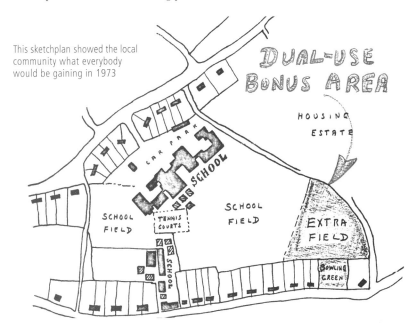

This sketchplan showed the local community what everybody would be gaining in 1973

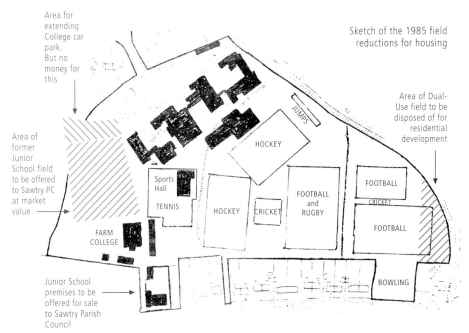

Sketch of the 1985 field reductions for housing

Area for extending College car park. But no money for this

Area of Dual-Use field to be disposed of for residential development

Area of former Junior School field to be offered to Sawtry PC at market value

Junior School premises to be offered for sale to Sawtry Parish Council

The Bowling Green

The dual-use recreation field of 1972 included an odd rectangle situated between a pub and a row of council houses. It could have, breathe it not, been sold off as a very lucrative building site. Fortunately the needs of the villagers, expressed though the Community Association, were heard first. A bowling green is not of much direct use to a school so, taking the narrow view, one ought perhaps to have advocated selling the land and buying more text books. In fact the Trustees of one nearby Voluntary Aided school did just that when a prime town centre site used as the town bowling green was sold off. It made way for an office block. But in Sawtry it was felt that promotion of goodwill in the adult community was a high priority – and anyway we realised that the credit on the land sale would never have reached our school capitation fund!

The official quotes for the development of the land as a bowling green were around £8000. This was quite beyond amounts which the local councils and the community were able to raise, and it looked as if that would be the end of the matter. However, the local District Council Recreation Committee was chaired by a most determined Alderman (Ald. Burgess) who saw a solution involving staff of the County Grounds Department. Their Organiser, Len Teague, was keen to give his men experience of this kind and so the work was planned as a part-county and part-volunteer job at a much lower cost. The price was acceptable to all councils and the work went ahead.

Throughout this development the college Community Association played a key role. The college was the custodian of the land and had links with all councils and agencies concerned. It also helped to found the Bowling Club, which would ultimately take full responsibility for the running of the green. Some critics might suggest that it would have been better for the entire initiative for developments of this kind to come from the club itself, leaving the school to get on with education. This is the way things like squash courts usually come about and, in an ideal world, it would be nice to rely on such initiative. Squash players tend to be youngish, affluent and rather pushing people who know their way around the worlds of councillors, planners and architects. But bowls players tend to be mostly older people looking for a quiet sport in a civilised and gentle environment.

Many of them may be in the evening of life and therefore not able to wield a pick at weekends or sign a seven year covenant. So they needed our help and we gave it. We never managed to raise a school bowls team to challenge them but one day it may happen! However, the school Groundsman, Derek Deller, was to become a vital and valued member of the club. And, although I never bowled, they made me their first President!

Sports field changes

In 1982 the Sawtry Junior School vacated its 106 year old buildings and moved into new premises with an adjoining field. This freed the field behind the Swimming pool – used not only by the Junior school: it was also accepted unofficially as a general recreation field very popular with the young in the village. In fact so worn was the grass round the goal areas, the part they always go for, that we put up a supplementary goal for the casual kickers, thus leaving the main field for team use. That field was the only casual recreation space in the village until the Parish Council bought St Judith's Field in 1979.

When the Junior school moved out, the county advertised that this land was to be sold for the building of 30 – 40 houses, with road access via the school drive. The community was outraged.

Although we, as a school, had been growing, the sports field entitlement for all schools had been reduced as a national economy measure. Thus, although, on community grounds, we supported the retention of the junior school field for general recreation, the county could not spare the resources to retain it. They even hoped that the Sawtry Parish Council would buy it 'at market value'! They also planned to sell off the old Junior School Hall and classrooms... Sawtry Parish Council were interested in the latter but again the county wanted 'market value', which was quite beyond local rate resources.

The county offered a way out. They would retain for us the junior field but in return we must give up part of the Dual Use sports field for housing! But they could not do this unilaterally because it was still jointly owned by school and the local councils! However, since the Parish Council now had a strong interest in purchasing the old school at a favourable rate they were 'asked' by the county to rescind their Dual-Use rights in exchange for a 'deal' over the old school. Do they call it blackmail?

Thus we gained one rather second-rate ridged and sloping smallish field and lost one good football pitch and 'half' a cricket pitch. Levelling of the former put it out of use for over a year. From a teaching point of view the school gained nothing, and a sports lesson now had to be split between two non-contiguous areas. All community rights, either on paper or by custom, were extinguished on both fields. You win a few. You lose a few.

Let me add a personal comment on the negotiations around these changes. Nationally and locally, people were outraged at the decision to reduce school playing field entitlements. Our case, where we were living with some of the benefits of that Dual-Use arrangement, was complex. What was our true 'school' entitlement and how far did our present acreage match it? I reckoned that, even under the new regulations, we were being discriminated against on some ten counts. In the *Eventsheet* and in Parents' Newsletters I gave full vent to the issue. There was to be a final council meeting to resolve the issue of which field was to be given up for housing and this was tied up with the associated issue of the Bowling Green who were also part of the original Dual-Use agreement. The meeting was, to my dismay, fixed for the Friday of the autumn half term 1983.

I had already fixed to visit my daughter who was working in Switzerland. *"So he won't be there to ask awkward questions"* they must have felt. But, come the Thursday, my wife and I cancelled our last days abroad, booked a different flight, flew back early and, like a bad penny, I turned up. Of course it did not affect their decision but I recall that, after the meeting, I was called aside by two senior county councillors and told to *"Lay off."* I didn't.

The Library

Henry Morris saw Village Colleges as centres of learning within which a library would form an essential component. He called it a Nominal Cosmos. Did he mean a school library or a county (public) library? The logic of a combined school and public library was one that had never before been pursued in Cambridgeshire so our proposals in 1976 for a joint scheme broke new ground. There had been a public library cohabiting within our library since 1964, but the school extensions of 1976 enabled us to think laterally. Not only could we have a room big enough to house the enhanced school library; it could also offer the County Library Service the extra space they needed to supply the needs of the fast-expanding local population. And to do this with a fully merged stock and expanded hours of availability would bring benefit to all sides. Thus the school got the biggest 'school' library in the county, greater than those to be found in all the larger Comprehensives, and the county got the biggest ever 'public' library. The effect? To quote from a report to the Governors:

(As a result) our pupils became 'County-library-minded' at an early age. Again, we have a Sawtry project which typifies what we hope is an underlying village college philosophy: by seeing that pupils' education is not something carried out in isolation from the community, but in close involvement with the community, with all its pressures and spinoffs. After all it is one of the chief aims of all education to lead people towards responsible literate citizenship.

```
JOINT LIBRARY PROPOSALS

The Joint Library idea is fundamental to the philosophy of a Village College
as a centre of education and recreation for the whole community.  By pooling
resources one is able to get best value for money, e.g. Swimming Pool.
Bowling Green, Health Clinic, Evening Class premises.  This is particularly
true in times of financial stringency.  The advantages of joint use to the
community as a whole far outweigh the minor disadvantages to the school.
The new extensions to our Comprehensive School present   a rare opportunity
which has to be seized quickly or not at all.
```

Advantages to the School	Advantages to the Public
1. A continuously manned library run to County Library standards.	1. Permanent premises about 2½ times as big as the present Mobile building and furnished to County Library standards.
2. Supervision and guidance throughout school opening hours.	
3. A doubling of bookstock from about 7,000 to 14,000 books.	2. A doubling of bookstock with room for further increases as school and village grow.
4. Improved reference library facilities. Wider selection of periodicals.	3. Improved reference facilities including Britannica. Wider selection of periodicals.
5. All pupils will become familiar with County Library resources and procedures, and so be more likely to continue as users when they grow up.	4. Opening hours at least as extensive as at present. (School classes would not visit the library at these times).
	5. Direct access from outside.
6. The opportunity to be treated as adults and learn that reading and study are also enjoyed by adults.	6. Parking space and grass area for prams, children and dogs. Easy access for the disabled.
ALL AT NO EXTRA COST	ALL THE ABOVE AT SAME COST AS NOW.

Disadvantages to the School/College	Disadvantages to the public
1. Loss of exclusive sovereignty over a large room, i.e. it cannot be used for school purposes at times when the public are present.	0. Apparently none. But if there are any then we would hope to see them removed by willing co-operation from everyone involved.
2. Loss of guaranteed access to books (other than reference books) since these might be borrowed by the public.	
3. Loss of a room for certain evening meetings.	
4. A commitment to staffing the library throughout the hours of school use.	

The Bar

In any community college with a thriving social life it is clear that the biggest turnover of money is at the temporary licensed bars arranged by the various clubs at Dinners and Dances. Most sports clubs and centres, residential education centres and working men's clubs rely a great deal on the income from bars to improve their amenities and benefit their communities.

At Sawtry, in 1976, the Community Association felt that they should bid for a similar setup. Their interests were not entirely financial. Under-age drinking is a national problem and one of the ways of dealing with it is to be vigilant at the point of sale. When a bar is run by an outside organisation that organisation can only judge age by appearance. But when that bar is run by the community in which the youngsters are known you have a much better chance of enforcing the law. The Friday question: *"Please sir, who's running the bar tonight?"* told us All.

Of course any school that involves itself in drink sales is open to criticism, and not only from the press. Should education be something that is confined to isolated academies, or is all life and every place an appropriate context for education? Is it better that a school should say *"No drink will ever cross our doors"* and the pupils then go and get drunk at the nearest town dance hall? Or should pupils/young people be welcomed in to the regular social events at school under closely supervised conditions?

For some years the College had had 40 to 60 'drinking' events a year, each of which had to be covered by a separate occasional licence. What was proposed in 1976 was an arrangement that could put these under a single control. In terms of accommodation the unsatisfactory temporary bars of folded board tables, 'bucket hygiene' and weekly lugging in and out of the total stock plus glasses, optics, etc., would all be replaced by a discreet well-built, and community financed, bar facility in a sealed-off bay of the Adult Common Room.

The County Council agreed to allow our bar licence application to go to the magistrates, treating it as a test case for colleges in general. No Cambridgeshire village college had such a licence. Police were fully consulted at all stages though they would not commit themselves in advance. They were told that one of the principal aims of the licence application was to create an environment which would encourage lawful conduct. It was never the intention of the licence to stimulate increased drinking. So I, as the incumbent, was summoned to appear in the dock and put our case.

In the event the licence was opposed not only by the Licensed Victallers Association, as expected, but also by the county police. The latter's case was apparently based on the fact that they felt it inappropriate for the Head of an educational establishment to be involved in and associated with drink. I had to face the music in the county court. Collapse of stout party. So, academe dies hard.

We ended up, however, with a good British compromise. The Community Association went ahead and built its permanent bar, counter, store, sinks, etc in association with the skills of the college Practical Studies staff. Administration of the bar was devolved exclusively to an appointed Bar Manager, who oversaw bookings, and an approved publican. The publican then split the profits three ways between himself, the hirer and the Community Association. The publican would apply for the licence each time and keep everything except drinks in the well-equipped bar. Community dances would then bring in a reasonable income, which was all ploughed back into college improvements. Some while later the Community Association extended the logic of supervision to alcohol-free Youth Discos by appointing a Disco Manager, who promoted this popular entertainment in the name of good order and fund-raising.

Our own school bus

Parents Newsletter • 15 September 1977

Actually it is a second hand 44 seater bus which, after much negotiating, we were able to acquire at reasonable cost. With the rising cost of hiring buses we had to find a way of maintaining our activities, sports and visits without using up too much of our limited money. We still have to raise all the necessary purchase money. Use of the bus depends upon the skill and enthusiasm of members of the school staff who have volunteered to run the bus. We are fortunate to have many experienced drivers on the staff who can take this on and I am sure we shall be able to make exciting use of this, our latest 'Mobile Classroom'.

A survey showed that the annual mileage on trips was around 10,000 miles. The bus did 13 mpg and the average number of passengers per journey was 32. Thus the coach does the job of two minibuses at a running cost of one minibus. Journeys include: trips to sports fixtures, theatre visits, exhibition visits, and trips to Huntingdon Technical College for the Link Courses. Then there are many other trips involving community groups, from Brownies to Pensioners, plus much use out of term for school expeditions at home and abroad. In one year the bus travelled to Germany, Sweden, France, the Lake District and Wales.

Parents Newsletter • 11 April 1979

A note to show that staff never accepted defeat.

School Bus

Recently we had a serious mechanical failure in our school bus, and prospects for its use in the coming weeks looked bleak. This included our Barry Island trip for over 80 pupils, the summer visit to Germany plus all our regular runs like that to Huntingdon Technical College. Thanks to a great deal of hard work by staff the bus will shortly be on the move again.

Parents Newsletter • 12 March 1981

A new school coach

At last we have found a suitable coach to replace our faithful Leyland Leopard at a price we can afford – just – thanks to a mammoth fund-raising effort over the last few months. It's another Leopard with 44 seats and we collect it next week.

For a school to have its own 'proper' bus was unusual. For it to then progress to a second bus must surely be unique! And we also had two minibuses, one complete with disabled access!

Swimming Pools update

The Swimming Pool continued to shine as an example of all that could be achieved in an active community college. But, after much heavy use, the shine was getting a little tarnished. Usage throughout the year was very intensive, and wear and tear was beginning to show. Voluntary help and shared responsibility had helped to keep down running costs but in some respects we were paying the price for being pioneers.

In 1980 the Huntingdon District Council came to our rescue and did extensive refurbishment and re-roofing, although this meant a long and frustrating closure. But soon we were back on course and again over 20 organisations made regular use of it.

Report to Governors • September 1973

Swimming Pool

The county architect's plan for new pool lighting has run into problems. £700 was allowed but the lowest quote was £930. The Director of Education suggests that the Swimming Club contribute the difference. In view of the fact that the Club have already contributed some £2000 in improvements over the past four years, and also lost some £300 of summer income because of architect's delays in the pump work, I would hesitate to make such a request.

Parents Newsletter • 12 January 1979

Pool Repainted

Pupils returning this term will find that the swimming pool has been repainted. This massive operation was carried out entirely during the Christmas break so that there would be no disruption of regular swimming during term time. The credit goes to our local community, the Swimming Pool Committee, who did this work voluntarily over the New Year Weekend. They painted the pool a year ago but, because we were sent inadequate supplies of paint, they were only able to put on one coat. However, they very generously offered to complete the job this year, when two further coats were put on in two days. This is a really fine example of community effort for the benefit of us all, and it shows once again that Sawtry is in the fore when it comes to getting things done.

Acting Warden's Report to Governors • May 1980

Pool

The roof had been removed and the pool cleaned out. (For summer use, sans roof?) As the pool had not been used for some time there were problems in getting the chemical content of the water right. The Public Health Inspector was called in weekly, but at that moment there were problems over getting a supply of chlorine. Tenders had been received from the Architect's Department for the improvements to the pool, but Mr Jones understood that these were higher than envisaged. Negotiations would have to take place between the Rural District Council and the Education Committee.

More Solar Heating for Pool

Work has just started on the installation of a much larger array of solar panels for the swimming pool. Those with long memories will remember that 18 years ago Sawtry had the first heated pool in the whole of Huntingdon and Peterborough thanks to community effort. Stage two, solar heating, ten years ago, was another 'first' in which the Sawtry Swimming Club were the prime movers in association with the county.

This latest scheme originated from the desire of users to see the temperature maintained and the efforts of Mrs Everett, the Swimming Instructress. It has taken almost two years to get the scheme off the ground since the county had to be involved at all stages. The total cost is around £5000 and, besides the proceeds from Mrs Everett's sponsored swim, in which many organisations took part, there will need to be other local contributions. However, the end product – a much more economic pool – will be well worth it.

The Sports Hall

In the 1970s sports halls were becoming a much sought-after provision in schools and communities. As a small school it was many years before we would, as a school, qualify for one. There was a time when our Community Association, ever keen to expand the place, was aiming to raise money towards one, as a joint school/community facility. We got a design and some pupils made an excellent Perspex model. But the project needed big money and this was out of their range. It was only when the school roll passed the 600 mark, in 1979, that the county could move towards providing us with a sports hall on school money. This is a good example of how the desire of a community for wider facilities depends, in the end, on there being, at the heart of that community, a thriving school. Which we were. However, by not including peripheral facilities, like changing rooms, we were throwing out a challenge to others to add something on.

I had a vision for even wider use of that Sports Hall. I hoped for the whole of one end to be a climbing wall, and the other end to have a very large white surface for film shows. 100% blackout was no problem. And, in a growing school, the Sports Hall became the only indoor space big enough to contain all the pupils. And what a venue for a rock concert!

But hold on, Maurice: you've done enough damage!

Sports Hall

The new Sports Hall has been built entirely with 'school' money, a consequence of the steady increase in numbers of pupils coming to school here. Nevertheless it is part of the village college complex and will therefore be fully available for community use...

There are no changing rooms and the reason is that we had to choose between a smaller hall with changing rooms, or a larger hall. In choosing the latter we have left you, the community, with the chance to provide changing rooms later.

Community Printshop

This is an interesting example of the active cooperation that existed between agencies, and the way in which we made use of economic crises. The venue was the recently shut-down Homecraft Centre and the 'driver' at our end was Peter Davies, our Community Tutor.

Print Training Workshop. At last the Manpower Services Commission have agreed to the formation of the Print Shop… It is sponsored by Cambridgeshire Community Council who are contributing £2000 of the annual £2600 running costs and doing much of the administrative work. Our Community Association is also putting time and money into the project. Some eight trainees, unemployed youngsters, will work on the project… In future all printing for community groups will be printed there and not in our office.

The link to the Cambridgeshire Community Council is an interesting one. Community Councils were formed after the First World War to promote community development. They helped found many village halls, something for which Henry Morris disliked them. He saw village halls as rivals to his village colleges. Now, in the 1980s, the Community Councils were attempting to tackle rural unemployment. We already had some links to the Council. They came to Sawtry for their conferences, and my wife, Marjorie, was a Vice Chairman. She was also a WRVS county organiser, which helped.

The next year, post-recession, this project was phased out. But it paved the way for the CARESCO printshop, which soon developed into a thriving volunteer-led activity.

21 **Return to General Philosophy**

*Dear Maurice, This is to say that I saw that unpleasant letter from 'Very Angry'
in yesterday's Hunts Post and have no doubt that it must have hurt you, as it
would have done me. Don't let it upset you... The letter is simply a rage against
Time, for having gone past. Hugh*

I don't recall what was worrying 'Very Angry' but it was nice of Hugh to write.

The Community's Education. A Memorandum for the Eighties

This is a summary of the points in the final chapter of my book *The Village College
Way*. I note that shortly afterwards, in 1982, the county produced a rather similar
Memorandum with the same title. No comment.

I wrote it in the style and the spirit of the original 1924 Memorandum of Henry
Morris. I include it here because it illustrates how we were trying to formulate
all we did at Sawtry into a scheme that could have wider relevance. The full text
of that final chapter is reproduced in Section 28 of this work.

*The last 30 years have seen tremendous improvements in state education. The
Comprehensive school is the first senior school to cater for the whole community.*

*By grouping and co-ordinating all the other necessary statutory services around
the school, a New Institution can be formed. Co-ordination is good economics and
good social sense.*

*To this New Institution can be added self-run community activities – something
which is seen as a Partnership in Lifelong Education.*

*Relatively modest additions to premises can bring flexibility and allow greatly
increased use. Further additions should be encouraged.*

*There must also be some staffing additions to organise and co-ordinate additional
use. If such use is to be related to school then the school Head is an essential member
of the team.*

*Statutory services associated with the village/community college could include: the
Secondary School, the Primary School, the Youth Club, the Library, Careers Service,
Health Service, Social Services, Recreation Facilities of County, District and Parish,
Local Council Administration, Citizens' Advice Bureau.*

*Facilities that could be ADDED to a college either by the above Services or by local
initiative include: Swimming Pool, Additional Playing Fields, Bowling Green, Play
Areas, Theatre facilities, Recreation rooms, Refreshment facilities, including a Bar.*

*The design of colleges should recognise that while a great deal of space can be in
common use and adapted for many purposes in the course of a week, there is also
a requirement for exclusive space for storage and for specialist equipment. This
is chiefly a school need though it also applies to community groups. Storage facilities
should be offered to them but preferably on a payments basis.*

Government of colleges should be as far as possible in the hands of a governing body of the users. This includes LEA, District and Parishes, but also staff, parents and the many voluntary community groups. Also representatives of the associated statutory services.

Local autonomy and financial devolution are to be encouraged. The checks and balances of local involvement should ensure sensible resource allocation: the County's role is ultimately reduced to that of providing the initial global finance. Decisions relating to use of premises, letting charges, running costs, caretaking and cleaning should be local, bearing in mind the total community need and its resources.

... and back to the curriculum

Despite our many and various concerns as a Comprehensive village college, it was *Curriculum* that was to become the key debating issue in my last year as Warden.

Curriculum questions were increasingly coming into the public debate. In 1983, prompted by a Guardian article by journalist Maureen O'Connor, I carried out a survey with all the staff to seek their reactions to the current turmoil. The results of this survey are in an internal booklet *Curriculum Questions and Answers*. A few copies may still be available. Their very useful replies helped me to write to The Times Educational Supplement.

Since then, national government has stepped in and required all schools to work to a prescribed curriculum. However, I guess that our curriculum was not far out on what ended up as a national curriculum. This letter of 3rd Feb 1984 was my contribution to the oncoming curriculum debate. And just look at the turmoil that followed!!!

My letter to the Times Educational Supplement.

Curriculum : How can a good formula be bettered?

Sir, When all the high thoughts about this new curriculum have been expressed and people have to get down to being precise about what is to be taught and what is to be discarded I wonder where we shall end up? I suspect we shall remain on familiar ground.

What is it that the world wants of us that we are not providing? Greater competence in simple English and Mathematics? There is no clear evidence of any decline in these skills. In fact, bearing in mind the massive school growth and upheaval of the last 25 years, the results are surely creditable.

More Science? Again the science knowledge and skills found among Comprehensive pupils must be streets ahead of that of a quarter of a century ago, even in the Grammar schools.

Awareness of the world about us and of modern problems? I would say that today's children are as aware of the world, including the Third World, as are the majority of adults. Furthermore, many of them are not just academically aware; they are prepared to respond positively to the needs of others.

The Arts? Despite considerable exam pressure, schools today have, I would say, a record of excellence in the Arts, which must be unequalled.

Craft, Design and Technology? In many cases schools can claim that their approach to a subject which should be pointing towards the heart of British industry is in advance of the requirements of that very industry. But while the requirements of the professions and the universities continue to favour traditional subjects we sometimes wonder if our approach was worth it.

Motivation? Very little has been said about the motivation for pupils under the new curriculum. If we are educating pupils to take their place in the adult world of work, then will the adults please give these young people some assurance that they want them to work? If we rejig our curriculum towards what will in effect be employment for the minority, then we are doing the young as big an injustice as in those days when much of secondary education was based on a diluted form of Grammar school education.

What is it that we are to be asked to drop? English Literature? But the traditional texts contain as many relevant discussion points for modern living as any 'Lifeskills' course. Ancient History? Again, a well-taught study of the struggles of man against man, of idealism and barbarism is as valuable as trying to keep up with some contemporary news item. Geography? Man and his world-wide relationship to his environment, his use or over-use of resources, is surely just what we need. Drama? How better to learn to speak up for yourself, or for your weaker neighbour? Religious Education? If we forget to ask why we are here, then we remove what to many must be the greatest work motive.

I do not wish to seem complacent. There is always room for improvement in the content of education and in the methods of teaching. But I do not believe we are as far off the mark as is being suggested.

When things get in a mess then it is natural to look around to place blame. But without wishing to pass the buck I wonder just what evidence there is to indicate that our economic decline has been a result of a failure of schools to produce properly-educated young people? All the evidence I know seems to point to factors far outside the schoolroom: oil crises, monetary snarlups, political posturing, demise of empire, lack of modern business acumen.

I have been a Head for over 20 years. I shall continue in my tracks, God willing, since, judging by results, the pupils educated by my skilled and devoted staff seem, by and large, to be: (a) happy, (b) willing to work for its own sake, (c) sufficiently competent in the traditional skills, (d) willing to go all out for whatever opportunities the world presents and (e) sufficiently philosophical to occupy themselves in a civilised manner when life is not all roses.

We have a good formula, based on the wisdom of the past, plus the technology of today. When I am convinced that someone has a better one I will scrap it.

Henry Morris put it better than I could:

"It is the intrinsic worth of the life that the adult leads, the working philosophy by which he lives, the politics of the community he serves in his maturity, and the amount of efficient action he contributes to that community, that should be the main concern of education"

Maurice Dybeck, Warden, Sawtry Village College

My last full School Assembly

I still have my notes of this occasion - I kept everything - and here are just some of the points made.

World today, this December, seems to be a gloomy picture. 'Peace on Earth?' Is this all someone else's problem – nothing to do with us here in Sawtry? Something that we leave for 'them' to sort out?

But who are these someone else, these super-persons who work it all out? And do they think differently from us ordinary folk?

In the last few months I have been at meetings with former Archbishops, Chairmen of big commercial companies, MPs, Leaders of large Trade Unions, & senior Royalty. I get around!!!

I concluded that they all have strong and weak points… just like us. But none of them can go far in their tasks in the world without the general support of ordinary folk. And that's where we come in!

Kipling may seem over-patriotic, in these 'universal' days. But he could, rightly, expect all people to be proud of their heritage, and loyal to the groups to which they belong. He knew all about the fears and hopes of ordinary people and the importance of care for others and responsible living. A message for all of us.

With that in mind listen to Kipling: 'Land of Our Birth'.

> Land of our Birth we pledge to thee
> Our love and toil in the years to be;
> When we are grown and take our place
> As men and women with our race.
>
> Father in Heaven who lovest all,
> Oh, help Thy children when they call;
> That they may build from age to age
> An undefiled heritage.
>
> Teach us to bear the yoke in youth,
> With steadfastness and careful truth;
> That, in our time, Thy Grace may give
> The Truth whereby the Nations live.
>
> Teach us to rule ourselves alway,
> Controlled and cleanly night and day;
> That we may bring, if need arise,
> No maimed or worthless sacrifice.
>
> Teach us to look in all our ends
> On Thee for judge, and not our friends;
> That we, with Thee, may walk uncowed
> By fear or favour of the crowd.
>
> Teach us the Strength that cannot seek,
> By deed or thought, to hurt the weak;
> That, under Thee, we may possess
> Man's strength to comfort man's distress.
>
> Teach us Delight in simple things,
> And Mirth that has no bitter springs;
> Forgiveness free of evil done,
> And Love to all men 'neath the sun
>
> Land of our Birth, our faith, our pride,
> For whose dear sake our fathers died;
> Oh, Motherland, we pledge to thee
> Head, heart and hand through the years to be!

It's better than *IF*. I defy anyone to read it without being moved

School Numbers Summary 1963 to 1984

Here is the history of our 21 years of growth in a nutshell. Two nutshells, actually. Having read this far you should be able to pass a test on the significance of all the various bumps on these graphs. The first graph shows the total pupil roll. The second graph: the annual First Year intake.

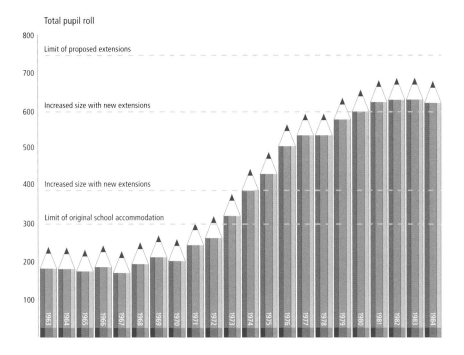

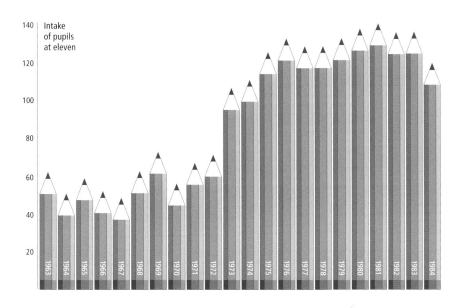

22 **Further Study**

The Village College Way by Dybeck, 1981.
Research into the relevance of the Cambridgeshire Village College philosophy to the Community Education Movement. *270 pages plus inserts*

Sawtry Pages Annotated local extracts from the above. *60 pages*

Educator Extraordinary by Rée, 1973.
The life and achievements of Henry Morris. *163 pages*

The Henry Morris Collection His writings. ed. Rée 1984. *146 pages*

We Built our Pool Duplicated full account, updated to 1984. *56 pages*

Seven 1970. A Report on the college's first seven years. *24 pages*

Comp-One 1971. The school at the end of Comprehensive Year One. *22 pages*

College for All 1972. Annual Report covering both School & Community. *32 pages*

Guide to Secondary Education at Sawtry 1981/84. *54 pages*

The Challenges of Community Education by Fletcher 1983. *316 pages*

Cambridgeshire Communities Film 30 minutes 1977. *Now in DVD*

Sanderson of Oundle 1923. *366 pages*

The Story of a Great Schoolmaster by HG Wells, 1924. *150 pages*

Going Comprehensive Dybeck (in Times Educational Supplement) *21 Aug 1970*

Pitfalls of Parental Choice Dybeck (in Forum for Education Issues) *Summer 1971*

Village Colleges Today Basic facts prepared for the '50th' Conference 1980. *40 pages*

Transporting Village College Concepts to a Wider Use Dybeck
(in Secondary Heads Review). *December 1983*

What Village Colleges can offer the Local Community Dybeck
(in County Councils Gazette). *April 1984*

The Story of CARESCO by Marjorie Dybeck, Foreword by John Major, 1998. *190 pages*

CARESCO Cares 20 minute film, 1991

College Annual Brochures Giving all regular events, 1963 ff.

Parents' Newsletters Nos 1 to 200 Covering 1963 to 1984

Eventsheets Nos 1 to 52 Covering 1971 to 1984

Part four
School Facts

23 **Chronology**

1963   Sept: Opening of Sawtry Village College
        The Secondary Modern School
        12 staff, 220 pupils, 8 classes, covering
        4 Years
        19 evening classes. 230 enrolments
        Oct: Official Opening by Chris Chataway MP
        Oct: Formation of PTA
        Nov: PTA dance in aid of proposed swimming
        pool

1964   Opening of adjoining County Agricultural
        Centre
        March: Senior Youth Club Residential
        Weekend in college
        June: Outdoor Activities Week
        Sept: Formation of Fifth Form
        Dec: Inaugural meeting of Hunts &
        Peterborough County Council at Sawtry

1965   Feb: Formation of Film Society
        April: Swimming pool in use
        Parent Representative on Governing Body
        Purchase of 'Arcon' building for Rural Studies
        August: American Day Camp
        PTA becomes joint, with Primary school(s)
        Introduction of Certificate of Secondary
        Education (CSE)
        School Pantomime

1966   First residential week at Kings Cliffe
        Ladies Afternoons
        First annual Form Drama Festival
        July: First Residential Art Week in college
        Homecraft Centre opened as part of the
        Agricultural Centre
        Swimming pool heating installed (diy)
        Housing shortage. Two staff in caravans on
        site
        County proposal for Sawtry to become 11-13
        Comprehensive

1967   Nursery School begins in Youth Centre
        County (amended) Comprehensive Plan: Sawtry
        to be 11-16
        80% of pupils can now swim
        First 'Meet the Staff' evening
        Fifth Form pupils sit GCE in six subjects

1968   July: Speech day postponed because of floods
        Quadrangle paved (diy)
        Formation of Scout Group. M Donne
        Sept: GEJ Chaney – Community Tutor

1969   Space crisis. '13 classes but only 6 ordinary
        rooms' First Mobile
        Inaugural meeting of Community Association
        Approx 62 'non-school' activities every week.
        1200 participants

1970   Publication of 'SEVEN'. Review of first 7 years
        Whole school walks the fields to Little Gidding
        church
        Start of transition to Comprehensive
        Education (11-16)
        Three more Mobile Classrooms
        Introduction of Year Tutors
        21 evening classes. 340 enrolments
        Dec: Festival of Nine Lessons & Carols

1971   Spring: Start of 'EVENTSHEET'
        May: 'Sawtry into the '70s' Convention.
        Biggest ever event
        June: Field Studies Week at Brathay
        Publication of 'COMP ONE' - Review of first
        'Comprehensive' year
        July: College Open Day. Over 500 attended
        Oct: Sawtry Harvest Weekend: 'Sa Ha We'
        First Year Outweek at Stibbington Res Centre
        Pool: showers, toilets, & spectator gallery.
        Club-financed
        Built by Gaynes Hall Borstal
        Opening of Sawtry Infant School
        Nov: First PTA Folk & Fireworks evening
        Dec: 'Toad of Toad Hall'

1972   First national fuel crisis. Most activities closed
        First school extension (ROSLA) Music suite on
        to Youth Centre
        April: Launch of Achievement Award Scheme
        May: 'HMS Pinafore'. Only five months after
        'Toad'!
        Publication of 'College for All'
        July: First Sawtry Show
        School Roll 300
        Maths for Parents. Mr Billson
        Youth Club attendance: 100 per night
        Oct: Glenn Richards (age 11 in 1963) accepted
        for E. Anglia University
        Proposal for additional (Dual-Use) sports field
        Nov: First Winter/Autumn Fair

1973   'Old Sawtry' exhibition. Led to formation of
        History Society
        Primary schools' concert/drama evening
        Tenth Anniversary.
        Fully illustrated EVENTSHEET
        July: 1200 attendances at Sawtry Show
        First A level successes
        New Playgroup started. Sec: Mrs Atkinson
        Major new school extensions to increase
        capacity 300 to 450
        Dec: 'The Thwarting of Baron Bolligrew'

1974   Second fuel crisis, except at Sawtry. We bought
        fuel to be self-sufficient!
        Additional & improved swimming changing
        rooms. Paid for by club
        HMI Inspection. 'Very encouraging and
        complimentary'
        Second minibus bought
        Raising School Leaving Age (ROSLA)
        Roll tops 400
        Floodlighting of playground for Youth Club
        (diy)
        Formation of new county of Cambridgeshire
        Outdoor play area formed for Playgroup (diy)
        The Sawtry Lectures
        Outdoor climbing wall
        Iceland Expedition - Glacier Survey
        Establishment of TV/Drama Room in old Art
        Room
        Eighteen pupils in Sixth Form
        FE Student reps on Community Association
        Plans for further building extensions
        (450 to 600)
        Autumn: Cage Bird Show
        'A Christmas Carol' Dickens

1975 Third national fuel crisis - except at Sawtry
Community Association Rep. on Governors.
Mr Custance
'Sawtry Visual' Multi-room films evening
May: College May Ball
June: *'Contemporary Hangings'* Exhibition
July: Fully Comprehensive School 11-16
Cessation of A level work. Older pupils must
move 'elsewhere'
Many big school outdoor trips. Over 50% of
pupils participate
'Village Voice' . Precurser of *'Sawty Eye'*
'Safe on a Moped' filmed for County Road
Safety Committee
Good Neighbour scheme
Dual Use sports field in use
Exchange link to Marburg, Germany
100 pupils in sponsored swim. 68 swam mile
Upper school Heads: Mr Billson & Mrs Burton
School has computer link to Tech. College at
Huntingdon
Purchase of Video Tape Recorder (Betamax)
Formation of Parents' Association mainly to
campaign for Sixth Form
Formation of Army Cadets Mr Paterson
Sawtry Parish Directory published
Hut provided for Army Cadets
Health Visitor based at the college

1976 Governors now have 2 parents and a staff rep
Jan: Roof blown off
First year Residential Weekends in school
increased to three
March: Ladies Hockey club formed
April: *'Pied Piper of Sawtry'* written by
parent Tim Rollo
May: Start of Governors' college visits
Bowling Green complete
Permanent Bar facility set up by Community
Association
Morocco Expedition
Archaeology Society formed
Self-budgetting for FE classes. Pilot scheme
for county
Hire fees now come direct to college
Youth Clubs at Gidding, Stilton, Folksworth,
Alconbury & Holme
Sep: Additional community tutor: Roger
Hemming
Anglo-American Dinner-Dance (Beavers)
Sawtry School of Dancing for age 4 plus
School roll now 500+
Dec: Gilbert & Sullivan: *'Trial by Jury'*
Dec: Two day residential for canoe-building

1977 Making of the film: *'Cambridgeshire
Communities'*
School now has computer links to two
Technical colleges
May: Application for own bar licence turned
down
Eventsheet circulation now 2000 copies
Sept: Purchase of 44 seater bus
School roll approaching 600.
Seven classes in mobile huts
Second – brief – HMI Inspection
Nov: Staff Revue!
School Play *'King John Lackland'* written by
Rod Fitzpatrick & Graham Whitehead
Dec: Regular *'Youth News'* pages in
'EVENTSHEET'
Dec: New extensions on the field (450-600)
complete

1978 Feb: New Joint Library opens. Over 10,000
books
Order for the Annual Brochure doubled to
4000 copies
Christine Wynne gets into Oxford University
Sponsored spell-in
Traffic Education – a CSE subject
Permanent Bar facility completed
13 students from Marburg. Twinning visit
July: Tony Gow edits *'EVENTSHEET's'* 'Society
News' pages
Sawtry population: 3000
Motor Cycle (Youth) Club. 53 members.
Fred Cossey i/c
Nov: Young Explorers' Trust National
Conference
Dec: Extracts from the Musical *'Oliver'*
Dec: Christmas Drama in church

1979 Jan: Pool repainted in 2 days by community
First edition of *'Leaves'* pupil magazine.
Ed: A Clifton
Bi-annual Careers Convention
June: *'Beat the Bounds'* sponsored walk
Summer Playscheme for c100 children
Proposed Foyer extension (ref.1985)
July: Motor cycle safety evening. With film:
'Safe on a Moped'
Aug: Warden reports on Australian Community
Education Conference
Sep: School Roll tops 600
Oct: First *'Youth in Action'* concert
Oct: Parents help purchase first mini-computer.
PET, @ £500
Nov: Archaeological Society rescue dig at
St Judith's manor site
Dec: *'Turkey in a Pear Tree'* production
Dec: 'Ice' skating in gym

1980 PT Jones: Acting Warden for year
Design Council Award to B Parkin
Offset litho replaces Roneo duplication
Pool refurbished by District Council
Pupils' RE Exhibition in Peterborough
Cathedral
Youth Club have one hour on Radio One's
'Talkabout'
School Meals: end of 'Family Service'. Most
schools gave this up long ago
County Conference for 50th Anniversary of
Village Colleges
Publication of *'Village Colleges Today'*. Basic
facts on all Cambs colleges
1000 young people in youth activities.
60% takeup, against national average 20%
Sawtry commended in Gov't Report:
'Craft, Design, Technology'
Oct: Extensions to lower block opened.
School capacity now 750
Sawtry Venture Scout Unit founded
Dec: *'The Ghost Train'* by Arnold Ridley.
Postponed to January

1981   March: Purchase of second 44 seat coach
June: ex Sawtry pupil, Hazel Farrington,
Head Girl of Kings, Peterborough
Summer: Sports Hall opened
Closure of Homecraft Centre
June: Champion Netball team
June: Community Day: Showcase for
organisations
July: Swimming pool overhaul & re-roof
complete at last!
Disabled persons' toilet in main block
Publication of 50 page *'Guide to Secondary
Education in Sawtry'*
Malcolm Baines gets into Selwyn College,
Cambridge
Lecture Room fitted out with hob etc for
community events
Publication of Dybeck's research: *'The Village
College Way'*
Good exam grades achieved by 25% of
pupils. National norm: 9%
Average CSE grade: 2.8. National norm:
grade 4
Severe cuts in education expenditure
Disruptions due to Industrial Action
Dec: Production of *'Humbug'*

1982   Igloo Building for BBC Blue Peter TV
Pupils in BBC TV debate
Jan: Formation of Choral Society. Peter
Davies
Foundation of CARESCO
Revival of First Year residential weekends
in school
Sports Travel Award from Wrigleys
Rock Concert. Andrew Clifton fecit
Nine pupil university degrees. More than
double national average
Sawtry Junior School moves to new premises
Jackie Perry gets into Cambridge University
Steven Simlo accepted for post-graduate
Masters Course in USA
Threat of 30-40 houses on ex-junior school
field
'Let's Look at Christmas' Joint Production
with Juniors
All FE class records now on computer. A
'first' in Cambs.

1983   Chief Scout, General Walsh, visits local
Scouts twice!
Jan: School Rock Concert
Print Training Workshop in former
Homecraft Centre
'EVENTSHEET 50'. Design & printing by
Sawtry Printshop
Oct: Major refit in Youth Centre. On own
finances
Junior School building to be sold to Sawtry
Parish Council
Junior School field transferred for college use
Part of Dual-Use field sold off for housing.
Dual-Use ceases

1984   First school to have a fully equipped
'Computer Laboratory'
Sawtry population: 4500
Feb: Update/reissue of our *'Guide to Sawtry
Education'* (1981)
Senior Citizens' clubs on 3 days a week
run by CARESCO
Over 80 FE classes and Enrolments of 1200
Exchange students from Marburg. Biggest
ever group
O Level results: over double the national
average
Summer Playscheme includes Special Needs
children
Community Association: 61 groups.
c15,000 members
New Solar panels for heating swimming
pool
General Prospectus for all users produced
Sep: Old Students Reunion. 21years on.
250 came
School Roll 645. 38 teaching staff

1985   Jan: Mr J Stewart MA appointed Warden

24 **Pupil Numbers**

Some of these figures are not always accurate because they have been extracted from a variety of sources and at different times of the year. But the overall trend is correct. (Compiling this has been a bit like doing Sudoku!)

Year Sept	School Roll 11-16							
	Year1	Year2	Year3	Year 4	Year 5	Yrs 1-5	VI Form	Total
1963	60	43	62	57	0	222		
1964	48	61	44	63	5	221		
1965	54	46	62	47	5	214		
1966	49	58	45	61	11	224		
1967	46	46	60	46	12	210		
1968	62	42	48	56	15	226	6	232
1969	70	58	40	48	25	240	10	250
1970	53 (*)	68	58	40	28	241	4	245
1971	63	61	72	58	28	282	5	287
1972	69	67	65	76	32	309	4	313
1973	104	72	67	62	69	374 (R)	4	378
1974	108	107	73	73	60	421	18 (A)	439
1975	121	106	106	70	70	473	3	476
1976	130	121	114	108	72	545	2	547
1977	125	125	119	110	106	585	0	
1978	126	125	120	108	106	585	0	
1979	130	125	125	120	118	618	0	
1980	135	130	125	125	119	634	0	
1981	139	134	134	130	124	661	0	
1982	132	135	131	135	134	667	0	
1983	125	132	135	129	133	654	0	
1984	118 (*)	125	132	135	129	644	0	

(R) = ROSLA Raising of compulsory school leaving age from 15 to 16

(A) = Cessation of remit to do A level courses. The 'Comprehensive Plan'

(*) = A time of falling rolls, nationally. But our decline is not simply due to fewer pupils in the area, but to take-up by parents of the opportunity to go to neighbouring 11-18 schools, which now had vacant spaces.

Graphs of the above figures are to be found in the main text. Page 149

25 **College Staff**

This is derived mainly from the lists in the Annual Brochures and so might miss out any changes that happened mid-year. I have included some part-timers.

1963

Warden	MW Dybeck MA		JAC Cowling BA
Deputy	PT Jones		Mrs HM Yates
Youth Tutor	DS Marshall		Mrs JA Harris
			Miss PA Pettifor
Staff	RE Claiden		Miss PA Chaney
	JC Yates		
	RG Tuplin	Secretary	Mrs MJE Curtis
	MGS Shaw	Caretaker	WF Fyfe
	MP Coulson	Cook	Mrs B Crowson

1964

Warden	MW Dybeck MA		Mrs HM Yates
Deputy	PT Jones		Mrs CMB Hillman
Youth Tutor	DS Marshall		Miss PA Pettifor
			Miss PA Chaney
Staff	RE Claiden		Mrs A Anson
	JC Yates		Mrs Newbould
	RG Tuplin		
	MGS Shaw	Secretary	Mrs MJE Curtis
	MP Coulson	LabTechnician	A Walker
	F Wiseman	Caretaker	J Cullup
	RI Davies	Cook	Mrs B Crowson
		Groundsman	A Thompson

1965

Warden	MW Dybeck MA		Mrs C Hardy
Deputy	PT Jones		Miss PA Pettifor
Youth Tutor	DS Marshall		Mrs PA Shaw
Staff	JC Yates	Secretaries	Mrs MJE Curtis
	RG Tuplin		Mrs C Thompson
	F Wiseman	Cook	Mrs B Crowson
	Mrs B Baxter	Lab Technician	E Dexter
	JH Gillis AKC	Caretaker	J Cullup
	MGS Shaw NDD	Assistant Caretaker	C Nickerson
	MP Coulson	Groundsman	A Thompson
	Mrs HM Yates		

1966

			Mrs M Girling
Warden	MW Dybeck MA		Miss PA Pettifor
Deputy	PT Jones		Mrs PA Shaw
Youth Tutor	DS Marshall		Mrs JM Lister
Staff	JC Yates	Secretaries	Mrs MJE Curtis
	RG Tuplin		Mrs S Wallis
	F Wiseman	Cook	Mrs B Crowson
	Mrs B Baxter	Lab Technician	E Dexter
	JH Gillis AKC	Caretaker	J Cullup
	MGS Shaw NDD	Assistant Caretaker	C Nickerson
	MP Coulson	Groundsman	A Thompson
	M Olssen BA		

1967

Warden	MW Dybeck MA	Social Studies	Mrs PA Shaw
Deputy	PT Jones	Remedial	Mrs J Atkinson
Youth Tutor	vacancy	Girls PE	Mrs J Tattersall
Head of Maths	JC Yates	Needlework & French	Mrs HMN Ilott BA
Head of English	F Wiseman	Needlework	Mrs C Hardy
Head of Science	J Atkinson	Secretaries	Mrs S Wallis
Senior Mistress	Mrs B Baxter		Mrs S Williams
Rural Studies	RG Tuplin	Cook	Mrs B Crowson
Music	Miss PA Pettifor	Laboratory Technician	E Dexter
RI & PE	JH Gillis AKC	Caretaker	J Cullup
Art & Metalwork	MGS Shaw NDD	Assistant Caretaker	WA Wright
Woodwork & TD	MP Coulson	Groundsman	A Thompson
English	M Olssen BA		
	Mrs B Mitchley		

1968

Warden	MW Dybeck MA	General Subjects	Mrs JR Burton
Deputy	PT Jones LCP	Social Studies	Mrs PA Shaw
Community Tutor	GEJ Chaney MBE	Girls PE	Mrs J Tattersall
Senior Mistress	Miss PA Pettifor	French	Mrs HMN Ilott BA
Head of English	F Wiseman	Geography & Maths	E Sharman
Head of Maths	JC Yates	Maths & PE	IM Tait
Head of Science	J Atkinson	Secretaries	Mrs S Wallis
Domestic Science	Mrs M Robson		Mrs S M Williams
Needlework	Mrs C Hardy	Cook	Mrs B Crowson
Rural Studies	RG Tuplin	Laboratory Technician	E Dexter
RI	JH Gillis AKC	Caretaker	J Cullup
Art & Metalwork	MGS Shaw NDD	Assistant Caretaker	WA Wright
Woodwork & TD	MP Coulson	Groundsman	AR Thompson

1969

Warden	MW Dybeck MA	Domestic Science	Mrs M Robson
Deputy	PT Jones LCP	Needlework	Mrs C Hardy
Community Tutor	GEJ Chaney MBE	Art & Metalwork	MGS Shaw NDD
Senior Mistress	Miss PA Pettifor	Woodwork & TD	MP Coulson
Humanities Dept	NT Pope BA	Girls PE	Mrs Walls
English	F Wiseman	Maths & PE	IM Tait
History	Mrs PA Shaw	Secretary	Mrs SP Cattell
French	Mrs HMN Ilott BA		Mrs SM Williams
RI	JH Gillis AKC		Mrs BC Wisker
Remedial	Mrs JR Burton	Cook	Mrs B Crowson
Science	J Atkinson	Laboratory Technician	EK Dexter
Maths	JC Yates	Caretaker	J Cullup
Geography	RG Tuplin	Assistant Caretaker	WA Wright
Practical Studies Dept	BM Parkin	Groundsman	AR Thompson

1970

Warden	MW Dybeck MA	Practical Studies Dept	B.M.Parkin
Deputy	PT Jones LCP	Domestic Science	Mrs M.Robson
Community Tutor	GEJ Chaney MBE	Needlework	Mrs C Hardy
Senior Mistress	Miss MF Clarke BA	Art & Metalwork	MGS Shaw NDD
Humanities Dept	NT Pope BA	Woodwork & TD	MP Coulson
English	F Wiseman	Girls PE	Mrs Walls
History	Mrs PA Shaw	Secretary	Miss M Bruss
French	Mrs HMN Ilott BA		Mrs CE Laxton
RI	Mrs J Gillis		Mrs BC Wisker
Remedial	DJ Houghton	Cook	Mrs B Crowson
	Mrs JR Burton	Laboratory Technician	Mrs J Kightley
Science	J Atkinson	Caretaker	J Cullup
Maths	AJ Billson	Assistant Caretaker	WA Wright
Maths & PE	IM Tait	Groundsman	AR Thompson
Geography	RG Tuplin		

1971

Warden	MW Dybeck MA	Geography	RG Tuplin
Deputy	PT Jones LCP	Practical Studies Dept	BM Parkin MCC DLC
Community Tutor	GEJ Chaney MBE	Needlework	Mrs JR Burton
Senior Mistress	Miss MF Clarke BA	Woodwork	MP Coulson
		Art	J Parfitt NDD ATD
Humanities Dept	Mrs J Stuart BA	Domestic Science	Mrs M Robson
English	F Wiseman	Needlework	Mrs C Hardy
Religious Education	Miss MF Clarke BA		
Languages	Mrs HMN Ilott BA	Secretary	Mrs RI Pilgrim
Music	Miss PA Pettifor	Assistant Secretaries	Mrs CE Laxton
History	Mrs PA Shaw		Mrs BC Wisker
French Assistante	Mlle J Dubois	Cook	Mrs V Crowson
Remedial Dept	DJ Houghton	Laboratory Technician	AE Woodward
Sciences Dept	GC Bowman MA	Youth Leader	JE Green
Mathematics	AJ Billson	Assistants	Mrs J Gillis
Science	J Atkinson		A Clark
Maths	Mrs JMD Gordon	Caretaker	J Cullup
	PT Jones LCP	Assistant Caretaker	WA Wright
Maths & PE	IM Tait	Groundsman	D Deller
Biology and PE	Miss S Farnsworth		

1972

Warden	MW Dybeck MA	Maths & PE	IM Tait
Deputy	PT Jones LCP		Mrs JA Dorling BSc
Community Tutor	GEJ Chaney MBE	Practical Studies Dept	BM Parkin MCC Ed DLC
Senior Mistress	Miss MF Clarke BA	Needlework	Mrs JR Burton
		Woodwork	MP Coulson
Humanities Dept	Mrs J Stuart BA	Art	J Parfitt NDD ATD
English	F Wiseman	Domestic Science	Mrs J Gillis
Religious Education	Miss MF Clarke BA		
	Rev THW Swan MA	Secretary	Mrs RI Pilgrim
Languages	Mrs HMN Ilott BA	Assistant Secretaries	Mrs CE Laxton
German	Mrs H Smart		Mrs BC Wisker
Music	Miss PA Pettifor	Cook	Mrs J Forbes
French Assistante	Mlle CO Marlot	Laboratory Technician	A Woodward
History	Mrs PD Bainbridge BA	Youth Leader	JE Green
Remedial Dept	DJ Houghton	Assistants	Mrs J Gillis
Sciences Dept	GC Bowman MA		A Clark
Science	J Atkinson	Caretaker	J Cullup
Geography	RG Tuplin	Assistant Caretaker	LT Trudgen
Biology & PE	Miss S Farnsworth	Groundsman	D Deller
Mathematics Dept	AJ Billson Grad IME		
Maths	PT Jones LCP		

1973

Warden	MW Dybeck MA	PE	Miss J Wilkinson
Deputy	PT Jones LCP	PE & Maths	IM Tait
Community Tutor	GEJ Chaney MBE	Maths & PE	PT Jones LCP
Senior Mistress	Miss MF Clarke BA	Practical Studies Dept	BM Parkin MCC Ed DLC
		Needlework	Mrs JR Burton
Humanities Dept	Mrs J Stuart BA	Woodwork	MP Coulson
English	F Wiseman	Art	J Parfitt NDD ATD
Religious Education	Miss MF Clarke BA		Mrs C Francis
Languages	JW Lemon BA	Domestic Science	Mrs J Gillis
	Mrs HMN Ilott BA		
German	Mrs H Smart	Secretary	Mrs RI Pilgrim
Music	Miss PA Pettifor	Assistant Secretaries	Mrs CE Laxton
French Assistante	Mlle JM Lambert		Mrs BC Wisker
History	Mrs IC Cambridge		Mrs J Newell
Remedial Dept	DJ Houghton	School Nurse	Mrs J Tucker
	Mrs A Allnutt	Cook	Mrs J Forbes
	Mrs B Elshaw	Laboratory Technician	AE Woodward
Sciences Dept	GC Bowman MA	Youth Leader	JE Green
Science	NJ Andrews	Assistants	Mrs J Stringwell
Geography	RG Tuplin		A Clark
Mathematics	AJ Billson Grad.IME	Caretaker	J Cullup
	RA Osmond	Assistant Caretaker	LT Trudgen
		Groundsman	D Deller

1974

Warden	MW Dybeck MA	PE	Miss S Farnsworth
Deputy	PT Jones LCP	PE & Maths	IM Tait
Community Tutor	GEJ Chaney MBE	Maths & PE	PT Jones LCP
Senior Mistress	Miss MF Clarke BA	Practical Studies Dept	BM Parkin MCC Ed DLC
		Needlework	Mrs JR Burton
Humanities Dept	Mrs J Stuart BA	Woodwork	MP Coulson
English	F Wiseman	Art	JParfitt NDD ATD
Religious Education	Mr J Oria BA		Mrs C Francis
	Miss MF Clarke BA	Domestic Science	Mrs J Gillis
Languages	JW Lemon BA		Mrs J Costin
	Mrs JA Britten BA		
Music	Miss PA Pettifor	Secretary	Mrs CE Laxton
French Assistante	Mlle JM Lambert	Assistant Secretaries	Mrs V Saunders
History	Mrs IC Cambridge		Mrs BC Wisker
Remedial Dept	Mrs A Allnutt	School Nurse	Mrs J Newell
	Mr FR Hutchings BA	Cook	Mrs M Thomson
	Mrs J Atkinson	Laboratory Technician	AE Woodward
Sciences Dept	GC Bowman MA	General Technician	A Booth
Mathematics	AJ Billson Grad IME	Youth Leader	JE Green
	Mrs B Elshaw	Assistants	Mrs S Keyworth
	RA Osmond BA		Mrs JS Stringwell
Science	J Atkinson	Caretaker	J Cullup
	NJ Andrews BSc	Assistant Caretaker	LT Trudgen
Geography	RG Tuplin	Groundsman	D Deller

1975

Warden	MW Dybeck MA	Geography	RG Tuplin
Deputy	PT Jones LCP		Mrs JE Hubbard BSc
Community Tutor	GEJ Chaney MBE	PE	Miss S Farnsworth
Senior Mistress	Miss MF Clarke BA	PE & Maths	IM Tait
		Maths & PE	PT Jones LCP
Humanities Dept	Mrs J Stuart BA	Practical Studies Dept	BM Parkin MCC Ed DLC
English	Mrs JV Bull BA	Needlework	Mrs JR Burton
Religious Education	Mrs JE Jackson	Woodwork	MP Coulson
	Miss MF Clarke BA	Metalwork	NW Bicknell AMI Mech E
Languages	JW Lemon BA	Art	J Parfitt NDD ATD
	Mrs MA Maddern BA		Mrs C Francis RAS Cert
German	Mrs H Smart	Domestic Science	Mrs J Gillis
Music	Miss PA Pettifor	Child Care	Mrs C Costin
French Assistante	Mlle H Arland		
History	Mrs IC Cambridge	Secretary	Mrs RI Pilgrim
Remedial	Mr DJ Houghton A DipEd	Assistants	Mrs CE Laxton
	Mrs A Allnutt		Mrs BC Wisker
	Mrs J Atkinson	School Nurse	Mrs J Tucker
	Mr FR Hutchings BA	Cook	Mrs M Thomsom
Sciences Dept	GC Bowman MA	Laboratory Technician	AE Woodward
Science	J Atkinson A DipEd	Youth Leader	JE Green
Mathematics	AJ Billson Grad.IME	Assistant	Mrs J Stringwell
	Mrs B Elshaw	Caretaker	DP Short
	Mrs AE Carlill BSc	Assistant Caretaker	LT Trudgen
Science	NJ Andrews BSc M InstP	Groundsman	D Deller

1976

Warden	MW Dybeck MA	Maths & Computer	Mrs B Elshaw
Deputy	PT Jones LCP	Geography & Environ	RG Tuplin BA
Senior Mistress	Miss MF Clarke BA	Geography	Mrs JM Brooker BA
Head of Upper School	AJ Billson Grad IME	Practical Studies Dept	BM Parkin BA MCC Ed DLC
Community Senior Tutor	GEJ Chaney MBE	Needlewk & Child Care	Mrs JR Burton
Assistant Tutor	RB Hemming BTech	Design	MP Coulson
		Metalwork & Maths	DO Crewe
Humanities Dept	Mrs J Stuart BA	Art	JParfitt NDD ATD
English	Mrs JV Bull BA		Mrs C Francis RAS Cert
	JA Whitehead		
English & RE	Mrs JE Jackson	Domestic Science	Mrs J Gillis
Languages	JW Lemon BA	Child Care	Mrs C Costin
	Mrs MA Maddern BA	Practical Studies	Mrs KH Blissett
Music	Miss PA Pettifor		Mrs M Crewe
French Assistante	Mlle M Brun	PE	Miss J Wilkinson
History & German	Mrs IC Cambridge		IM Tait
History & Europ Stud	JC Phillimore BA Dip AD	Secretary	Mrs CE Laxton
RE & Classical Stud	Miss MF Clarke BA	Assistant Secretaries	Mrs BC Wisker
Religious Education	Mrs CA Anderson		Mrs V Saunders
Social Studies	GEJ Chaney MBE	Medical Assistant	Mrs J Newell
Remedial Dept	DJ Houghton A DipEd	Cook	Mrs M Thompson
	Mrs A Allnutt	Laboratory Technician	AE Woodward
	Mrs J Atkinson	General Technician	A Booth
Sciences Dept	WR Fitzpatrick BA	Youth Leader	JE Green
Science	J Atkinson A DipEd	Assistants	Mrs J Stringwell
	AJ Lloyd BEd		Mrs J Keyworth
Mathematics	AJ Billson Grad IME	Caretaker	DP Short
	Mrs S Brown BSc	Assistant Caretaker	AR Dawson
	PT Jones LCP	Groundsman	D Deller
	A Allmark		

1977

Warden	MW Dybeck MA	Geography	RG Tuplin BA
Deputy	PT Jones LCP		Mrs JM Brooker BA
Senior Mistress	Miss MF Clarke BA	Practical Studies Dept	BM Parkin BA MCC Ed DLC
Head of Upper School	AJ Billson Grad IME	Needlewk & Child Care	Mrs JR Burton
Community Snr Tutor	GEJ Chaney MBE	Design	MP Coulson
Assistant Tutor	RB Hemming BTech	Metalwork	D Crewe
Humanities Dept	Mrs J Stuart BA	Art	J Parfitt NDD ATD
English	A Clifton BA		Mrs C Francis RAS Cert
	Mrs JE Jackson	3D sculpture	Miss SM Patterson BA
	GA Whitehead	Domestic Science	Mrs J Gillis
Languages	JW Lemon BA	Practical Studies	Mrs KH Blissett
	Mrs MA Maddern BA		Mrs M Crewe
	Miss S Rix BEd	PE	Miss S Farnsworth
Music	Miss PA Pettifor		IM Tait
French Assistante	Mlle G Agen	Secretary	Mrs CE Laxton
History & German	Mrs IC Cambridge	Assistant Secretaries	Mrs BC Wisker
History	JC Phillimore BA DipAD		Mrs V Saunders
English & Social Studies	Miss MF Clarke BA	Medical Assistant	Mrs J Newell
Religious Education	Mrs CA Anderson	Cook	Mrs M Thompson
Remedial Dept	DJ Houghton ADipEd	Laboratory Technician	AE Woodward
	Mrs A Allnutt	Laboratory Assistant	Mrs P Harradine
Sciences Dept	WR Fitzpatrick BA	General Technician	A Booth
Science	J Atkinson A DipEd	Youth Leader	JE Green
	AJ Lloyd BEd	Assistants	Mrs J Stringwell
Biology	Miss LJ English BA		Mrs J Keyworth
Mathematics	AJ Billson Grad IME		GA Whitehead
	Mrs J Atkinson	Caretaker	DP Short
	PT Jones LCP	Assistant Caretaker	A Dawson
	RB Hemming BTech	Groundsman	D Deller
	G Feakes BEd		
Maths & Computer	Mrs B Elshaw		
	A Allmark		

1978

Warden	MW Dybeck MA	Maths & Comp Studies	Mrs B Elshaw
Deputy	PT Jones LCP		A Allmark
Senior Mistress	Miss MF Clarke BA	Practical Studies Dept	BM Parkin BA MCC Ed DLC
Head of Upper School	AJ Billson Grad IME	Needlewk & Child Care	Mrs JR Burton
Community Tutor	RB Hemming BTech	Design	MP Coulson
		Metalwork	D Crewe
Humanities Dept	Mrs J Stuart BA	Art	MJ Ingram DipAD
English	A Clifton BA		Mrs C Francis RAS Cert
	Mrs JE Jackson	3D sculpture	Miss SM Patterson BA
	GA Whitehead	Domestic Science	Mrs J Gillis
Librarian	Mrs J Bibby	Practical Studies	Mrs J Fradley
Music	Miss PA Pettifor		Mrs M Crewe
French Assistante	Mlle M Marchais	PE	Miss S Farnsworth
History & German	Mrs IC Cambridge		IM Tait
History	JC Phillimore BA DipAD		
Geography	RG Tuplin BA	Secretary	Mrs CE Laxton
	Mrs JM Brooker BA	Assistant (Comm.Ed)	Mrs V Saunders
English & Social Studies	Miss M Clarke BA	Medical Assistant	Mrs J Newell
Religious Education	Mrs CA Anderson	Cook	Mrs M Thompson
Remedial Dept	DJ Houghton A DipEd	Lab Technician	AE Woodward
	Mrs A Allnutt	Lab Assistant	Mrs P Harradine
	Mrs S Gibson BEd	General Technician	A Booth
	Mrs M Edge BA	Youth Leader	JL Green
	Miss S Smith BA	Assistants	Mrs J Keyworth
Sciences Dept	WR Fitzpatrick BA		GA Whitehead
Science	J Atkinson A DipEd		F Cossey
	AJ Lloyd BEd	Caretaker	DP Short
Biology	Miss LJ English BA	Assistant Caretaker	Mrs P Robinson
Mathematics	AJ Billson Grad IME	Groundsman	D Deller
	Mrs J Atkinson		
	PT Jones LCP		
	G Feakes BEd		
	Miss S Chilton BEd		

1979

Warden	MW Dybeck MA
Deputy	PT Jones LCP
Senior Mistress	Miss MF Clarke BA
Head of Upper School	AJ Billson Grad IME
Humanities Dept	Mrs J Stuart BA, A Clifton BA, Mrs JE Jackson, GA Whitehead, Miss PA Pettifor,
	Mlle C Haupert, Mrs IC Cambridge, JC Phillimore BA DipAD, Miss M Clarke BA
	Mrs CA Anderson, Mrs AJ Allnutt, Mrs S Gibson BEd, Mrs M Edge BA,
	Miss S Smith, BA G Lewis MA DipEd (Australian exchange), Miss K Dobson,
Science Dept	WR Fitzpatrick BA, J Atkinson BA A DipEd, AJ Lloyd BEd, Miss L J English BA,
	AJ Billson Grad IME, Mrs B Elshaw, Mrs J Atkinson, PT Jones LCP, G Feakes BEd,
	A Allmark, RG Tuplin BA, Mrs J M Brooker BA, Miss S Chilton BEd, J Keil BEd.
Practical Studies Dept	BM Parkin BA MCCEd DLC, Mrs JR Burton, MP Coulson, D Crewe,
	MJ Ingram DipAD, Mrs C Francis RAS Cert, Miss SM Patterson BA, Mrs J Gillis,
	Mrs J Fradley, Mrs M Crewe, Miss S Farnsworth, IM Tait.

Community Education

Community Tutor	RB Hemming BTech	Community Ed Asst	Mrs V Saunders
General Assistant	Miss D Clark	Youth Leader	JL Green
Assistants	Mrs J Keyworth GA Whitehead F Cossey H Hitchman		

Administration

Secretary	Mrs CE Laxton	Assistant Secretary	Mrs G Jack
Medical Assistant	Mrs J Newell	Head Cook	Mrs M Thompson
Laboratory Technician	AE Woodward	Laboratory Assistant	Mrs P Harradine
General Technician	A Booth	Caretaker	DP Short
Assistant	Mrs P Robinson		
Groundsman	D Deller		

1980

Acting Warden:	PT Jones LCP
Deputy Warden:	Miss MF Clarke BA
Senior Master:	AJ Billson Grad IME

Humanities:	Mrs J Stuart BA, A Clifton BA, Mrs JE Jackson, Miss K Dobson, Miss PA Pettifor, Mlle C Haupert, Mrs IC Cambridge, JC Phillimore BA DipAD, Mrs CA Anderson, Mrs S Gibson BEd, Mrs M Edge BA, Miss S Smith BA.
Science & Geography:	WR Fitzpatrick BA, J Atkinson A Dip Ed BA, AJ Lloyd BEd, Miss LJ English BEd, AJ Stevens BSc, Mrs JM Brooker BA.
Maths & Computing:	Mrs B Elshaw, G Feakes BEd, A Allmark, J Keil BEd, Miss S Chilton BEd.
Practical Studies:	BM Parkin BA MCC Ed DLC, Mrs JR Burton, MP Coulson, D Crewe, MJ Ingram DipAD, Mrs C Francis RAS Cert, Miss AD Green DipAD, Mrs J Gillis, Mrs J Fradley, Mrs M Crewe.
Remedial:	DJ Houghton A DipEd, Mrs AJ Allnutt, Mrs J Atkinson.
PE:	Miss S Farnsworth IM Tait.

Community Education

Community Tutor:	RB Hemming BTech	Community Ed Asst:	Mrs V Saunders
General Asst:	Miss D Clark	Youth Leader:	JL Green
Assistants:	Mrs J Keyworth, GA Whitehead, F Cossey, H Hitchman.		

Administration

Secretary:	Mrs CE Laxton	Assistant Secretary:	Mrs G Jack
Medical Assistant:	Mrs J Newell	Head Cook:	Mrs M Thompson
Laboratory Technician:	AE Woodward	Laboratory Assistant:	Mrs P Harradine
General Technician:	A Booth		
Caretaker:	DP Short	Assistant Caretaker:	C Short
Groundsman:	D Deller		

1981

Warden:	MW Dybeck MA
Deputy:	PT Jones LCP
Senior Mistress:	Miss MF Clarke BA
Head of Upper School:	AJ Billson Grad IME

Humanities:	Mrs J Stuart BA, A Clifton BA, Mrs JE Jackson, Mrs KJ Chapman, Miss PA Pettifor (1st Yr Hd), Mrs IC Cambridge, JC Phillimore BA DipAD, Miss M Clarke BA, Mrs CA Anderson (2nd Yr Hd).
Languages:	Mrs M Edge BA, Mrs S Gibson BEd, Mrs S Houghton BA.
Remedial:	DJ Houghton A DipEd, Mrs SC Thomas.
Science & Geography:	WR Fitzpatrick BA, AJ Lloyd BEd, Miss LJ English BEd, SFV Thomas BSc, AJ Stevens BSc, Miss L Heslop BEd.
Maths & Computing:	Mrs B Elshaw, PT Jones LCP, G Feakes BEd, A Allmark, Miss S Chilton BEd, JW Keil BEd.
Practical Studies:	BM Parkin BA MCC Ed DLC, Mrs JR Burton (Asst Hd Upper Sch), MP Coulson (3rd Yr Hd), DO Crewe, MJ Ingram DipAD, Mrs CA Francis RAS Cert, Miss S Patterson BA, Mrs J Gillis, Mrs JE Fradley, Mrs ME Crewe, Miss D Green DipAD, Mrs J Messenger.
PE:	Miss CA Cook BEd, IM Tait.

Community Education

Community Tutor:	P Davies	Community Ed Assist:	Mrs V Saunders
Youth Leader:	JL Green	Assistant:	Mrs E Waby, Miss S Chilton, F Cossey

Administration

Secretary:	Mrs CE Laxton	Assistant Secretary:	Mrs G Jack
Medical Assistant:	Mrs J Newell	Head Cook:	Mrs M Thompson
Lab Technician:	AE Woodward	Laboratory Assistants:	Mrs P Harradine, Mrs S Radwell
General Technician:	A Booth		
Caretaker:	DPG Short	Assistant Caretaker:	C Short
Groundsman:	D Deller		

1982

Warden:	MW Dybeck MA
Deputy:	PT Jones LCP
Senior Mistress:	Miss MF Clarke BA
Head of Upper School:	AJ Billson Grad IME

Humanities:	Mrs J Stuart BA, A Clifton BA, Mrs JE Jackson, Mrs KJ Chapman, Miss PA Pettifor (1st Yr Hd), Mrs I Cambridge, JC Phillimore BA DipAD, Miss M Clarke BA, Mrs CA Anderson (2nd Yr Hd).
Languages:	Mrs M Edge BA, Mrs S Gibson BEd, Mrs S Houghton BA.
Remedial:	DJ Houghton A DipEd, Mrs SC Thomas.
Science & Geog:	WR Fitzpatrick BA, Miss LJ English BEd, AN Wood BSc, SFV Thomas BSc, AJ Stevens BSc, Miss L Heslop BEd.
Maths & Computing:	Mrs B Elshaw, PT Jones LCP, G Feakes BEd, A Allmark, Miss S Chilton BEd, JW Keil BEd.
Practical Studies:	BM Parkin BA MCC.Ed DLC, Mrs JR Burton (Asst Hd Upper Sch), MP Coulson (3rd Yr Hd), DO Crewe, MJ Ingram Dip AD, Mrs CA Francis RAS Cert, Mrs J Gillis, Mrs JE Fradley, Mrs JM Messenger BEd, Miss D Green DipAD.
PE:	Miss CA Cook BEd, IM Tait.

Community Education

Community Tutor:	P Davies	Community Ed Asst:	Mrs V Saunders
Youth Leader:	J L Green	Assistants:	Mrs E Waby, Miss S Chilton, F Cossey

Administration

Secretary:	Mrs CE Laxton	Assistant Secretary:	Mrs G Jack
Medical Assistant:	Mrs J Newell	Head Cook:	Mrs M Thompson
Technician:	Mr E Gay	Laboratory Technician:	Mrs S Radwell
Laboratory Assistant:	Mrs P Harradine	General Technician:	A Booth
Caretaker:	DPG Short	Assistant:	CR Short
Groundsman:	D Deller		

1983

Warden:	MW Dybeck MA
Deputy:	PT Jones LCP
Senior Mistress:	Mrs MF Jones BA
Head of Upper School:	AJ Billson Grad IME

English:	PA Hind BA, A Clifton BA, Mrs JE Jackson, Mrs G Thompson BA, Mrs Bull BA.
Humanities:	Miss PA Pettifor (1st Yr Hd), Mrs IC Cambridge, Mrs CA Anderson (2nd Yr Hd), Mrs Beaven BA, AJ Stevens BSc, Miss EP Webber BSc.
Languages:	Mrs M Edge BA, Mrs S Gibson BEd, Mrs S Houghton BA.
Remedial:	DJ Houghton A DipEd, JW Keil BEd.
Science:	WR Fitzpatrick BA***, Miss LJ English BEd, AN Wood BSc, SFV Thomas BSc.
Maths & Computing:	Miss S Chilton BEd, G Feakes BEd, A Allmark, Miss J Kitchen BA, Miss LM Morton BEd.
Practical Studies:	BM Parkin BA MCC Ed DLC, Mrs JR Burton (Asst Hd Upper Sch), MP Coulson (3rd Yr Hd), DO Crewe, MJ Ingram DipAD, Mrs J Gillis, Miss DE Marsh DipAD, Mrs JM Messenger BEd, Miss D Green DipAD.
PE:	Miss CA Cook BEd, IM Tait.

Community Education

Community Tutor:	P Davies	Community Ed Asst:	Mrs V Saunders
Youth Leader:	Carole McGee, Sue Chilton	Assistants:	Fred Cossey, Bob Kelly

Administration

Secretary:	Mrs CE Laxton	Asstitant Secretary:	Mrs G Jack
Medical Assistant:	Mrs J Newell	Head Cook:	Mrs M Thompson
Technician:	Mr E Gay	Laboratory Technician:	Mrs S Radwell
Laboratory Assistant:	Mrs P Harradine	General Technician:	A Booth
Caretaker:	DPG Short	Assistant Caretaker:	CR Short
Groundsman:	D Deller		

1984 ———

Warden:	MW Dybeck MA (Retired December 1984)
Deputy:	PT Jones LCP
Senior Mistress:	Mrs MF Jones BA
Head of Upper School:	AJ Billson Grad IME

English:	PA Hind BA, A Clifton BA, Mrs G Thompson BA, Mrs Bull BA
Humanities:	Mrs PA Tuplin (1st Yr Hd), Mrs IC Cambridge, Mrs CA Anderson (2nd Yr Hd),
	AJ Stevens BSc*, JC Phillimore BA DipAD, Miss EP Webber BSc.
Languages:	Mrs J Harris BA BEd, Mrs LM Tetley BA, Mrs S Houghton BA.
Remedial:	DJ Houghton A DipEd, JW Keil BEd.
Science:	AN Wood BSc, Miss LJ English BEd, P Jackson BSc BEd, Miss JMA Gammon BEd.
Maths & Computing:	N Smith BA**, G Feakes BEd, A Allmark, Miss J Kitchen BA,
	Mrs C Bowler BSocSc BEd, RG Tuplin BA.
Practical Studies:	BM Parkin BA MCCEd DLC, Mrs JR Burton (Asst Hd Upper Sch),
	MP Coulson (3rd Yr Hd), DO Crewe, MJ Ingram DipAD, Mrs J Gillis, Miss DE Marsh DipAD,
	Mrs JM Messenger BEd, Miss DGreen DipAD.
PE:	Ms A Togher PE, IM Tait.

COMMUNITY EDUCATION

Community Tutor:	P Davies	Community Ed Asst:	Mrs V Saunders
Youth Leaders:	Fred Cossey, Jill Cossey		

ADMINISTRATION

Secretary:	Mrs CE Laxton****	Asst Secretaries:	Mrs G Jack, Mrs C Chisnall *****
Medical Assistant:	Mrs J Newell	Head Cook:	Mrs M Thompson
Technician:	J Brooke	Laboratory Technician:	Mrs S Radwell
Laboratory Assistant:	Mrs P Harradine	General Technician:	A Booth
Caretaker:	DPG Short	Assistant Caretaker:	CR Short
Groundsman:	D Deller		

The following staff from my years are still (2010) active in the college.

Mr Stevens*	is Head of Community and Extended Services.
Mr Smith**	is Head of one half of the College - St Judith's School.
Mr Fitzpatrick***	(left 1983) is now back in a volunteer capacity supporting Duke of Edinburgh
	Award Scheme and the Outward Bound Award.
Mrs Laxton****	is still in office as PA to the Principal and Clerk to the Governors, with over
	40 years service.
Mrs Chisnall*****	is still in the Community office, as PA to Sawtry Multitask Managing Director.

26 The Governing Body

1963 ———

County Councillor	RF Hoefkens	Chairman & Chair of County Education Committee
County Councillor	W Grindley	Vice Chairman
County Councillor	CR Dell	LEA Representative
County Councillor	Mrs WA Hunting	LEA Representative
County Councillor	TER Parsons	LEA Representative
County Councillor	Mrs WM Price	LEA Representative
County Councillor	DV Robinson	LEA Representative
County Councillor	H Williams	LEA Representative
	GL Grey Esq	Huntingdon RDC Nominee
	JH Newton Esq	(Sawtry Parish Council)
	The Rev EA Bishop	Norman Cross RDC Nominee
	Fl Bliss Esq	Co-opted
	R Taylor Esq	Co-opted

1964 ———

County Councillor Grindley becomes Chairman, exchanging with County Alderman Hoefkens.

1965 ———

Mr RA Young is co-opted as PTA Representative.

1966 ———

County Councillor JH Pinner and Mr ED Green replacing Mr Newton.

1967

Mr Newton returning as an LEA rep, replacing Mrs Hunting.

1968

Mr EC Bond replacing Mr ED Green, and Mr Newton.

1969

PTA rep now Mr J Bates, replacing Mr Young

1970

Mr BL Hughes replaces Mr Bond. Plus County Councillors JD Williams & RM Attwood

1971

Mr Pinner is replaced by County Councillor Mrs PH Spiller.

1972

County Councillor	W Grindley	Chairman
County Alderman	RF Hoefkens	Vice Chairman
County Councillor	CR Dell	LEA Representative
County Councillor	H Williams	LEA Representative
County Councillor	JD Williams	LEA Representative
County Councillor	Mrs PH Spiller	LEA Representative
County Councillor	RM Attwood	LEA Representative
	Mr DV Robinson	LEA Representative
	Mr GL Grey	Huntingdon RDC Nominee
	Mr BL Hughes	Huntingdon RDC Nominee
	Mr LT Lough	Norman Cross RDC Nominee
	Mr Fl Bliss	Co-opted
	Mr R Taylor	Co-opted
	Mr J Bates	PTA Representative

1973

Mr Grey becomes Chairman. PTA Representative: Mr JK Rivett, replacing Mr Barter

1974

Now part of Cambridgeshire. All Governing Bodies reorganised

County Councillor	Mrs PMH Spiller	Chairman
County Councillor	Mrs J Willmer	Vice Chairman
County Councillor	TEJ Crofts	LEA Representative
County Councillor	AG Sturt	LEA Representative
	Mr H Williams	LEA Representative
	Mr KF Rivett	LEA Representative
	Mr BL Hughes	LEA Representative
	Mr T Corbin	LEA Representative
District Councillor	LT Lough	Huntingdon District Council
District Councillor	JD Williams	Huntingdon District Council
Parish Councillor	MW Baines	Parish Council Representative
Parish Councillor	V Toulmin	Parish Council Representative
Parish Councillor	A Grocock	Parish Council Representative
	Mrs D Baines	PTA Representative
	Mr AJ Billson	Teacher Governor
	Mr H Custance	Adult Student Representative

1975

Losing Mr Corbin & Mr H Williams.
Mr Custance now referred to as Community Association Representative

1976

District Councillor	Mr JD Williams	Chairman
County Councillor	Mrs J Willmer	Vice Chairman
County Councillor	TEJ Crofts	LEA Representative
County Councillor	AG Sturt	LEA Representative
	Mr PJ Smart	LEA Representative
	Mr KF Rivett	LEA Representative
	Mr BL Hughes	LEA Representative
District Councillor	CW Bridge	Huntingdon District Council
Parish Councillor	MW Baines	Parish Councils
Parish Councillor	CH Marshall	Parish Councils
Parish Councillor	A Grocock	Parish Councils
	Mr J Scorer	PTA Representative
	Mr AJ Billson	Teacher Governor
	Mr H Custance	Community Association Representative

1977
Mr Hughes now Vice-Chairman. Losing Mr Crofts and gaining Mrs Baines and Mr J Wilson.

1978
Mrs M North replaces Mr Wilson. Mrs Lee-Smith replaces Mr Custance as CA Representative

1979
As above but without Mr Rivett.

1980
Mr BL Hughes becomes Chairman. Mr PJ Smart Vice-Chairman.

1981

District Councillor	BL Hughes	Chairman
	Mr P Trolove	Vice Chairman
	JD Williams	
County Councillor	Mrs J Willmer	LEA Representative
District Councillor	PJ Smart	Huntingdon District Council
Parish Councillor	CH Marshall	Parish Councils
Parish Councillor	MW Baines	Parish Councils
Parish Councillor	Mrs M North	Parish Councils
	Mr J Scorer	
	Mr GM Henderson	
	Mr DJ Williams	
	Mr J Green	
	Mr ATC Guyatt	
	Mr IDA Thomas	Parent Governor
	Mr MP Coulson	Staff Representative
	Mr PW Bratby	Community Association Representative

1982
As above but without Mrs North.

1983
Mr RG Tuplin now Community Association Representative.

1984

District Councillor	BL Hughes	Chairman
	Mr P Trolove	Vice Chairman
County Councillor	Mrs J Willmer	County Council Representative
	Mr J Scorer	County Council Representative
	Mr DJ Williams	County Council Representative
Parish Councillor	J Green	County Council Representative
	Mr ATC Guyatt	County Council Representative
	Mr KJ Clarke	County Council Representative
District Councillor	PJ Smart	District/Parish Council Representative
Parish Councillor	CH Marshall	District/Parish Council Representative
Parish Councillor	MW Baines	District/Parish Council Representative
Parish Councillor	GM Henderson	District/Parish Council Representative
	Mr JD Williams	District/Parish Council Representative
	Mr IDA Thomas	Parent Governor
	Mr MP Coulson	Staff Representative
	Mr PW Bratby	Community Association Representative

Part five
Community Education Articles

27 Articles written for 'NETWORK'

Between 1980 and 1988 I wrote fairly regularly for NETWORK, the journal of the Community Education Development Centre, which had a wide circulation among certain types of school. All are based upon Sawtry experience though sometimes I felt it wise to change names.

What do you do for money?
Part one

There's nothing focuses the mind so clearly as money, be it short or be it, as here, up for grabs.

Our Community Association finance meeting, when over £9000 was allocated, revealed, more than any philosophical debate, what community was all about. In the same way that you can learn a lot about a person from the way they earn and the way they spend so too you can assess a community's sense of values from the way it arranges its budget.

Let's start by looking at their income. Our Community Association is based on a village college and its main function is to promote and encourage community activities. Many of these activities take place at the college, and the county council, in their wisdom, recognises the valuable work done by local organisations and so offers very favourable terms to affiliated groups. And how do the locals make their income from this? Although they are required by the county to charge a reasonable fee they can retain much of that fee for their own purposes.

The system is complicated, being a mixture of levies, capitation fees and social event surcharges but there is great interest in running it smoothly since the more you raise the more you will have to distribute at the end of the year. And if people come along and ask for cheap rates 'because we are doing good work' *(aren't we all?)* their pleading has to be weighed against whether we can afford passengers. We often can.

Fund Raising. To many people fund raising means jumble sales, sponsored larks or just plain begging. While some people might be willing to do this, and possibly find great personal fulfilment in it, it has been felt that the energies of our Association are primarily needed for running activities. It is interesting to note that in a government survey of Community Centres in 1944:

'*The aims to which we attach importance in fostering the establishment of community centres would be almost entirely frustrated if they (the users) were to be compelled by poverty to concentrate their efforts on whist drives and similar expedients for raising money to the practical exclusion of all other developments'*

So, how do we get our Nine Grand a year? Retained fees and levies bring in about £4300. The next best source is catering. Out of a tiny annexe, the refreshment canteen for evening class breaks, has grown a comprehensive catering service which will provide anything from conference tea to a full-blown dinner for 200. Income has been ploughed back to pay the helpers and increase the facilities but even so a healthy surplus is put into the Association general funds each year.

Even more healthy is the profit from the bar. It's not a fully-licensed bar - they wouldn't allow us that - but it is fully equipped and let on a franchise to an approved local licensee, who takes out 50 or more occasional licenses a year. So not only do the Association and the publican benefit: a share of the profit also goes directly to the community group running the particular event.

Recently the biggest money-spinners have been Discos. We were aware that local clubs made good profit from these events which they held at the college. This was right and proper since they needed the money and our role was to help them flourish. But not all clubs were good at running discos. So, to help the young, and our own funds, and to set a high standard to which all were required to conform, the Community Association decided to appoint a Disco Manager plus stewards to run Discos. They were able to fill some vacant weekends and actually increase this form of jollification for the young. In the first year this brought in almost £2000!

And the rest of the income? Profits from the New Year's Eve Dance, which the Association always runs (the most popular event of the year) advertising in the annual brochure, and insurance fees made up the balance.

What do you do for money?
Part Two

Our Community Association is centred on a Village College. There are sports clubs, youth clubs, Scouts, playgroups, wine-makers, drama groups, and churches. And the school governors, parents, staff and students all have representatives. The council elects an executive of 16.

In allocating money they are bound by just two rules: *'To promote the welfare of the community'* and, in return for the county's concessionary rates, they are obliged *'to spend 20% of the income on improvements to the school.'*

With over 50 member organisations interested in a slice of the current year's £9000 profit you might imagine that the business of allocation could become an unseemly scramble. Not a bit of it. All organisations are invited to put in bids. They should state how much their project would cost and how much they will contribute themselves.

This year the Bowling Club were aiming to build a pavilion (£25,000) and asked for £1000. The Parish Church needed a new organ (£4000) and asked for £750. The Drama Group wanted £750 for props. The Print Shop (an MSC project) asked for £500 towards £1500 of equipment. And CARESCO (our welfare group) asked for £500 towards their budget of £7000.

All this batch of requests, if acceded to, would take money away from the college. No bad thing, you might say, if the Association exists to promote local welfare. And all these organisations clearly did that in their various ways. The Association decided to give all of them a portion of what they asked for and, in so doing, had to judge the relative 'worthiness' of each request. You need the judgement of Solomon to divide fairly but, I would submit, local decision makers with local knowledge of the groups themselves and the persons running them can make better judgements than a remote committee in a distant town. If they get it wrong plenty of neighbours will call them to account. But if they get it right, not only will the groups benefit: they will also be able to serve their community the more effectively.

The above grants to groups disposed of about a third of the money. The rest was spent on improvements at the college itself. This is far more than the 20% required by the County although, as they realise, it helps not just the school. This is because so many of the school facilities are openly available to the community. But handing over the money to the school did not happen without some astute bargaining here and there. The library: a joint school and county library, badly needed new furniture. Cost £1000. The County were prepared to pay 50%, but only over three years. But you cannot refurnish a room by dividing the bill into six and waiting ages. Blow you, says the Community Association… and pays the lot. It's our library, so let's have it nice now! Then

there was a straight request from the school for £1000 for additions to the computer room. Granted, and soon the school had the best-equipped room in the area. That computer room is also regularly used for adult classes, for community groups, and life-skills training for the lads in the Print Shop.

Then there was a protracted negotiation over resurfacing the tennis courts, the school playground. This had not been done since the college opened 19 years previously. Strictly speaking it was a job for county maintenance but they showed little interest. The Association reckoned they could do this for £2500 and offered to do the work. County reacted and said it would cost their people £5000. After some arm-twisting both sides paid 50% and a good job was done.

Not everyone gets all they ask for in these annual handouts. But they all go away having gained something. Being part of a community school means more than just a warm feeling inside. It means MORE CASH, to do what we want to do!

Community people

I was asked to produce some character sketches of people in community. Identities herein are a little concealed though all the facts are true.

Eric the Caretaker

"I've replaced those broken coat pegs". There had been a rather boisterous club do at the weekend and three pegs had got wrenched off. As Head, I hadn't even had time to notice but Eric knows that I fume if damage remains in evidence for a school day. Actually he doesn't really have to put the pegs on at all. But the official repair procedure would take a long time and Eric, like the rest of us, doesn't like to be caring for an unnecessarily tatty building. And never, oh never a basin plug missing! Do we trade on such people's goodwill? Does devotion mean doing more than you are paid for? No employer has the right to say yes. But often it's not the employer, in County Hall, who benefits or who suffers because of the way Eric does his job. And does the community 'pay' him for the extras? Not so many bottles and 'boxes' for him in these democratic days. But the equally rewarding 'payment' of appreciation and goodwill. People can thrive on that. If you care, Eric cares.

Sylvia the Swimmer

For many years the percentage of swimmers she sends us from the junior schools has been approaching 100%. Not content with that she goes on to persuade our community tutor to let her run a mums and babies class. *"I can fit it in at lunchtimes between my other work"*. So, after a quick sandwich in the car, she's back in our pool to teach tots who not long before had left the waters of the womb. A practical problem: financial 'freezes' meant that the pool was not all that warm. Sylvia saw a way out by proposing that we add some solar heating. She got round her engineering friends and worked out a scheme. She then set up her own fund raising, involving all the 15 or so user groups, and she ran a sponsored swim. Mind you, she left me, as Head, to tackle the bureaucracy. But that's as it should be. Now, thanks to Sylvia, we shall be not just warm, but economically warm.

John the Deputy

Even the best-run community schools run the risk of being misunderstood. *"What are that lot doing in there? We always have that room!"* Not surprisingly the more you encourage some groups the more independent and outspoken they get. Ironically, it was John, now the rightful defender of the school's position, who in early days was the principal founder of many of these community groups. He helped revive the cricket club. He and fellow teachers started the Winemakers, and the Scouts. He even got golf going. It is sad that people's memories are often short. They forget their founders and claim an independence which, had it not been for such as John, they would never have reached. We both now sometimes find ourselves in the position of the democrat who says *"I disagree with what you say but will defend your right to say it."*

Mike the Bus

This is really an amalgam of one or two people but to save argument about shares I'll make it one. We'd had a school minibus for years but his suggestion was still a surprise. *"Why don't we buy a proper bus?"* At that time few people, even in community schools, dared to think that far. Worries about licences, driving skills and maintenance crowded the mind, to say nothing of possibly putting the local bus proprietors out of joint. However, in our case, all were good friends.

Mike had an answer to all these points. He had already driven buses and they would form a group and learn up to PSV standards. Over a quarter of the staff, male and female, were persuaded to take on this seemingly considerable task. *"Actually it's as easy to drive as a car and trailer"* he told us. And, boy, were they proud of their new badges! As for maintenance, well what's a school Craft Department for? Plus a few 'helpful arrangements' with the authorities.

The advantages of Mike's 44 seater bus need not be underlined. Sports visits are so much easier and cheaper. And we have, for any school subject, often on call at a moment's notice, a rather different but much more exciting form of 'mobile classroom'. In five years we ran our first bus into honourable old age. But, thanks to Mike and his team's enthusiasm and commitment, we are now well into the life of our second bus. This year alone it's been to Germany, Sweden, France, the Lake District and Wales. For the Swedish trip, to save fuel costs, he put in a supplementary fuel tank so that they didn't need to buy any fuel abroad. Then he discovered that diesel was much cheaper in Sweden! You can't win 'em all!

Jean the Tuckshop

Years ago the county used to pay ancillary staff to run the small canteen that supplied refreshments to Evening Class students. But all that went in one of the earliest of the Cuts. Jean, who used to be a school meals cook but was now working in town ten miles away, offered to take over. She and a colleague had for some years been running our Community Association catering service for weekend functions and so they had built up a good reputation. Running a tuckshop as well was almost a doddle. But it was not, as far as assistants were concerned, a voluntary job. Jean arranged proper payments and a proper rota, though I suspect she took nothing for her own services.

Now she runs the tuckshop at a fair profit, for the further benefit of the community. In fact last year when the question arose whether or not she should open on quiet, loss-making evenings, she was the one who strongly advocated opening. *"We can't disappoint the few who come on quiet nights. It's not their fault they are not here on a busy evening…"*

Tom the Crafty

Some community schools have well-appointed County funded special rooms. Others have almost nothing. At least we had two rooms, single plain spaces, but with no comfortable facilities. *"If they won't give them to us we'll have to get them/make them ourselves"* said Tom. So, the Adult Room got its wood panelling. This was no school project done in school time with an educationally doubtful apportioning of staff/pupil labour input. It was done at the weekend as a community project. Tom and his voluntary staff team were in charge and the local Young Farmers' Club were the labour force. Cost of materials? All met by the YFC. So, thanks to Tom, we, the community school, have, for the benefit of everyone, a really pleasant-looking comfortable room. All at no extra cost to the ratepayers. And why did the Young Farmers throw in their lot so generously? Because, every other Tuesday evening, it was not just the place they met in. It was their room. Community does not mean losing your identity; it means reinforcing it, in partnership with such as Tom.

Feelings from the front line

When you see a school with a newly-smashed window, what are your reactions? Do all those platitudes about a caring community recede into the background? Catch him, bounce him, charge him. Must maintain standards, you know.

There had been a Friday night football club disco in the school hall. At about midnight a front window in the school office had been broken. It was promptly boarded up and, by the rules of the game, it should have been repaired over the weekend. But the weekend was stormy and the glass was an odd size and so it had to wait until Monday. An English Teachers' Course on Saturday had to find its way down a bloodstained corridor to its rooms. And Monday, for the office staff, began cold and dark. What price community, you may feel, if this is how you have to start the week.

That's one view and a very narrow one. The picture changes as soon as you fill in the background.

"Yes, I was here when it happened." says the Community Tutor. Community Tutors don't miss much. *"There was no fight: just a former pupil, long since left, but a little the worse for drink. He'd been out in Northern Ireland in the army. In some trouble out there his jaw had been broken and it was still wired up. The evening had not gone well for him and his girlfriend had left him. He'd just gone out and was on his way home and things had become too much for him. So the school window got it."*

"Sorry about Friday" says the Senior Master between lessons. He is chairman of the local Football Club and has done tremendous things for village sport. According to the rules of our game the school's only dealings with him in relation to Friday should be to send him the repair bill. But in a community school there are layers of concern that cushion the hard case of financial equity. I asked him if the lad had been injured by the glass. *"Yes, he cut his hand and I offered to dress it but he wouldn't have it. It wasn't bleeding too profusely and he just went off. He knows*

he'll have to pay and there's no hard feelings."

Though we can't condone the fact that a window had been deliberately broken, a knowledge of what really happened, and why, makes it all the more bearable. It is not difficult to retreat into a corner and condemn: the young, the Irish, drink, slow builders, football clubs, or even the education system. Yes, it's very hard to stay upright in the middle of life's slippery skating rink. But being a community school at least gives you support and understanding. And keeps you in touch with life as it really is.

A disabled person's toilet

We used to call it the disabled toilet, as if someone had been mean enough to vandalise this rather important piece of community equipment. It took some getting and by the time we eventually got it, anyone who dared to harm our hard-won facility would probably have found themselves temporarily added to the ranks of the disabled.

It all began five years ago to provide for the basic needs of a Day Centre which ran in the Adult Common Room of this community college. But, in these days of economy, how do you acquire a disabled person's toilet?

Solution No 1

The school was about to get an extension for its expanding pupil numbers and it had become a requirement that all extensions should have toilet provision for disabled persons. But we didn't want it in a remote extension; we wanted it in the main block near to the adult rooms. But, say They, this is a school extension and we have no brief to look at your non-school needs. But, say We, surely it is best to have your one and only disabled toilet in a central spot. However, as we had no disabled pupils at that time we could not press the point. So the school disabled toilet was built in the school extension. To this day it has remained un sat-upon.

Solution No2

Enter the college Community Association, a body which unites all fifty user groups, levies rates from users, and spends much of this money for the benefit of the college generally. A scheme to convert a cleaners' store in the main block into a disabled person's toilet was worked out by them, costed and approved. They would pay the full cost of £220. A local builder quoted the job at this low price because, knowing funds were limited, he wanted to use his skills as his contribution to local welfare.

28 The Community's Education

Meanwhile the Social Services, who ran the Day Centre, said that they might be able to come up with part or all of the cost but could not confirm that for some weeks. Naturally, the Community Association did not want to spend their own money on a facility which could be paid for by a statutory body, so they waited for a reply. Financial stringencies cut in, and the Social Services were considerably longer in coming up with an offer of money. We waited almost a year and finally they said that they could only pay part of the cost (£125).

Now since the Social Services, as a statutory body, were to be involved in payment the project now became an official scheme and so the county authorities had to draw up their own specifications and call for tenders. Thanks to the year's delay, inflation, and the tendering process the lowest quote was now £739. It looked as if our toilet was receding faster than the wheelchairs could reach it!

Solution No3
So we had a scheme but not enough money. The Community Association were not prepared to give up. Living close to these disabled persons helps concentrate the mind wonderfully when it comes to 'answering their calls'. The Association was still prepared to put in its first offer even though this would now cover less than a third of the cost. Social Services agreed to contribute its original offer (£125) and it was left for the college and others to scratch around for the remaining money. This came from the Area Community Education Department, (£164) and the Education Dept sites & buildings estimates.(£150)

It was a complex solution to a seemingly simple problem. But a solution we are increasingly being driven to seek, as major funds become harder to tap. In all this what is not costed is the time consumed and the trouble involved in such a piecemeal operation. And this was not really about money. The chief obstacle was the difficulty of persuading others of the importance of a scheme which did not fit into their view of how things should be done. As Eric Midwinter said in his book: 'Education and the Community' *'Community Development calls for an immense simpatica amongst departments'* One day we might get there.

In 1980 I spent a year at the Cambridge Institute of Education examining the role of village colleges. In the last chapter of my subsequent thesis I attempted to sum up what I saw as the way ahead for the concept of community education. In so doing I was drawing heavily on the experience and practice of Sawtry Village College. In fact what I wrote could be regarded not just as a pattern for the future but also as a rationale for all that had been developed at Sawtry over the previous two decades.

Whether this pattern is still valid (in 2010) is for others to decide. But it is heartening to see that a primer of 2008: 'Regenerating Schools' by Groves, draws heavily on current Sawtry experience. And it refers favourably to the 1984 Cambs County Council Policy document entitled, surprise, surprise, 'The Community's Education'. While changed circumstances might demand changed approaches I would aver that much of what we did in those early years laid the foundations for the future success of Sawtry Community College.

What follows is much of that final chapter.

'Education is committed to the view that the ideal order and the actual order can ultimately be made one.' Henry Morris: 1924 Memorandum to the Cambridgeshire County Council.

Henry Morris' Memorandum suggested a way forward in education for people of all ages. His plan was launched at a time of depression and crisis not unlike today; unemployment was high and morale in education was low. In this, my own *Memorandum for the 'Eighties'* I have tried to copy his style but relate it to current practice, my own experience, and the work of Sawtry Village College.

Schools of Today
The immense development of the state system of education over the past thirty years has been so successful and so complete that it is sometimes difficult for those closely associated with it to appreciate the progress that has been made. Class sizes have improved dramatically and the overall pupil/teacher ratio in secondary schools has changed from 1:22 (1950) to 1:17 (1978). The number of teachers has almost doubled from 232,000 to 445,000. This has happened during a period when school populations rose from six million to nine million. The school leaving age rose to 15 in 1949 and to 16 in 1970. The school

building programme was so extensive that over 72% of pupils are educated in post-war buildings. All these influences combined to produce a rise in the number of secondary school classes from 56,000 (1950) to 170,000 (1978)

It is alleged by some that educational standards have fallen. But the numbers entering higher education have, over the three decades, risen threefold and the number of people taking GCE O levels has risen tenfold. The population rise of the relevant age groups over this period was about 25%. At the level of general education and basic literacy and numeracy comparative studies are rare and limited in scope. But recent indications are that there have been all-round improvements. This, in spite of the demands of greatly increased numbers in education.

The transition to Comprehensive education, which began in the '60s, has greatly enlarged the opportunities available to the average child. Many teachers have faced and accepted the challenge of teaching pupils over the full ability range and their results stand comparison with those of the few remaining Grammar schools.

But against this general success of the post-war schools must be set the problems of inequality which still exist and which threaten to dominate educational thinking in the chillier times ahead. While Henry Morris saw inequality in terms of poor rural areas and rich towns, today the differences lie elsewhere and are more subtle.

The 1944 Education Act put forward the idea of 'parity of esteem' among schools. Pupils, after an objective examination at eleven plus, would be put in the school most suited to their performance in that examination. But few parents felt that if their child 'failed the eleven plus' he would get an equally good education in the Secondary Modern school. Few education authorities staffed or financed their schools on an equal basis, giving the lie to any concept of equality. Comprehensive schools could not be born overnight and it will take a generation to forget their non-selective or selective past and become the New Institutions they are intended to be.

A New Institution
'There must be a grouping and co-ordination of all the educational and social agencies which now exist in isolation in the countryside: an amalgamation which, while preserving the individuality and function of each, will assemble them into a whole and make possible their expression for the first time in a New Institution, single but *many sided, for the countryside.'* Henry Morris 1924 Memorandum.

To the public, and especially to parents, the local Comprehensive school should offer all that they require of one particular stage in education. Gone are the days when the ablest children were obliged to travel many miles away from their home community to a Grammar school.

The New Institution has, or should have, the ability and the resource to become the neighbourhood school. For the first time in history we are developing within our community a secondary school to educate the children of the whole community. If education were chiefly a matter of learning skills and concepts unrelated to the local community then this new development would be unimportant; little more than a device to cut down transport costs. But education is concerned with the community and our greatest hope for this New Institution is that it will make young people aware of their environment and their responsibilities to it. They should do this not by merely studying it in textbooks, but by being directly involved with the people in that community as fellow citizens, as traders, as mentors, as future employers and of course as parents. If we are educating for life then school must overlap life. For a school to be involved in its community in this way requires no extra finance. Simply the right attitudes.

The Community College
'But if England is to have the education it needs, and the social and recreational life it deserves, more is required than a reorganisation of education'. Morris.

Some of the statutory agencies at present operating in the community are:

1 Schools, Primary and Secondary
2 The Youth Service
3 The Library Service
4 Health Services, especially Ante-natal Clinics, and Child Health services
5 Social Services, especially Day-Care centres for the disabled and elderly
6 District Councils, providing recreational facilities
7 Local Councils, requiring meeting rooms
8 Careers office.

All the above services are bound to be provided in some form or other by the statutory authority. If use of a service is continuous then it is probably economic to build independent premises. But if, as is often the case, use is intermittent then much money can be saved by some form of sharing. For example if a Youth Centre lies dormant in the daytime it can double up as a Child Health Clinic at minimal extra cost. Or a library, which the county cannot afford to staff for more than half a week can, if doubled up with a school library, be opened for the whole week. Again, a district council which provides its recreation field next to the school is doing the community a double service. It should be emphasised that all of the above could be achieved at no extra cost. In fact the cost can be less and could bring great overall benefits to the community. At present there is little or no co-ordination of county council services in this way. County services often see themselves as based in important central units, with outposts among the people; of these services the Wolfenden Report (1978) says: *'There is recognition of the need to decentralise, but little happens.'*

A Home for Activities

If education is seen as lifelong then this New Institution must find ways of extending its facilities to people of all ages. One way would be to open up its existing daytime classes to any who are able and willing to attend. The biggest barrier to such developments at present is the lack of official recognition of the experiments which have taken place.

But the main demand for adult classes is of course in the evenings. Much of this demand can be met by the use of school classrooms and part-time tutors. Such classes cost very little to fund since, if twelve or so people are willing to join a class, the amount they are prepared to pay should cover the principal cost, which is the tutor's salary. If that class is held in a school alongside other evening activities then the further running costs: heating, lighting, cleaning & caretaking, should not be very great.

There is one aspect of community college evening classes which has not been explored. This regards evening classes not just as isolated events but relates them to the mainstream of that school's work, with the school's Heads of Department in charge. Thus anything that happens in the Art Room, day or evening, is the responsibility of the Head of Art. Typing classes could come under the Head of Commerce or English. *(This was written in 1980. In 2010, I am told that typing would come under IT.)* Not only would this provide pupils, the younger community, with a sense of continuity when they come back as adults: it would also enable adults, who include parents, to savour something of the education given to their children. Thus a unity of educational purpose can be built into the system and the isolated

school, with all the narrower conceptions associated with it, will be abolished. All would be absorbed into a Larger Institution.

Self-run Activities

Besides formal evening classes there is a host of educational and recreational activities which the community college can encourage and stimulate. Why should it bother? And if it does bother, why should it do any more than simply permit these activities to take place on its premises? The justification for involvement of a community college, or any school for that matter, can be examined under three headings: Physical, Educational and Social.

The ***physical*** justification starts from the fact of the premises. Although schools were built for the education of one age group they are not occupied by most of those people for more than 8 hours a day in 38 weeks of the year. Any business or hotel or shop that used premises at such a low intensity would soon be bankrupt. No restaurateur would ever contemplate fitting out a kitchen to serve one meal on only 180 days a year. With no extra capital cost, school premises could be made available for many extra hours. Even after deducting time for cleaning and maintenance the usable hours could be at least doubled. Schools are public buildings paid for with public money. If the public, through its organised groups, has need of these premises and if that need is compatible with secondary education, then those needs should be met. And they *can* be met at relatively little extra cost.

The ***educational*** justification is similar to that within schools when one is seeking to justify pupils' clubs and hobby groups; these are activities which are complementary to basic learning. They enhance the participants' education, physique or well-being. As in schools, the role of the host organisation is one of encouragement rather than close involvement. Provided the proposed activity is legal and wholesome, and if it is sufficiently popular to attract a sufficient number to be viable, as it usually is, then it is not an expensive or complicated matter to allow it to develop. Its association with the community college is one of mutual trust. It is seen as a partner in education providing one or two more stones in the mosaic of life for those who care to tread in that direction.

The ***social*** justifications for encouraging community activities have positive and negative aspects. If Life is Meeting then this meeting is usually done in the context of an activity. The context may range from drinking in a pub to voting in a factory union meeting. By offering meeting places a community college is encouraging people to meet, interact and become more involved in the lives of others. These benefits are often of far greater importance than the activity itself, which can be anything from winemaking to judo.

The negative aspect of the social argument is that people who do not have the chance to meet others may be lonely, depressed or sick. We ignore these people at our peril. They are a liability not only to themselves but to society. To a lonely mum, an afternoon's fellowship meeting, with crèche, can be more than a pleasant experience. It may be a lifesaver. Again this is something that can be achieved at little or no cost. The world is full of people needing help; it is also full of people willing to help others. The role of the community college is to bring these groups together.

Using existing premises?

So far it has been argued that the non-statutory activities proposed can take place within existing school premises. However, it is prudent not to press dual use of such a limited base too far. A school, though it may only be in occupation of the premises for part of the available hours of use is, nevertheless, likely to spread its equipment and its books and its displays throughout these premises, as is its right. It would be understandable if some schools saw use by others as an intrusion, involving at best the need to keep the place tidy and, at worst, ending in teachers leaving outraged notes: *"Please do not put fag ends in my desk!"* If a school is to open its doors to adults it is best done on something more than altruism.

One Extra Room

The best starting point is to provide one room over and above the schools's normal entitlement. This has many advantages to both the school and the community. When it is not in use by the community it gives the school one extra room to teach in. In a full school such a bonus is not just the room itself; it is the flexibility that one extra space allows. As in the 'fifteen' puzzles, where 15 blocks can be moved through 16 spaces in any combination, so now the school has the freedom to move all its classes around.

The second advantage of the extra room is that there is now additional space available, when required, for daytime adult activities. These need not take place in the extra room itself; it could, say, for a typing class, be in a specialist room in the school. The school need not feel turned out since, in return, it has gained the extra room.

By definition the extra room will probably not be something provided by the education department. In the early village colleges the Adult Common Room, as the extra room was called, was provided by benefactions. This was fortuitous but it did not accord with the principle of community self-help, which was at the core of Henry Morris' original scheme. If the community want full and flexible use of school premises it should be on the basis that they are prepared to contribute something towards those premises to make this flexible use possible. They should bring a dowry to the marriage so to speak. In practice this contribution could be the result of local fund-raising and independent building. More likely, in these days of falling rolls, the contribution could take the form of 'buying in' a surplus classroom.

Once the community have brought some contributions to the premises they can begin to negotiate as partners rather than merely as tolerated occupants. In the same way as the extra room gives the school flexibility of use so too it gives the community a bargaining platform from which to move, as of right, to other parts of the premises: the hall, the gymnasium, the craft rooms and the classrooms. But this is putting it at its lowest. One hopes that once the educational and social advantages to community and school are understood, there will be no limits other than time and space to the fullest possible use by everyone.

The Personal Addition

It must be recognised that any use of premises involves negotiation, and negotiation takes time. While a school may be willing to open its doors to the community it must be remembered that it is not staffed with persons who are given time to do this work. Some community use may be in the school's direct interest, eg football coaching, and this could be easily negotiated. Similarly, negotiations of use by regular users who simply want a room every week and leave it tidy present few problems. But if a school is to be open for the amount of activity it can physically hold, which could conceivably equal the total school use, then additional staff are needed.

The extent to which such a person is paid by the county authorities will depend upon the importance that the authority puts on this work. In terms of general social benefit, particularly in areas of social need, he can probably justify his salary. The test of his worth could be the extent to which other agencies are prepared to underwrite his appointment.

Other additional space

The argument for linking various statutory bodies to the community college needs to be understood. It can be stated in terms of common core facilities and accessibility. Any public building put up in isolation requires money to be spent on certain common items such as car parking space, heating plant, caretaking and cleaning. If the core building, a school, is put up in conjunction with others there will be considerable financial economies.

Accessibility is gained because so many of the people using these premises are also associated with other parts of these premises. For example if a child health clinic is near the public library one journey can serve for both. If the doctor's surgery is near the school a pupil might save half a day's absence. More important to the school is the *educational* advantage of having access to these caring services usable as a factor in their teaching. Far better for pupils to *see* old people in an adjoining day care centre that just to hear or read about them.

The advantages of a service being near a familiar building are insufficiently understood. Many young people would never go to a public library if it meant a walk to somewhere new. But if this library was the same as their school library they would, almost without knowing, make the transition to becoming a regular adult user. Similarly when they grow up and become pregnant, a child health clinic on familiar youth centre premises is much better that an isolated building on the corner of some remote housing estate.

If we think we are being bold we should look back to the vision of Henry Morris:

'A clubroom or hut for the very young people of 15-17 who have just left school... a home for Scouts and Guides... a simple observatory, as accessible as the local inn, in which the local lad or girl and the older enthusiast can become universe-minded and acquire a valuable interest with as much naturalness as they learn to dance... a place for silence and meditation.'
From Rural Civilisation p.7 1936.

The total complex

Thus we can have on site and at no extra cost a complex of premises as follows:
... and most of these have existed within the overall Sawtry campus.

1　A Comprehensive school. 11-16 or preferably 11-18. If the educational arguments permit a Sixth Form this is to be encouraged since older pupils can be an important part of the community jigsaw.

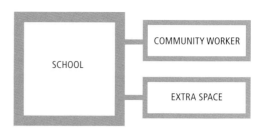

Expressed diagrammatically this is the basic provision for a community college.

2　A Primary school. Proximity would have many advantages particularly if the complex included library and swimming facilities.

3　A youth club. Even if this is only one extra room it gives them the entrée to school facilities such as the gym and the sports field. In return the school gets an extra space, or the space is available for a playgroup.

4　The 'extra room'. Henry Morris' basic extra provision for community use. Sawtry has two such rooms: the Adult Common Room and the Lecture Room.

5　A Library. Totally integrated with the school library, with dual funding, so that access and hours are maximised.

6　Health services. All schools have medical rooms, which are necessary but usually underused. These could become the focal point for area medical services, community health worker etc., whose work is often with school children and their parents. If more space is available for occasional ante-natal clinics, and money is not forthcoming for a permanent extension, then they could use the youth centre, the 'extra room', or the school hall. A school hall is a natural venue for Blood Donor sessions.

7　Social services. An increasing concern is with the elderly and the provision of day-care centres. Their requirements are simple: a warm room with easy access and tea-making facilities. This use doubles up well with the 'extra room' for which they could pay part of the capital cost. They could also add a disabled persons' toilet.

8　Recreation facilities. In recent years District and local councils have spent considerable sums on such facilities, ranging from playing fields to complete leisure centres, including complexes with prestige halls, theatres and committee rooms. Such centres are least used during school hours and a merging of requirements would therefore seem logical. This would go some way towards meeting the very high running costs, and subsequent hire charges. From a school's point of view the advantages are obvious, costing nothing extra if they are going to be built anyway. Among the advantages would be occasional access to a large hall, an item fast disappearing from school design.

9   Local councils. Since local government reorganisation, parish and town councils have been given increased powers. They could, in response to local demand, raise considerable sums to support local welfare. It might be towards supporting a publicly-used swimming pool, or extensions to a school playground for adult tennis, or even the salary of a community worker appointed to seek out local needs and organise economical forms of self-help. All this could logically and economically happen in close association with the school: the traditional home of their council meetings.

10 Careers service. All secondary schools have a careers room but little staff time to maintain it. There is usually an excellent careers service... located elsewhere. To combine these facilities and link them with the work of the Employment Exchange would benefit everyone, particularly young people in times of high unemployment. Such a centre, knowing the need and being in close touch with the school, could be the place from which training schemes to alleviate unemployment could originate. The Sawtry Print Workshop is one example. (See page 144) They could also provide a school-linked focal point for employers to meet and express their views on education to schools staff, and vice versa.

11 Citizens' Advice Bureau. Increasingly school and community education staff find themselves drawn into general matters of social welfare. The proximity of a CAB office, or at least the occasional visit of an adviser, would greatly benefit all sides. One county spent thousands of pounds equipping and maintaining a Mobile Advice Centre, which spent half its time, 9-5, travelling. It stayed 1.5 hours every fortnight in each village for the sake of one or two patrons. The use of a village college base would have enabled it to reach far more clients, sometimes in the evening.

Further additions

Besides the 'extra room' for the community and the necessary buildings for the statutory services, local groups can make their own additions to the premises according to their needs, enthusiasms and resources. And as a quid pro quo, they can then claim right of use of core facilities that already exist. Examples of such additions which have happened at Sawtry include:

12 Swimming pool. Provided by a contribution of education, local and district council funds plus local volunteer labour. Administered for community use by volunteers who plough back their assets into further improvements.

13 Dual-use field. An additional recreation field provided by Parish and District Council money but maintained by County Council.

Expressed diagramatically we could envisage all these services linking in to the school at the centre.

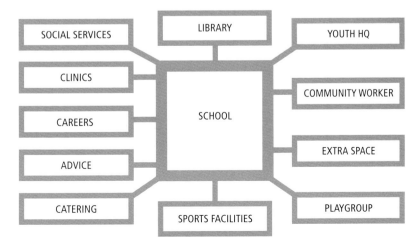

14 Bowling Green. Paid for as above plus local fund raising. Run by local bowling club who financed all further additions to the buildings, and did all maintenance.

15 Play area for playgroup. Materials paid for by playgroup but built and painted by senior pupils as a community project.

16 An Adventure Playground in an odd corner of the field.

17 Bar. Built by school staff within the 'extra room' but paid for and run by Community Association from bar profits.

Storage

Many groups who meet regularly are quite content to use already-existing space for their activity. But many have a problem with storage. Playgroups are the extreme example but any club indulging in practical work will be incommoded. Of course one could insist that everything is taken away every time, and a timid group, grateful for the crumbs of accommodation, may struggle on in this way for years. Another answer is for them to quietly leave their items in the corner, in an ever-growing pile, to the inconvenience of other users whose goodwill may be severely tested. A third answer is to propose that any user requiring permanent storage space provides it themselves. This may take the form of a cupboard, although this in itself does not create the extra space required, unless it is well-planned and occupying 'dead' space. Alternatively the extra space is created as something additional to the building: an annexe or a loft. The advantages of such an addition are not only practical; the organisation thus has a stake in the premises, a small right to be there and a feeling that something is theirs not just in the usual we-are-the-ratepayers sense.

Architecture

'Let us say to the architect... will you think out a design (for) an Institution that will touch every side of the life of the inhabitants...' Morris.

The village college approach to building starts with the school since every town and every large village must have its educational base. That school must satisfy the basic educational needs of the area but should be so designed that it can also be the core to which other elements can be attached. The hall should be as large as possible and kept simple so as to invite later furbishing. That hall is not only a large meeting place; it should also be the space that people cross or pass on their way to various activities.

The first supplement to the school must be a base for the co-ordinator of activities: the tutor. This base should be both near the entrance and near the hall. Thus he is accessible to new arrivals and also near the heart of the action. Needless to say if the school and community administration are one, the two offices should be linked. The second supplement, a comfortable common room, open to all groups, should adjoin the hall. So should a refreshment counter.

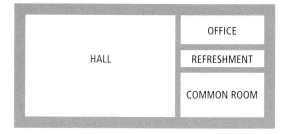

The physical design that is developing is very similar to the earlier schematic diagram:

The Hall should also be so placed that further additions can be made alongside it: a library, a gymnasium, an exhibition area, a health clinic, a citizens' advice bureau. If, to reach these activities, people are funnelled through one entrance, their chances of becoming aware of people doing other things are greatly increased. Separate entrances might be needed when the hall is booked for some special function, but this should only happen exceptionally. Every opportunity should be taken to discourage the tendency towards unnecessary separation with its attendant fears and prejudices. See all, understand all and welcome all.

Eating and drinking are supremely corporate activities and the refreshment facilities of a community college need very careful planning and an understanding that food and drink can be partaken of at many different levels. If the facilities are well planned and well run they will always pay their way and often bring in profit.

(a) Full dining facilities. These could be coterminous with the School Meals provision requiring no extra construction: merely negotiation.

(b) Light refreshment bar. A simple tea making and biscuit selling facility mainly for breaks in adult events, evening classes, concerts etc.
But in the daytime it can also serve as the school's break tuckshop. For school use there could be a simple outdoor outlier, so that the youngsters can

combine queueing for crisps with the benefits of fresh air!

(c) Further facilities for light refreshments. While these could be provided via the school kitchen, management and supervision rules often make this uneconomic. A better alternative is to establish a small unit that can be run by approved members of the community. Such a unit could be financed by the community and sited, but boxed in, in one of the adult rooms. Or this could be the same as (b) above.

(d) A specialised licensed drinks bar. (See page 138)

Surrounds. Many of the community will be interested in using the playing areas. The core of these will be what is provided for the school: the football/hockey/cricket//rounders field, the tennis/netball courts, the swimming pool. There should be opportunities to ADD to these with community money both in area – giving extra fields – or in intensity by creating all-weather pitches, floodlighting, or even a sports hall. If sports halls are already provided on school money they should be large and simple, allowing for additions, such as changing rooms, gallery, squash courts, or pavilion to adjoining field, later on. School changing rooms need to be so sited that they can, if necessary, be sealed off from the rest of the school, so that they can serve teams using the fields out of school hours.

The site. Ideally, the community school should be sited in the heart of the community and not on the fringe. But to get such a site may involve careful advance planning and pooling of resources. Sometimes, with imaginative design, good use can be made of second hand sites. In Kensall Green, London, one show primary school of the '30s was built on the foundations of a redundant gasholder; hence its circular design. In Massachusetts, USA, a community school is built almost entirely underneath a road and railway embankment, taking people literally from both sides of the tracks.

Residential Space? A final twist to the way we used the premises: at Sawtry our school use of the building went far beyond that of almost every other school, in that we regularly used the premises for Residential Courses over the weekends and in the holidays over whole weeks. In practical terms these made no extra demands on the building. All that was needed, bar the beds, was already there, and any school could easily follow this example if it chose to do so. These experiences are described elsewhere, on page 39ff.

The Message. In the same way that any good work of art can influence its viewers, so too a community school should be seen as a work of art with a capacity to move people. Not only its structure but also its contents and its displays by child or adult can speak to all who pass by or who work in its presence

In all this we need to say (in the manner of Henry Morris) to our architect: *"Come to us without any preconceived ideas as to what is best for us. Come to us prepared to fully understand our many and various needs"* Out of such a partnership we shall gain worthy buildings which express, in their form, the values of partnership.

Government of Community Colleges

'The object of the village college will be to enhance and not diminish freedom. (The village college is to be seen as) a theatre for the free and unfettered activities of the Voluntary Association. Voluntary Associations will have direct representation on the governing body.' Morris.

It is important that all organisations contributing funds to a joint scheme should be represented on the Governing Body. That body, while recognising the rights of these organisations, should have the power to use the total resources in the best interests of the local community. To put this principle into practice effectively it is essential that persons nominated to the governing body – even when representing county organisations – are local people. The principal organisations represented on the governing body would normally be:

(a) County Council, as the LEA controlling the school.

(b) District and Parish councils within the school catchment area. But if there is a proliferation of parish councils it would seem reasonable to restrict representation to those with a vested financial interest.

(c) County, District and Parish councils where they are suppliers of council-funded services eg Library, Social Services, Youth/Community service, Recreation field. nb Not all the above need be councillors, though the two-way link that they provide can be valuable. Better a loyal local nominee who attends regularly than a councillor who rarely turns up.

(d) The principal users: teachers, parents, adult students, youth, school pupils.

(e) Community Association, as representing the voluntary organisation users.

Management Committees

The Governing Body would be mainly concerned with ensuring a fair balance of resources and operations and would probably meet only twice a year. Sectional operations would be in the hands of management committees as follows:

(i) School Management committee
(ii) Youth Management committee
(iii) Community Association
(iv) Statutory Services committee, where needed

Meetings would as far as possible be open. There would inevitably, and usefully, be cross-representation and cooption. Throughout it is essential that all committees see education as a seamless garment and their subdivisions as merely artificial ones designed to expedite business.

Local autonomy

Within the limits of safety regulations and necessary employment regulations, the Governing Body should be given as much autonomy as possible. This autonomy should extend to initiating further development schemes in the community interest. From the trust and sense of responsibility and the encouragement of enterprise thus engendered, one can hope to see an upsurge of local leadership and community awareness that can bring nothing but good. In these developments the role of the higher authorities would be one of general guidance and encouragement. Their role as administrators, checking the minutiae of day-to-day local activity should diminish, with a consequent saving in cost. The 'watchdog' role is taken over by the local committees to whom all activities are accountable.

Loss of sovereignty

It must be recognised by all participants in a shared scheme that their involvement will involve some loss of sovereignty. This may be the principal reason why in the past statutory bodies, used to running their own departments in their own way, have been reluctant to join such schemes. The counterbalances for loss of sovereignty are two:

(i) Those who merge into a joint scheme will gain access to greatly enhanced facilities, or even to some facilities rather than none. Or they may gain the same facilities but at greatly reduced cost.
(ii) They will have the checks and balances of representation on the joint management. Such a body may at first seem restrictive. But it will offer participating organisations the contact with other 'caring' organisations, which they often claim to desire. Better that they meet on decision-making bodies of this kind than on the emasculated 'advisory bodies' that seem to proliferate these days.

'Where there is no public vision the Statutory Authority perisheth.' Morris.

Staff

Experience in a variety of multi-purpose establishments indicates that for maximum efficiency and optimum use of plant there must be unitary control. The village college Warden approach has stood the test of time though at no village college has he been asked to supervise the more extensive provision of services that is now suggested. Alternatively, if there is to be team management, eg Headmaster, Leisure services Director, and Community Services Director, then it is essential that the team is united under a single authoritative chairman. Arrangements involving a permanent carve-up of control in terms of space or time are to be avoided at all costs. All staff within a community college complex are to be encouraged to see their roles as partners, promoting the well-being of the whole community.

Maintenance of premises

Premises should be looked at as a whole in matters of maintenance since, overall, this will result in considerable economies. All contributory partners however, must pay their share of the costs. Arrangements for heating, lighting, cleaning and caretaking should be unified and based upon the total expected use of the premises. The concept of the 'school' caretaker treating all non-school work as an extra, paid on a one-off basis, or as overtime, is unrealistic and expensive. If a college is to be open 100 hours a week then 2.5 caretakers could spread their basic week over that time. This is normal practice in most service industries. Cleaning practices need scrutiny. If eight successive school classes can use a room before it is cleaned why does it need a further clean after one evening class? If community use is not to be priced out, account should be taken of groups' offers to leave the place as they found it. Costs can sometimes be lowered, and appearances improved if local craft resources are used to repair minor damage. All these arrangements presuppose a strong local negotiating body to protect local interests and to encourage local support. Such arrangements will help to encourage local pride of ownership in 'our' establishment.

Hire of premises

One aim of the community college is *'to become the community centre of the neighbourhood, to provide for the whole man and to abolish the duality of education and ordinary life.'* Henry Morris

To translate those aims into categories for the purpose of letting, some 'educational', some 'social' and some 'outside lettings' is not only impossible; it makes unwarranted assumptions about the motives of users. If the premises are already paid for completely by the ratepayers then no payment to the county in respect of capital costs should be required. Nevertheless, it would be prudent for most users to be charged a fee according to their ability to pay so that the income raised could be invested in improvements to the premises. The amount to be charged should be a matter for local arrangement bearing in mind their responsibilities to other college users and the laws of supply and demand. Running costs for heating, lighting, cleaning and caretaking are another matter. At present most of these are calculated centrally by county on a one-off basis, which is expensive to users and complicated to administer. How often does it cost more in clerical time to deal with a £2 fee than to collect the fee itself? Again there should be room for arrangements to be made at a local level. The present cumbersome arrangements could be compared to trying to assess fees for a school on a use-of-classroom basis. And, in these days of auto-systems, to what extent do maintenance staff have to be present, and paid, all of the time?

More experiments?

When Gamlingay Village College, the eleventh in line, was opened in 1965, Lord Butler described it as *"Another lovely and gracious Experiment"*. Every urban community school opened in those times was also described as an Experiment; a one-off but not something accepted as the general pattern.

Village and community colleges are no longer experiments. They have been going for over fifty years. If those colleges are regarded as and proved to be successful then what is there to prevent a general development along these lines? Overseas, whole areas have adopted community college principles as general policy. The time is ripe for us to do likewise in our own land.

The ultimate resource

In any community scheme it cannot be emphasised too strongly that the foundation is neither capital nor premises. The ultimate resource is people. If people speak up, band together and collectively put their institutional and their personal resources into the community college, and are encouraged to do so, then nothing but good can arise.

'The village college would not be a spectacular experiment and a costly luxury... (but something) ...bringing together a New Institution for the English countryside, ...as in all organic unities, the whole is greater than the mere sum of the parts. It would be a true social synthesis – it would take existing and live elements and bring them into a new and unique relationship. Morris, 1924 Memorandum.

'The school must enter the community of which it is part, associate itself with its people and its problems and become the resource centre from which these problems can be tackled.' C Poster: Village Colleges Today, in New Society 9 Oct 1969.

29 **Community Education in Huntingdonshire**

A Personal View

Maurice Dybeck – Warden of Sawtry
Village College 1963-1984

*This was to be one of six sections of a book
on community education to which I was
asked in 1981 to contribute. But not all the
other contributions materialised and so the
book was never published.*

I am starting my contribution within two
hours of hearing a proposal that all youth
and adult centres in the area should lose
their independence and become satellites
of one central co-ordinating body. The
argument is that central control – even of
places 20 miles apart – makes for greater
efficiency and better services. I maintain
a totally opposite view, and I do so in
company with the founder of village
colleges.

When Henry Morris launched the idea of
village colleges in 1924 he did so in a desire
to give deprived communities facilities
equal to those enjoyed by the cultured and
the affluent. In his day it was rural England
that was deprived and it was the towns
that thrived. Today it is sometimes the
reverse, but his point remains: those in
power have a duty to see that the cake of
social and educational facilities is divided
according to need. And the best way of
achieving this economically is to encourage
local autonomy and to put decision-making
into local hands.

In this contribution I want to identify some
of those needs, and illustrate how we, in
Sawtry, have attempted through the Village
College, to meet those needs. We have not
always succeeded. But I like to think that
by attempting solutions, instead of merely
preaching, we have at least made some
progress towards providing a better life for
our community.

People need somewhere to meet

This is a very practical justification for
public buildings. With domestic living rooms
getting smaller, and heating bills larger, the
need grows for public gathering places,
even a pub. Today, no-one can afford to
build places exclusively for meeting. So
why don't they turn naturally to the one
public building of any size to be found in
any community: the school? The school is
theirs. They paid for it through rates and
taxes, and it costs very little more to open
it for extended hours when the school is
not in session. As long as what they want
to do in it does not upset its main purpose

– the children's education – then people's
use of their school should, in my view, be
automatic, unquestioned and encouraged.

In Sawtry Village College there are (1980)
600 school pupils. Yet over double that
number of people use the place for some
purpose or other during each week. In a
busy week there will be over 80 separate
gatherings of one kind or another over and
above the normal school classroom
activities. The list ranges from Parish
Council Meetings to Play Rehearsals to
Evening Classes to Judo. In the corner of
the Library there might be an adult getting
help with reading. Elsewhere a tiny baby
is weighed by the Ante-Natal Clinic nurse.
In the Staff Room, evening oil is burned
over school reports and in the gym the girls
of the Youth Club are pounding the five-
a-side football. And it all happens because
the school has space, which it makes
available to others.

People need to feel they belong

In opening the doors of a school we are not
just providing space, shelter and warmth.
We are encouraging people to express
among each other their deepest need: a
sense of belonging. It is no platitude to talk
about one big family, for that is the ideal
towards which we aim. Like a family we
cannot choose our relations but we
recognise our obligations to them and our
loyalties. We acknowledge the need of all
members for recognition, symbolised in
the welcome they get not only from the
'in group' whose meeting they are attending,
but also from the wider group of the
community.

At Sawtry, we try to express this welcome
in many ways. Architecturally, it is done
by making the place visually pleasant and
reassuring. Henry Morris once said that he
didn't like village colleges to look like
schools. But that was in the days when
schools probably had far more sombre
associations than they have today. I would
not want to apologise to adults that they
are having to come into a school since today
a school, at its best, ought to be somewhere
which people, children or adults, are happy
to enter.

We can also welcome people by just being
around. The office is not just the place
where you pay your fee. Unofficially it's
the local advice centre, information bureau,
sometimes even the confessional. Like the
refreshment counter it is there for one
reason but serves many.

People need to test themselves against others

With accommodating and belonging goes testing, and this applies to both school and community. People are not fully themselves unless they are able to grow to the limit of their capacities. For some, this development will be through sports clubs: tennis, football, darts or bridge. For others, their skills may lie in becoming efficient and useful members of some committee and, however reluctant to stand at the AGM, they will secretly welcome the chance to do well and receive the approbation of the community

At Sawtry, we offer both challenge and opportunity for service in the many activities of the Community Association. All our 50 regular user organisations contribute to the general well-being of the community. The Association makes demands on people – tests them – by constantly reminding them that living together demands give-and-take, tolerance, plus a positive dynamic to work towards better things. Soon they come to realise that, given the will, they can, collectively, 'build the pyramids'. Only this is not through slave labour but willing cooperation. For 'pyramids' one should read, in Sawtry, a covered heated swimming pool, built by collective community effort 16 years ago. Now, thanks to collective *political* effort, it is being renewed and improved by County, Parish and District Councils. All part of the same continuum of skilful collective effort towards a common good.

People need to celebrate

It usually happens that those who set prices on community use of schools vary the charges according to the nature of the use. Thus if a school is to be used for a gathering deemed 'educational' the charges are low. But if the use is 'social' or, heaven forbid, 'commercial' then the charges are high. Social events held to raise money for charity tend to throw disorder into such a tidy scheme, and when someone proposes a light entertainment *'to raise money for school textbooks'* the logic totally collapses. The reality is that you can never put community activity into categories and attach price tags. What is entertainment for one may be a life-saver for another. A government booklet on community centres once spoke of *'the educational value of jumble sales'*.

I believe that our role in relation to community activity is to try to be all things to all men. We try to be the citadel of culture for those who want culture. But we can also offer the plastic ice rink for those who want thrills and spills. While we would like to see every evening class filled with ever-so-serious students, we also have an obligation to help the less-serious to be less serious. That great community centre of the Middle Ages, the church, used its naves for much celebration of what we would now call a 'secular' nature. They gave the word Festival a wide meaning: one which helps to give focus to community aspirations at many levels.

In Sawtry we encourage people to celebrate, and we try not to categorise what they do. For to categorise is to kill. Like analysing a joke or asking what a painting is made of. Celebration is the field of activity where community and school can begin to meet: a school Nativity Play brings in the community. The Community Summer Show brings in, as helpers, all sides. The Parts begin to become One.

Let's look now at some of the needs of that particular group of adults in the community who are most closely connected to this building they call a school: the parents.

Parents need to be involved in education

A local school is a local school is a local school. This contortion is a reminder that the school is there by virtue of the wishes of the local people, as voters and taxpayers. The school is theirs not only as a place. It is theirs as an organisation deputed to carry on their - the parents'- duty of education. It is not something remote, apart from the community, an academic ivory castle dispensing gleaming tablets of knowledge. Rather, it is an extension of that community, expressing its highest desires in relation to what the next generation should be. Sadly, the steady centralisation of education throughout this century has led people to think of education as something provided by 'them', and something over which they have no influence.

One benefit that is coming out of the present crises in education cuts is that parents are banding together to try and 'save education'. If they want standards to remain high in education they must say so and use their influence on the decision-makers. It is not enough for them to apply first aid locally, buying textbooks to patch up the effects of the cuts. They need to question the whole basis on which the cuts are being made. In so doing they will need the support of the generality of voters since all, and not just the parents, have to share the cost of education.

What has all this to do with community education? In my view, everything, though from the way most counties organise community education people could be forgiven for thinking that school and community were separate entities.

All education is community education in that it is nothing more and nothing less than a series of activities which the community has, through its rates and through its institutions, decided that it wants. School education is of course the most important of these activities, but it is only one among many. School education is community education because we are educating pupils not just for themselves or for their parents but for life in the community. Pupils can then go on and add, by choice, any amount of what we call Further Education.

Parents need confidence in their local school

In some quarters it is now fashionable to regard the concept of catchment areas as bureaucratic tyranny. Parental choice is encouraged and those who can afford to travel out of their community have the pick of the county before them. This is to treat education as if it were nothing more than a commodity, like soap powder, cornflakes, or a furniture suite. Public education is what we make it, and if it is not to our liking the reaction should be not to shop around but to *improve* it. Education is not someone else's product. It is the community's product: ours.

At Sawtry, I believe the fact that we are a community school can do much to increase parents' confidence. It is not just a matter of enhanced facilities, though this helps. More importantly, in my view, is the matter of accessibility. A community school has no walls round it, no gates and no secret gardens. People can see us for what we are. While this can at times be embarrassing - we would all like a few cupboards for our skeletons - on balance it is good. If we are all trying to be one family it would be unreal to expect it always to be one happy family. But it is no less a family for that, and if people are invited to share not only our successes but also our problems then community begins to take on a real meaning.

Parents need lifelong learning

Like the colours in a tartan, parents are a key thread that runs through the community on two directions: in *space* and in *time*. In *space* they, through their children at the school, the power house, can reach out into the whole community in a communications network that can bring all into contact with the source of power.

They are also a thread in *time* since their own family and its interests may well span the years from birth to old age. At all these levels a thriving community will have something to offer them. A family can plug into the college in countless ways. Perhaps it is just a 'two-pin plug' one link to the school and one to mum's evening class. Or nowadays it might be a 'multiplex' with countless pins linking to many and various activities.

At Sawtry, some of those connections into which they might plug are as follows. In age order: the Ante Natal Clinic, the Playgroup, founded here but now expanded into its own premises in an old telephone exchange which we helped them acquire, Swimming classes at the pool for Infants School, Junior Schools, and our own Comprehensive school giving 11-16 education for all pupils, Youth clubs for different groups from age 11 to 25 plus, Sports clubs of all kinds covering ages from 7 to 70, adult classes both in the daytime and evening, a joint school and County Library, a Bowling club, a day centre for handicapped people and an over 60s club.

The Library

Of the above activities the one which is perhaps the most lifelong and which, after the school, most interests parents is the library. In a library all are equal. A good library can provide such a wide range of information that it can draw to itself almost everyone. It is, in Henry Morris' words: a *'Nominal Cosmos'*. Like a community college, a good library can instruct, inspire and entertain. And, like a community college, a good library in a rural area can only come into being through cooperative effort.

The Sawtry library is a *totally integrated library* in which the book resources of a school library and a county library are combined to give double the expected stock. This is then available to all comers. The library is staffed professionally thanks to contributions from school and county, the latter to the level allowable for a village of our size. Thus not only is the stock doubled but the time it is open is also, potentially, doubled.

Thus, like the college itself, the library spans the range of human need; it opens its doors to all, it makes good use of existing resources and is not dependent upon special favours. And it can appeal to all ages. Furthermore it came into being not as a result of a plan from on high but as result of local wishes.

Local or central control?

County authorities have a duty to ensure that resources are allocated equitably according to local needs. Beyond that it is my view that as much decision-making as possible should be in local hands.

We have, of late (1980) seen some moves in the direction of devolution of responsibility for self-budgeting schemes in education. This is good, but unless these are accompanied by some fund-raising power they are likely to be seen not as devolution but abdication. Genuine devolution of power and decision-making, which is really what all education is about, is born of trust. Trust people to do a good job... and they will.

Case Study: A Community Association in action

These notes are extracted from one set of 1980 Sawtry Community Association Minutes. If an ounce of practice is worth a pound of theory then here are ten 'ounces' to start you off. Explanatory notes follow each item.

1 **New members.** Mr DB and Mr CB, the newly-elected school student members were welcomed to the meeting. Mrs K of the Folksworth Mums & Toddlers Group was welcomed and explained the work of her group. Agree to ACCEPT them into membership subject to ratification by the governors.

There are over 50 member groups and membership confers privileged rates for use of the college premises. But it also entails paying quite a high affiliation fee as decided by the Association. In fact the Mums group was not after premises: simply advice and moral support. The school student reps were, at the time, aged 15.

2 **Handicapped Persons' Toilet.** The Warden suggested that it might be expedient to offer to pay for this project and leave the Social Services to grant aid the larger foyer development.

This was a project arising out of the needs of the weekly Day Centre started in the college by the Social Services for handicapped people. In the event the costs were shared but the initiative had come from the Community Association.

3 **Foyer Development.** In view of the possible grant-aid from Social Services, District & County Councils, and the Jubilee Trust plus possible manpower from Job Creation Schemes and Gaynes Hall (Borstal) it was AGREED 13 for 6 against to obtain working drawings for the project.

This was a major project of ours to extend the area at the back of the school hall to make an additional adult room. The architect was a school parent. In the event it never happened.

4 **Charitable status.** The secretary reported that our application for registration with the Charity Commissioners had been turned down. The National Federation of Community Associations was as surprised as we were and were following up our case.

This refusal stemmed not from any irregularity in our conduct or intentions; simply that a school-based community association did not fit into anyone's accepted category of institution. It was later ACCEPTED and paved the way for other schools to act likewise.

5 **Pantomime.** It was felt that the Community Association ought to re-emphasise its stipulation that the Sawtry Little Theatre should not produce pantomimes to clash with Stilton Playscene productions.

Not quite a storm in a teacup but the tail end of a dispute between two equally enthusiastic drama groups as to which had priority. Such matters can never be resolved to the satisfaction of everyone. The important fact is that, through a community association, the case can be argued openly and not left to be decided by officials behind closed doors.

6 **Firework Evening.** The Sawtry Young Farmers representative reported that his club would be prepared to take on the organisation of this event.

One of the most popular events in the college year. Run for over a decade by the joint PTA of the local Junior and Secondary schools, initially as a safety move to deter children from using their own fireworks. Costs escalated, it ceased to be a money-maker and the number of helpers dropped.

7 **Annual Brochure.** AGREED that Community Association funds contribute £50 towards the cost of the Brochure.

This was the main mouthpiece of the college. In more prosperous days it was county-funded. Now it has become entirely self-supporting thanks to this grant and advertising. A copy goes to every household in the catchment area.

8 **Bar Door and Shelves.** The bar manager reported that the bar account stood at £450. It was unanimously AGREED to go ahead with the bar exterior door and shelves.

The final phase of equipping the bar for the many weekend social functions. Entirely paid for by the Association and bar profits. The exterior door would obviate supplies movement through the college.

9 Common Room Curtains. A curtains sub-committee was formed of Mrs K, Miss P and Mrs P AGREED they should compare quotes and samples and decide on curtains to be ordered up to maximum of £280.

All the common room furnishings including fitted carpet, panelled walls and furniture have been paid for entirely by the community.

10 Any Other Business. The existence of Sawtry Music Makers was advertised. Agreed that they could pay Community Association hire rates pending an expected membership application.

Some groups die. Others take their place. The Association is receptive and encouraging towards all new ideas. In return members are receptive and encouraging to each other.

This is what community education is all about.

30 Hunts Verses

Dr Colin Fletcher, an old Community Education colleague, steered me through my year of research at the Cambridge University Institute of Education in 1980.
One day he sent me this poem. The source of it is unknown to me. I responded.

Huntingdonshire
by DR Peddy

If anyone asked what there is about Hunts,
I should have to proclaim myself a dunts.
The name itself is practically useless for rhyming; I don't dispute
That there are punts, stunts, shunts, and even Lunts,
But how to drag them in is a point which is moot.
It isn't a garden of England like Kent, nor does it foucester
Young ladies of the type found in Gloucester;
Nobody writes songs about Hunts-by-the-sea, I fear,
Nor about Hunts, Glorious Hunts, or that they come up from Huntingdonshire.
Yorkshire, now, has a pudding, and bred the sisters Bronte;
And is the largest conte;
That's what I call hot stuff,
Unlike that Oliver Cromwell and quads-at-St Neots stuff
What Hunts needs, beyond all doubt, is some chap
To put it on the map.

Hunting Still A reply

Some chap to put old Hunts on the map?
No doubt some day that may well hap.

Meanwhile, it's not so mean a place as some may think.
There's famous cheese named after Sawtry's neighbour Stilton
But there's a rhyme that's hard to use unless you think we have a Hilton.
Not our style, for humble homes are mostly our concern,
With Comprehensive Community Schools where All can Live and Learn.

At Gidding, Little, TS Eliot wrote verses erudite and, some would say, obscure
But people still flock there, both sinner and saint
though the inmates now are decidedly fure

The greatest of books in the British Museum
Were housed quite near here, but you'll not now seum.
Conington Castle, their home, has now gone
Though its church I spy still as it shines in the sonne
'Cottonian Manuscript' ascriptions would say
But, for libraries now, you must come down our way.
At Sawtry we have county's largest, for schools,
Thanks to Joint-Scheme which gives us our much-needed tools.

There's a big Base for planes at Alconbury,
Press Red Alert and they're away in a hurry
Flight path over Sawtry brings far too much noise
And that's not much fun when you teach girls and boise

Then there's boffins galore working up at Monks Wood
Their eyes on environment, and checks on its mood
They feed their computers with facts gleaned world-wide
We learn from their lessons and follow their gide

But the best place in Hunts is undoubtedly SAWTRY
Though, for rhyming, I find it impossible. Ought we
To flee somewhere else and lose our identity?
That makes matters worse, and might bring in emnity
We don't want her here; it's bad enough with Maurice
Forget the whole lot and refer back to 'Henry'!

MWD

Index

For reference to Chronology, Staff lists and Governors, go direct to Part Four.